THE DEVIL'S SNAKE CURVE

The Devil's Snake Curve

A Fan's Notes from Left Field

Josh Ostergaard

COFFEE HOUSE PRESS
MINNEAPOLIS
2014

COPYRIGHT © 2014 Josh Ostergaard
COVER AND BOOK DESIGN by Linda Koutsky
COVER AND INTERIOR ILLUSTRATIONS © Andy Sturdevant
AUTHOR PHOTO © Ruth Ostergaard

Coffee House Press books are available to the trade through our primary distributor, Consortium Book Sales & Distribution, cbsd.com or (800) 283-3572. For personal orders, catalogs, or other information, write to: info@coffeehousepress.org.

Coffee House Press is a nonprofit literary publishing house. Support from private foundations, corporate giving programs, government programs, and generous individuals helps make the publication of our books possible. We gratefully acknowledge their support in detail in the back of this book.

Visit us at coffeehousepress.org.

LIBRARY OF CONGRESS CIP INFORMATION
Ostergaard, Josh.
[Essays. Selections.]
The devil's snake curve : a fan's notes from left field / Josh Ostergaard.
pages cm
SUMMARY: "*The Devil's Snake Curve* offers an alternative American history, in which colonialism, jingoism, capitalism, and faith are represented by baseball. Personal and political, it twines Japanese internment camps with the Yankees; Walmart with the Kansas City Royals; and facial hair patterns with militarism, Guantanamo, and the modern security state. An essay, a miscellany, and a passionate unsettling of Josh Ostergaard's relationship with our national pastime, it allows for both the clover of a childhood outfield and the persistence of the game's service to those in power. America and baseball are both hard to love or leave in this, by turns coruscating and heartfelt, debut. Josh Ostergaard holds an MFA in creative writing from the University of Minnesota and an MA in cultural anthropology. He has been an urban anthropologist at the Field Museum and now works at Graywolf Press." —PROVIDED BY PUBLISHER.

ISBN 978-1-56689-345-9 (pbk.) — ISBN 978-1-56689-346-6 (e-book)
1. Baseball—United States. 2. Popular culture—United States.
3. Baseball stories, American. 4. Alternative histories (Fiction)
I. Title.
PS3615.S636A6 2014
813'.6—DC23

PRINTED IN THE UNITED STATES
FIRST EDITION | FIRST PRINTING

814
OSTERGAARD

THE DEVIL'S SNAKE CURVE

Contents

It wasn't true. But nobody cared.
They all laughed. They thought it was true.
They wanted to believe it was true.

—PHIL PEPE,
The Wit and Wisdom of Yogi Berra

Now he and I are
watching some men with a ball.
No matter the shape or size of the ball, what
team or for what country the men fight.
The TV is showing men with a
ball so we're watching.

—MARY ROBISON,
Why Did I Ever

CHAPTER I

Origins

Long Ago, in Kansas

The clover in deep left field was delicious. I crouched for a better look, laid my glove on the thick green grass. My shoe was untied. A cluster of purple flowers gleamed, each blossom a mid-inning snack. I picked the best one—not the biggest, because their nectar has usually dried, but the darkest purple bud. I stood, tucked my glove under my arm, plucked the long purple threads, placed their white stems between my teeth, and pulled. Sweet nectar spread across my tongue. Coach called my name. I looked. The inning was over. My teammates were already in the dugout.

Winter Sunshine

It was the worst part of winter: the dark, dead stretch between the end of the World Series and the day pitchers and catchers reported for spring training. At eleven years old, it was my season in hell. Days were short and temperatures steadily dropped, nothing to do but throw snowball strikes. But one day was different—in the basement I conjured sunshine.

A few months before, during the hottest part of summer, I had spent my allowance on two blank cassette tapes and stolen my older sister's tape recorder—a black-and-silver machine the size of a shoe. She always taped songs off the radio, like "Wake Me Up Before You Go-Go." We'd lie on the floor of her bedroom and listen. But I had a new plan. The Kansas City Royals played every night in our living room. The announcers kept us company, reciting the details of the games, sharing memories of past seasons. One sweltering evening, recorder in hand, I crept through the living room to our ancient family stereo and turned up the volume on the game. I placed the machine next to a speaker and pushed Record. The tape rolled slowly forward. I left the room to light the grill and ignored the game, hoping to remain ignorant of the score. I returned only to flip the tape.

Now it was winter, and even on a rare sunny day the light in Kansas was dim and thin, like air breathed through a heavy scarf. It was bitterly cold, and dirty snow was piled high on the edge of everyone's driveway. My older sister was busy with band practice, and my younger sister was busy reading *Lord of the Flies.* I could not take one more day of winter. I dug the tape from the nest of junk that was my bedroom, stole my sister's tape player, and darted down to our unfinished basement. It was dark, cold, and I was alone. Spring would never come. I settled in a corner, under a blanket, near a heat vent. I pushed play, the wheels turned slowly, and I heard announcer Denny Matthews say, "We'll be back in a few minutes with the lineup for today's game against the White Sox."

I sat and listened, and though I could hear the wind moaning outside our house as it whipped the branches of our giant cottonwood trees, the basement seemed to fill with sunlight and warmth. I listened to the announcers banter back and forth and call the play-by-play, and suddenly it was a hot July day, the peak of summer, with months still left in the baseball season. It was staying light until nine, the Kansas City Royals had hopes of winning, cared about winning, tried to win. In the emptiness of winter it seemed possible as I listened to Bret Saberhagen, Bo

Jackson, Kevin Seitzer, and George Brett keep the Royals aloft in the league standings.

Universal Reverence

On my first visit to the Baseball Hall of Fame, I looked for the plaque awarded to Royals legend George Brett. While I was growing up in Royals country, Brett was one of the best players in the nation, keeping us in contention year after year, and he is the only player inducted wearing a Royals uniform. But his career is more than just a smattering of memories—it's a reminder of what became of the Royals after he retired. They lost 100 games in 2002, and in the year of this visit, 2004, they were on their way to losing 104.

Bronze plaques lined the wood-paneled walls. I did not see George Brett. I was surrounded by Yankees: Babe Ruth, Reggie Jackson, Whitey Ford, Yogi Berra, and on and on, everywhere I looked. The Royals' rivalry with the Yankees—my rivalry with the Yankees—bloomed in the late seventies and eighties, when the Royals fielded contending teams and actually beat them in the playoffs. Years later, disgust for the Yankees lingered in the Kansas City air like a stench from a rendering plant. As I stood in the Hall of Fame, I looked at the Yankees enshrined on the wall and felt anger zipping along the nerves in my arms and legs.

And then I found Brett's plaque:

> Played each game with ceaseless intensity and unbridled passion. . . . Hit .390 in 1980 MVP season and led Royals to first World Series title in 1985. . . . A clutch hitter whose profound respect for the game led to universal reverence

The next season, 2005, the Royals lost 106 games, and in 2006 they lost an even 100. Reading Brett's plaque and seeing it there with the other greats was a balm, and though it reminded me that Kansas City has a disadvantage by dint of geography and economics, it also proved that the system once allowed Podunk teams to compete.

Look. See.

Many baseball stories are about fathers and sons. This one is not, though it could have been. When I was a kid, my dad and I saw the Athletics, Dodgers, Padres, Twins, Cardinals, Mets, Royals, Cubs, White Sox, and Blue Jays play in their home stadiums. As father and son, we watched Ken Griffey Sr. and Jr. play together in the Kingdome.

Every summer, my dad and I played catch in our backyard. When he was out of town, my mom wore his glove. We created our perfect little world and there is no downside to that story. They went to my little-league games and encouraged me when I struck out. My dad and I collected baseball cards, and he let me open his half of our shared box of 1987 Fleer. He even let me inscribe the value of the cards on their back side with a ball-point pen, defacing the likes of Will Clark and Bobby Bonilla.

I could write much more about the side of baseball, and America, these stories represent. I've lived it. It's wonderful. The experiences my family and I had together through baseball were a magical part of my life as a kid. But as an adult, they turn my stomach sour. They don't reflect the world I live within and choose to see. The old way of seeing feels saccharine, though I realize it's more my feeling than hard fact.

I used to think baseball was a game of certainties. The pitcher and batter did their gritty work, and the blurred ball thudded into the catcher's mitt or bounced off the right field fence. The official scorekeeper recorded precisely what happened. Every pitch was tabulated, digested, and put to use in understanding what might come next. The hit-and-run. A double steal. A grand slam on a 2 and 0 count. The game was a controlled space of its own. Its boundaries were clear: foul lines, baselines, backstop, outfield walls, strike, ball, out, walk. A defined physical space where players played, and seemed to do what they wanted even as they followed rules. A space outside of time. There was no clock. The final inning could last an hour, or five minutes. The game was predictable, yet it birthed infinite stories about what happened in the past or could happen next. Even within these variations, it felt comforting to see the same pattern, game after game. It felt comforting to sing along before the first pitch with my hand over my heart and my eyes on our flag. It felt comforting to stand and stretch during the seventh inning, and sing again. It felt comforting to go to the ballpark and escape life for a while.

One of the great things about baseball is the breaks built into its flow. Three strikes are an out, pause. Four balls are a walk, pause. Every inning is split in half. Some innings are short, some are long, some are exciting, some are boring, but there is always an interlude. If the game is good, each pitch, each wipe of the brow between pitches, has drama and suspense. If not, there is time to let your mind wander while sitting in the bleachers.

Baseball rewards inattention. I eat a hot dog or two and drink a beer or two, and overhear snippets of lively conversation. The suburban couple in the row behind me have left their Doberman and their kitten home alone together. Will Kitty survive the game? I see a colleague in the next section, and wave, only to panic because I have just been caught faking a sick day. But so has she, and I relax and finish my third hot dog

and enjoy the freedom of throwing the wrapper to the ground.
I can eat six hot dogs in nine innings.

There's time to sing and stretch during the seventh: *Take Me Out to the Ballgame,* and in some stadiums, *God Bless America.* The next inning begins. The game can change at any moment. What began as a pitchers' duel may end with a home run. This book is like a day at the ballpark. Its stories are the murmurs between innings. They are the pitches that make up a game. They career off the wall and roll into dark corners. The game is played in fragments. Meanings accrue. Memories interrupt history. Each of us should be an umpire.

HE'LL SAVE CHILDREN, BUT NOT THE BRITISH CHILDREN
George Washington had rotten teeth and wore a wig atop his natural hair. At the time of his death, the United States was twenty-three years old and ready to have its way with the world. The sport of baseball was little more than a homunculus lodged in the brains of cricket-weary Revolutionary War veterans.

Two hundred thirty-one years after our nation's founding, a company that specializes in making children's toys purchased three strands of Washington's hair. Corporate executives had the hairs embedded, one by one, into baseball cards. Alongside Ryan Braun or Josh Hamilton, a lucky boy or girl might find a card bearing the likeness of our dear leader, and the words: "This card contains an authentic hair of George Washington, first collected by his adopted daughter Eleanor Parke Custis."

Lest we believe George Washington's follicular trinity bestowed moral authority to the sport of baseball, it is wise to remember our first president as poet Dobby Gibson has:

This and the fact that George Washington's dentures

weren't made of wood

they were constructed from his slaves' teeth.

Quantification

A man named Henry Chadwick is credited with inventing an improved baseball box score. He modified the system used by the English and their colonies to monitor cricket scores and statistics. The 1850s were the beginning of attempts to tabulate, in statistical form, what happened during baseball games. The accumulation of data. The hope of improvement. Science. Precision. Control.

Scorecards allowed the fans to participate in the game, and were first printed and made available to baseball throngs during the 1870s. One of the most vibrant of baseball's early entrepreneurs, Harry M. Stevens, helped popularize the use of scorecards among fans a decade later. As he hawked the cards, Stevens attracted attention in the grandstands by wearing a silk hat and a red coat while loudly reciting Shakespeare.

The Rules

But statistics beg for subversion. Mark Twain served as an umpire for a baseball game in Elmira, New York, in 1887 between the Unions and the Alerts. Twain didn't suffer from nostalgia. Insanity, maybe. Vision, definitely. He had a knack for the absurd.

The teams were made up of local businessmen and politicians. The mayor pitched for the Unions, and the Alerts had the county judge in centerfield. Bankers, telephone company staffers, lumber executives, and other "leading citizens" filled out the lineups for both sides. It was a friendly match, and umpires were chosen by the teams. The Unions hired Reverend Thomas K. Beecher. Nobody invited Mark Twain, but he showed up anyway and demanded to be made a general umpire.

As the game progressed, Twain imposed his own commandments:

- Any ball is a strike that passes within eight feet of the plate on either side of it.
- To wait for good balls causes delay and public dissatisfaction and is not going to be allowed on this occasion. The batsman will strike at everything that comes, whether he can reach it or not. In waiting intervals, pecking at the plate with the bat to see if it is there will not be allowed. The batsman is denied all professional affectations; he must stand up straight and attend strictly to business.
- The pitcher must not wipe the ball on his pants; neither must he keep inspecting it and squirming and twisting it and trying to rub the skin off it with his hands. He must not keep the public waiting while he makes allusory feints at reputable parties or first or second base. All these foolings delay the game and dull the excitement.

It was still only the first inning, and Twain's umpiring quickly grew more bizarre. He was irreverent. Rightly and blissfully so. The crowd and the teams turned on him when his proclamations skittered beyond reason.

- No more than fifteen men at a time will be allowed to leave their places to chase a foul or a fly or a bluebottle, and prevent the capture of it. The catcher will keep his nose out of the batsman's pocket and stand fair. Cripples will be removed from the field at once and substitutes put into their places. No public rubbings and rollings and restorings will be allowed. They cause delay. Presentation speeches by dumb people not permitted. Persons arriving at bases on their stomachs do not score. Parties who guy the umpire will be killed.

After making these demands, Twain declared the Alerts' inning was over, and an argument ensued among players and spectators that lasted over a half hour. Twain finally allowed Reverend Beecher to take his place as umpire the next inning, and when the game resumed, the "Unions scored sixty-four home runs in succession."

When a reporter later visited Twain at home, the famous author said he preferred theology to baseball and would allow younger men to umpire in the future. A week later the paper reported anew on Twain's umpiring:

> Realizing he was taking his life in his hands when he began to umpire a game at Elmira, he took with him also a dangerous-looking package which he carefully deposited near his post of duty. Before the game began he blandly informed the audience that he didn't propose to be mobbed by the aristocracy of Elmira, or any equally disreputable assemblage, and that he had written his obituary the night before. The mysterious package, he said, contained dynamite, and when his decisions gave dissatisfaction he coolly placed one foot upon it and the hubbub immediately ceased. To carry out his threat Mark Twain would have had to go up with the others in the explosion, but he was fully as anxious to go as anybody on the field.

PLAY

It was early July, the best time to live in Chicago, and I was on a kickball team for adults called the Blackout Brigade. We played in a park in the north central part of the city on public diamonds after the kids were gone. The hour before sunset, the light was pink and gold. Our team arrived, one by one, some on foot, some in cars, most on bikes. We laughed and wondered whether we would score any runs that night. A duffel bag was unzipped, hands reached for cold cans of Old Style. A bottle of Jameson appeared.

The other team wore short yellow shorts and tight green shirts, did calisthenics, and blasted the Rolling Stones through a small, staticky, battery-operated tape deck. They had their own ball, and used it to run drills. They wanted to win. Two shabby men were drawn in by the music. The Rolling Stones are chum for burned-out ex-hippies. They stopped and slipped their fingers through the chain-link fence. They leaned in to watch, and stayed the whole game.

Our pitcher rolled wide of home plate. Smoke had forced him to close his eyes, a cigarette dangled from his lips. By day he was an engineer for a steel mill south of the city. Another roll, and the batter kicked the ball to our third baseman, who had not been looking, so it toppled the can of beer at her feet. Two runs scored. The other team was serious. They stretched doubles into triples. They had the lead. It grew and grew and grew. They tried, we laughed.

TECHNOLOGY

Not long after Mark Twain's turn as an umpire, a pitcher named Pud Galvin, whose face was bejeweled with a mustache more luxuriant than the emperor tamarin's, put his faith in science and delivered into his blood a potion made from the testicles of critters such as guinea pigs, monkeys, dogs, and sheep. The neurologist Charles-Édouard Brown Séquard invented the potion, which seemed to be able to restore vigor to men whose vim had withered. On August 12, 1889, Pud Galvin received his injection, and the next day pitched a 9–0 shutout over Boston. In his long career, Galvin won 361 games and lost 308. He was later elected to the Hall of Fame, despite his use of testicular elixirs.

Horace Wilson's Seedlings

European traders introduced guns to Japan in the mid-sixteenth century. The Japanese used firearms for nearly a hundred years before they slowly abandoned them. Japan, a culture with advanced technology in other realms, refused to use guns for the next 250 years. It was a rare but inspiring thing in world history. A culture gave up the use of an "advanced" technology for a "simple" one. They reverted to swords. Among the reasons: war with guns was too impersonal for the samurai class and lacked the aesthetic fulfillment of swordplay.

The nation was closed to American influence until the 1850s, when Commodore Matthew Perry arrived and arranged the Treaty of Kanagawa. Perry's ship had sixty-four-pound guns. Japan had nothing close. They signed.

Twenty years later, an American named Horace Wilson, an English instructor in Japan, began to teach his students how to play baseball. The game became popular, and the two countries have been playing it ever since. Baseball didn't prevent them from becoming enemies. It didn't prevent Pearl Harbor or Tokyo in flames. Hiroshima and Nagasaki, going going gone.

Though some Japanese sought to reintroduce guns even prior to Commodore Perry's show of intimidating military hardware, the government didn't begin producing them until after the Americans had made contact. Guns, baseball.

In 1876 a new Japanese government forbade the samurai from "wearing their two swords." When they used their swords in a rebellion, the government responded with their newly acquired guns. It was an uneven battle.

Soon afterwards, the first Japanese baseball team was formed. Japan abandoned the sword and adopted firearms and baseball at precisely the same time. The swing of the instrument through the air, the precision needed to fight well, the timing, the close personal competition. Swords, bats.

Accumulation and Construction

Mass production of goods began in the United States in the mid-nineteenth century when federal armories manufactured thousands of rifles. Soon other industries began to mass-produce "watches and clocks, sewing machines, agricultural equipment, bicycles, and automobiles."

Over time the idea gained traction. In 1910, Henry Ford opened a manufacturing plant and soon began mass-producing cars. Ford advocated a "clean, sober, industrious life" for his workers. For the owners, it was the best way to increase production, profits, and wealth. It wasn't long before these principles took root in professional baseball as teams began to behave like factories.

BATTING NINTH

"Like butter," said the skinny kid as he stood in the on-deck circle. He was grinning and looking through the chain-link fence at the rest of us on the bench. We were horsing around. Our yellow mesh caps were turned inside out hoping he would get a hit and start a rally, though half of us didn't even know the score. "Like butter," he said again, swinging as he waited for his chance at the plate. His hands were an inch apart, and there was a hitch halfway through his swing that made it look as though he were trying to hit a butterfly. He had a mouthful of grape gum and blew a bubble so big it turned from purple to white. He was the only one not wearing a uniform—he wore blue jeans. During practice, despite the heat, he added an army green camouflage jacket. Night games were hard for him because his glasses were the kind that darkened automatically in the sun, and the lenses were so thick it took too long for them to return to normal once daylight faded. He was the most awkward kid in the league, the worst hitter on the worst team, but he carried himself like he didn't know it, or didn't care. "Like butter," he said, and he meant it. He had learned to let problems slide. On a team where all the other kids' dads were bankers, doctors, and lawyers, someone joked that his dad worked at Go Chicken Go. The rest of us would never even eat there. The on-deck circle and the batter's box were the only safe places on the field for this kid. There, he became one of us, one of the team, and we stopped mocking him for two minutes, three minutes, however long it took him to strike out. "Good luck," we said. He smiled and walked toward the plate, slowly, evenly, and the barrel of his bat drew a line in the dirt.

HOT AIR

Two baseball teams, the Chicagoans and an assemblage of players called the All-Americans, left for a tour of the world in 1888. Upon their return, a banquet was held in their honor at

Delmonico's in New York City. The papers reported it was the liveliest event ever held there, with over 250 guests feasting, drinking, and smoking cigars. Speeches were given by Al Spalding, Cap Anson, and Mark Twain, who by then had recovered from the trauma of serving as an umpire. Several politicians spoke. The partiers were intoxicated, and so was the rhetoric. A. G. Mills, the man whose committee falsely claimed that Abner Doubleday invented baseball, lauded the contributions made by the touring teams to "universal peace and good rule which Americans have always done most to promote."

Daniel Dougherty: "In all your wanderings you have been distinctly Americans and as such have tightened the ties of peace with distant people; have, perhaps, paved the way to new commercial relations, have widened the brotherhood of many. . . ."

Mayor Chapin of Brooklyn: "My recollection of base ball rests on twenty-five years ago, when the base ball nine of the city of Brooklyn stopped short the triumphal tour of the Cincinnati Red Stockings. If I was asked to name the two great events of that period, I would mention the assassination of Abraham Lincoln and the defeat of the Red Stocking nine by the Atlantics of Brooklyn."

Mark Twain: "And these boys have played base ball there [the Sandwich Islands]. Base ball, which is the very symbol, the outward, visible expression of the drive and push and rush and struggle of the raging, tearing, booming nineteenth century. . . . They have carried the American name to the utmost parts of the earth and covered it with glory every time. I drink long life to the boys who plowed a new equator around the globe, stealing bases on their bellies."

Railroad booster Chauncey M. Depew: "George Washington was a great and good man, but he never saw base ball games. Madison wrote the Constitution of the United States, and

Jefferson gave Democracy its birth, but there is no indication upon their tombstones that they were ever roused by the enthusiasm of a home run. . . . Athletic sports are the mainstay of civilization."

THE DEVIL'S SNAKE CURVE

A centerfielder named Billy Sunday visited Chicago in 1889 as an evangelist. He'd grown a red mustache since his last visit, and wore a black suit as he preached against Satan to a group of five hundred young men at Farwell Hall. It was his first visit to the city for his new gig as a preacher. His shtick was his career in baseball, and he pitched baseball metaphors at the men to save their souls.

The title of his sermon that day in 1889: "Is the Young Man Safe?" Sunday warned the men the Devil wanted them for his own. No man was secure in a big city—they were full of temptation. He mixed his baseball and religious metaphors and came up with an unsettling, though barely lucid warning for the young men who were present. Each good man should be careful: "He's the chap that the Devil in the box wants to pull on with a snake curve. Hold your base. Wait for your ball." The paper tallied his statistics that day: he "made a three-base hit" and racked up forty-eight converts.

A young man who'd listened to Sunday quipped, "Say, how he did line Old Satan's delivery out of the lot. . . . He hit the ball on the nose every time."

SAMPSON AND THE YANKEES

One day a man arrived at the Ruppert Brewery in New York and proposed a wager. The story has the tenor and significance of myth. It was 1896, nearly twenty years before Jacob Ruppert purchased the Yankees. The journeyman's name was C. A. Sampson. He bet young Jacob Ruppert, then in his twenties, a hundred dollars he could break a set of heavy chains with nothing more than his own muscles.

To prove the strength of the chains before the challenge, Ruppert and Sampson called for a team of horses. The chains were attached to a wagon loaded with fifty barrels of beer. It weighed seven thousand pounds. The horses pulled the wagon up a hill. The chains held. They were real. Ruppert agreed to the bet. Sampson placed the chains around his arm, flexed, and snapped them. Ruppert lost the bet and donated the money to charity. He didn't like to lose.

This is the origin of the Yankees' long and storied opposition to hair.

EVOLUTION

Nobody knows who invented the hot dog. Like baseball and people, they evolve, or devolve. It depends on whom you ask. Credit, for the hot dog at least, erroneously goes to Harry M. Stevens. He became the concessionaire for the New York Giants in the late nineteenth and early twentieth centuries. Legend holds Stevens was having a hard time selling lemonade and ice cream on a cold day at the Polo Grounds, so he put piping hot dachshund sausages into rolls and sold them instead. A sports cartoonist named Tad Dorgan is widely acclaimed as having captured the moment, and, since he couldn't spell "dachshund," he labeled the snack "hot dogs." That was purported to be in 1901.

It's a contested creation myth. Dorgan was a known prankster and a good friend of both Harry M. Stevens and Giants manager John McGraw. The myth spread casually until 1935, when it was printed in *Collier's*. After that, everyone believed the lie.

The earliest known usage of the term "hot dog" to describe the food dates to 1895. Until then, "hot dog" was used primarily by sports fans to describe a good athlete showing off his skills. People still use the phrase this way.

Baseball fans in the late nineteenth century were eating a food named after the players they watched on the field. Old-time fans were trying to consume the prowess of the athletes, ingest their strength, and carry it home in their blood. It was like killing a grizzly bear and making a necklace of its claws.

A ROYALS SANDWICH

Bologna is nothing more than a flat hot dog. A hot dog pancake. It was central to a forgotten old joke. I was in third grade, standing in the grass field behind my elementary school talking baseball. I had no idea what the World Series was. I had no idea why the Kansas City Royals were in it, or that decades would pass before they made it that far again. I didn't know much about the Royals or baseball, but I knew a version of a joke that sauntered around grade-school playgrounds: How do you make a Royals sandwich?

The proper answer has molded and decayed in my brain, but this remains: Two slices of White Brett, and a piece of Balboni. Put some Quisenberries on there too. Maybe some Biancalana.

Frank White was the Royals second baseman. Brett played third, and Balboni first. Quisenberry was a poet, and our star reliever. Biancalana was the shortstop. Now here's a joke: How would you make a Yankees sandwich? In Kansas, we believed the only ingredients were arrogance and money. We were bred to scorn the Yankees.

INVADING US, TAKING OVER, AND CHANGING THINGS ALL AROUND

A baseball team moved to New York City from Baltimore in 1903 and became part of the new American League. Everyone

called them the Highlanders. Their stadium was called Hilltop
Park, for reasons you would expect. After a while the papers
began referring to them as the Yankees. Their official name was
neither Highlanders nor Yankees. It was the New York
American Baseball Club.

I imagine a windowless old bar in Manhattan not far from
Hilltop Park, the kind of place where people ducked inside for
a quick double shot of rotgut and went on their way. A place
where newspapermen slouched after reporting the day's game.
I imagine a spittoon in the corner but most of the people too
drunk to hit it, or to notice the slop on the floor.

Inside, an old man sits drinking whiskey. His dark side-
burns are thick and threatening, like two snakes creeping across
his face and meeting under his nose. His chin is clean-shaven.
He's a veteran of the War of Northern Aggression. Probably
named Virgil. Left his tobacco plantation to fight at Fort
Sumter. Fired his rifle in self-defense as the battle erupted.
Narrowly missed hitting the Union general. After the war he
looked around, saw his land had burned, and moved to New
York City. I imagine him stopping by the bar every afternoon,
bathed, powdered, and ready to talk baseball. He's a Giants fan.
Likes John McGraw. Hates these Highlanders.

My Southern soldier speaks through me, the way I imagine
all Southern soldiers spoke: "Them Highlanders ain't nothin'
but Yankees, invadin' us, changin' things all around, takin' us
over." Every summer day it's the same. The term spreads and
soon the regulars all use it. It reaches the papers, then Boston,
Cleveland, Detroit, Chicago. The Yankee invaders.

THE FACTS

Big Bill Devery looked as though his father were a walrus and his
mother a musk ox. He'd been the police chief for the city of New

York during the 1890s, and a partnership with local politician
and saloon owner Big Tim Sullivan earned them an estimated
$3 million a year from graft. It was good career training.

Sullivan became a state senator.

Devery helped finance the Highlanders and also got
involved in politics.

In September 1902, a few months before the team's first season, he ran for the leadership of the Ninth Assembly District.
In those days, election betting took place at the Hoffman
House, a hotel that served as the "rendezvous" for the
Democrats. A man named Louis Bauer bet Richard Butler a
thousand dollars Devery would lose, which he did. The paper
elaborated, "Frank Farrell is said to have furnished the money
put up by Butler."

Farrell co-owned the Highlanders with Devery. He was a
professional gambler and bookmaker. He made money from
pool halls, horse racing, politics, and baseball. In 1903 the
Highlanders played their first season in New York and finished
72–62. A few weeks later Big Bill Devery ran for mayor of New
York as the anti–Tammany Hall candidate—a bad idea—and
garnered just over two thousand votes. Not much in a city of
millions.

The end of Devery's political career was a loss to New York
mainly because it meant he would be giving fewer speeches. His
language and erudition were a source of entertainment for
newspaper readers:

"If you fool me once that's your fault. If you fool me twice
that's my fault."

"No bald man has ever been president of the United States."

"I don't like orating. The people don't like it, neither. They
want facts hurled at 'em in chunks and right to the point."

Devery and Farrell began to work at the business of owning

the Highlanders. In 1906 Farrell netted $90,000 and expected profits to increase in the future. The Highlanders were never very good until after the pair sold them in 1915, but they made money despite their flaws. That was the point. Making money.

THE FARRELL COLT

Clark Griffith was a pitcher and manager for the Highlanders. He made headlines several times in 1906 not for his ability in baseball, but as the namesake for a horse owned by Frank Farrell, the Highlander owner.

The paper described one race: "The Farrell colt, named for the popular baseball player, already had won at Aqueduct in cheap company, and in yesterday's race got in light, though with a much higher grade of horses. . . . Clark Griffith trailed for a little more than three furlongs, then, making a move after Green Room, the pacemaker, took the lead about as he pleased."

In the midst of his success with the Highlanders and his horse, Clark Griffith, Frank Farrell drove his car into a telephone pole. The car was destroyed. Farrell survived.

On the same page as the newspaper story of Farrell's accident, a curious incident is described. A train company, the Pennsylvania, had issued a new rule: hirsute male passengers were henceforth forbidden from shaving their faces. The company collected fares using ticket books with photographs of riders, and men who shaved their winter beards were difficult for the company to properly identify.

It was April, and getting warmer every day. The commuters wanted to shave. They responded with an ingenious protest. They shaved, but created fake beards that they wore while traveling on the train. As they disembarked each morning, they removed their beards and let their smooth skin breathe.

Cleanliness and Democracy

Reverend Billy Sunday became a celebrity in his new career, and in 1908 *Collier's* asked him to name his baseball all-star team. None were Yankees.

He included a passionate defense of baseball as a clean, honest sport, and implied it embodied America itself:

> My interest and love for the old game have ever been intense, warm, and true. I believe baseball to be the cleanest sport in America and I never miss an opportunity to go on record as its uncompromising friend. Gamblers have never been able to creep in and spoil the game. Men in control, both magnates and players, have always been united in the effort to keep the game clean. All this talk about baseball being crooked, the game being decided before it is played, is all bosh. Such a charge is an unmitigated lie. This is my conviction and I would back up my statement with my reputation and all I have. I love baseball and know the game is clean, and I will not allow to go unchallenged any false statements. Then, too, the game is not only clean, but democratic.

Sunday found an audience because people needed reassurance. They sensed the democratic game was not clean.

"Luck"

When the Tigers and the Cubs met in the 1908 World Series, the Cubs thought they had a secret weapon. According to legend, they kept a young boy they called Li'l Rastus as their mascot for good luck. *Rastus* is a derogatory slang term used against African Americans. One version of the story says the Cubs had acquired Li'l Rastus from the Tigers' star Ty Cobb, who supposedly kept him under his bed and rubbed his hair for luck

before he batted. The Cubs were the best team in baseball that
year with the famous infield of Tinker, Evers, and Chance. Li'l
Rastus watched from the bench, and the Cubs have not won a
World Series since. Over a hundred years. Northsiders choose
to blame a billy goat for their troubles.

KNOTHOLE

At the time Billy Sunday was crowing about the cleanliness of
the sport, baseball teams who visited the Yankees in Hilltop
Park complained their signals were being stolen through a
hole in the outfield fence. They couldn't prove it. In mid-July
1910, the White Sox took action. During that era, outfield
fences at baseball parks were used as advertising space.
Centerfield at Hilltop Park had a sign for Young's Hats. The
White Sox had noticed the *H* in the sign moved when the
Yankees were at bat. Two members of the Sox crept around
the outside of the park until they reached centerfield, where
they startled two men, who fled. The White Sox "detectives"
found the holes, but they were too high off the ground to be
reached without a ladder. No ladder was ever found, but the
Yankees were tainted.

HAL CHASE

The Yankees had a new leader during the 1910 city series, the
first-ever match between the Yankees and Giants. First baseman Hal Chase had been appointed player-manager weeks
before, when Devery and Farrell fired the old manager, who
had publicly accused Chase of throwing games for money.
Chase was considered one of the best defensive first basemen
of the time. His skills illuminated his rare mistakes. Ban
Johnson, president of the American League, intervened and
declared Chase clean.

Over time the deposed manager was proven right. Chase threw games and paid others to lie down as well. Rumor has it he also helped the White Sox throw the 1919 World Series. In the twenties he traveled west, as scoundrels often did, and played in a league near the Mexican border with blacklisted ruffians.

TEAM SPIRIT

People have always argued about the role of money in the sport, but professional baseball has always been a big business. An old-time writer, Edward Mott Woolley, discussed the huge profits made by owners even during the dead ball era. He was dismissive of money as being the most important factor in winning. Writing of the Detroit Tigers, he said, "But even millions cannot make a pennant-winning baseball team, and back of Detroit's success has been that mystic quality which no mere cash can create."

It was 1912, an era when the Yankees were mediocre. They had yet to rationalize their business model.

CASH MONEY

Reverend Billy Sunday's fame and influence as an evangelist spread. Baseball, God, and America were his golden calf. He drew huge crowds and won the adoration of baseball fans and elected officials.

Sunday was a self-styled Mr. America. He collected thousands of souls and even more dollars. But a letter to the editor offered a dissenting perspective on Sunday:

> In the matter of financial profit evangelizing has
> got baseball playing forced out at first, second,
> third, home and then some, notwithstanding
> baseball players of class are pulling pay for their

efforts these days that make bank Presidents weep because they took up banking instead of baseball. Billy is no doubt doing good work, but he certainly isn't doing it according to New Testament rules.

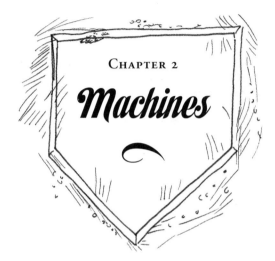

CHAPTER 2

Machines

The Way Forward Forever Amen

*B*illy Sunday ascended not to heaven, but to the White House. President Wilson recognized his clout and said, "God bless you and your work." In Washington, Sunday asked a herd of legislators where Jesus would find them upon His return: "Would He find you shrieking your head off at a Sunday ballgame? I'm for baseball; I played it professionally for eight years; I have played in this city. It is the cleanest sport in America."

Clean is a curious word for a game in which men slide around in the dirt, spit, scratch themselves, and sometimes brawl. But Sunday meant baseball was an honest game, and that ballplayers were more respectable than in the past. In some ways he was right. Facial hair was going out of style. The sport and its players were being scrubbed, processed, and made cleaner in proportion to the ever-increasing amounts of money at stake. The sport was being equated with democracy, God, and America, and it helped Sunday launder the masses.

When he concluded a successful revival meeting in New Jersey, the paper printed his statistics as though he were still a ballplayer.

Total Collections: $62,741.49
For Campaign Expenses: $31,482.71

For Charity: $6,258.71
Billy Sunday's Share: $25,000.00

OH, TO BE A HAIRY HELLION

John Titus was known for three things: playing right field for the Philadelphia Phillies, the toothpick in his mouth, and being the last man in baseball to wear a mustache before he retired in 1913.

It looked like a small brown bat had taken roost under his nose and stretched its wings, only to have them freeze in place. In the nineteenth century, it was common for ballplayers to grow mustaches and live rowdy, unruly lives. Players were not expected to have discipline, look clean, or be virtuous. Nobody cared as long as they could hit.

A couple years before Titus retired, taking the mustache out of the sport, the Gillette Safety Razor Company began using players to advertise their products. Honus Wagner was the best fielding shortstop in the game and a top hitter. John McGraw was arguably the smartest manager. They looked clean. Both were pitchmen for Gillette.

The mustache vanished from players' faces for decades. Some teams even developed rules forbidding players from growing facial hair. Even today, the Yankees discourage it, allowing trimmed mustaches but not beards, as if bristles could devour dollars.

FEAR

Hair turned baseball and money into an awkward threesome. Hair hinted of animals, of the nineteenth century, of the chaos of the Civil War, of the orangutan-like display on General Burnside's face. Money is frightened by irrationality. Players depended on their physicality, their brute ability on the field wielding clubs, throwing balls, and running. Rules prohibiting facial hair suppressed and denied their animality. Their bodies were crudely on display, spitting, scratching, sweating, breaking, and bleeding. Forcing them to shave was like putting a collar on a dog.

WINNERS

The Yankees floundered under Devery and Farrell, losing more than a hundred games in 1908 and 1912. The team's failure was no surprise considering gambler Hal Chase was their boy. Victory was a novelty. The Yankees needed owners willing to spend money, and Colonel Jacob Ruppert and Tillinghast L'Hommedieu Huston bought the team and began obliging in 1915. They were determined to increase profits by selling food and drink, but also by winning games.

Ruppert and Huston paid $450,000 for the club, and immediately began buying the best players in America and corralling them in New York. Home Run Baker, the greatest power hitter in baseball, soon joined the Yankees. In his best season, he smacked twelve home runs.

Knickerbocker was the flagship beer of Jacob Ruppert's family brewery. Father Knickerbocker, a fictional pitchman for the brand, proffered beer in newspaper ads. Outfitted in Revolutionary War–era garments, he looked like Benjamin Franklin with less of a paunch.

In one advertisement, Father Knickerbocker stands on a long wooden dock next to the ocean. In his left hand he holds a tray graced with a bottle of beer. With his right, he extends a frothy glass to the Statue of Liberty. She holds the torch of freedom high above her crowned head, and with her left hand she reaches for her solace. She is grinning, and rightly so. The copy reads, "FATHER KNICKERBOCKER represents health, honesty and cleanliness—hence the good, healthful beer that bears his name."

In another, Father Knickerbocker stands next to Uncle Sam, who wears striped pants and a white top hat pocked by a broad band of stars. Sam is placing a wreath around a giant bottle of Knickerbocker beer. When people drank Knickerbocker, they were drinking the best. They were drinking America. They were drinking freedom.

And starting in 1915, they were drinking the New York Yankees. The Rupperts were industrious, and explained, "We search the hop and barley markets of the world and buy the best; we use every precaution and adopt every sanitary method known in the trade of malting, brewing, bottling and delivering; we only employ skilled and experienced men in all our departments; every department is equipped with the best and most modern machinery ever invented for the making of beer."

The Ruppert Brewery mechanized its brewing process, just as Henry Ford had written of his new "motor car," "It will be constructed of the best materials, by the best men to be hired, after the simplest designs that modern engineering can devise."

It worked for Ruppert's beer, and then it worked for his Yankees.

NICE, VERY NICE
Barnstorming continued to be a fad, and major leaguers sailed across oceans to play ball for people not fortunate enough to be Americans. The New York Giants and the Chicago White Sox traveled to France to play exhibition games in February 1914. Their tour also included stops in England, Rome, and Egypt. The world absorbed American goodwill and peace.

When the teams arrived at the field in Nice, France, five thousand spectators gaped. Before the game the ballplayers put on athletic displays. Jim Thorpe, the Native American star of the 1912 Olympics, had recently signed with the Giants and showed off his skills with discus and shot put. Herman Schaefer walked a tightrope. When Schaefer came to bat, John McGraw noted, "He wore a carnival false face with a mustache, which brought forth roars of laughter."

The United States government had an official presence at the game. The American consul threw out the ceremonial first pitch, and the White Sox beat the Giants 10–9.

The players had arrived in Nice for Carnival, and partied alongside the French. McGraw wrote: "Everywhere we went through the crowds the masqueraders greeted us with cries of '*Les Americans.*' We were in the midst of the battle royal of confetti, and the ballplayers attracted much attention."

McGraw concluded his dispatch with patriotism, and a lack of awareness of European tensions: "Our party will start for Paris to-morrow morning, and we plan to play a game there on Washington's Birthday if the weather permits."

A few months later, a man named Gavrilo Princip shot Archduke Franz Ferdinand of Austria. Europe exploded. Then the world.

PROTECTORATE

Millions died before the U.S. entered the war. Americans served in the British Army and introduced baseball to Palestine. In 1918, the Clark Griffith Ball and Bat Fund equipped four teams of soldiers with uniforms. Ex-patriots continued playing baseball after the war ended.

A decade later, Americans in Palestine held a large Fourth of July celebration in honor of it being the first year the State Department placed a consul general in the territory. Festivities included a reception, an Episcopal church service, and a baseball game. The new consul general threw out the first pitch and gave a speech: "Americans are watching with friendly sympathy the prosperous development of Palestine under the benevolent guidance of the mandatory for the benefit of all its inhabitants."

America was formally supporting Britain's nondemocratic rule at the expense of Arab and Jewish voices, and celebrated by playing baseball.

Pay Attention

Big Bill Devery never returned to baseball after selling his Yankees. He died in 1919 of apoplexy.

Two years before, Devery had rescued ten families from a burning tenement building on Thirtieth Street. He had become a hero.

The Hall of Fame's Mustache Collection

After too many hours hunched at a table in the Giamatti Research Center at the Hall of Fame, I was falling asleep over my notebook. My eyes were dry and bloodshot, my fingers sore from writing. I did not have the focus to finish reading old scrapbooks and journals about long-ago games. But then, as I stretched and paced around the little room, I saw a package of fake mustaches affixed to an office window. The package described its contents as "Self-Adhesive Stylish Mustaches," and as "a mustache for every day of the week!"

My fatigue vanished. My focus returned. The package in the Hall of Fame window had been altered, personalized. It was Tim Wiles's office, and he was known for dressing up in a baseball uniform and reciting the poem "Casey at the Bat."

The mustaches were labeled according to characters from the poem. There were mustaches for Mighty Casey; Cooney, the player who died at first; Barrows, who did the same; Flynn, who let drive a single; Blake, who tore the cover off the ball; and a gray mustache for the umpire who called Casey out on strikes.

On the package, a man wearing a fedora warned, "Don't be caught in public with a naked upper lip!"

BABE RUTH

Things changed for the Yankees when Huston and Ruppert began paying cash for talent. They wanted to win. The team improved, but it needed more, better, sooner, and for longer. A fellow who played for the Red Sox named Babe Ruth was a nuisance for the Yankees. Ruth struck them out, hit home runs, and instilled terror.

He appeared in New York in 1915:

> His name is Babe Ruth. He is built like a bale of cotton and pitches left-handed for the Boston Red Sox. All left-handers are peculiar, and Babe is no exception, because he can also bat. Between his pitching and batting at the Polo Grounds yesterday, the Yankees were as comfortable as a lamplighter in a gunpowder factory. When Babe Ruth finished the Yanks were clinging for dear life to the slim end of a 7-to-1 score.

Whenever the Red Sox were in town, headlines emphasized Ruth's prowess over the Yankees.

"Ruth Lets Yanks Have Three Hits."

"Babe Ruth Menace Breaks Out Again."

"Left-Hander Ruth Puzzles Yankees."

Ruth was in New York in September 1919 when he surpassed Ned Williamson's record of twenty-seven home runs in a season. The paper proclaimed him "the batting sensation of all time," and the Yankees owners lusted. They paid $100,000 to the Red Sox for Babe Ruth and became nearly invincible for decades. Anything they feared, anything that humiliated them, anything that beat them, the Yankees pacified or acquired.

YANKEE KILLERS

Like Babe Ruth in his early years, certain players had a knack for thrashing the Yankees. Christy Mathewson was among the first, but he beat them in 1910, before the Yankees were a worthy opponent. During periods when no team could beat them, when the Yankees were the unquestioned kings of the sport, lone and often lowly players were able to excel when no one else could. Papers in the early decades of the twentieth century called them Yankee Killers. People love an underdog.

They didn't level the playing field, they didn't change the course of baseball history, but Yankee Killers managed to win a few games and their fans saw them as heroes. They were merely shin splints for Achilles, annoying insurgents against the efficient New York machine. Yankee Killers slowed them down, tripped them, stung them, bit them, hit them, and gave hope to the other teams in the league. If mediocre hurler Willard Nixon could beat the Yankees, maybe the Washington Senators could, maybe the St. Louis Browns could, the Brooklyn Dodgers, and so on, forward through baseball history all the way to the abysmal twenty-first-century Royals. These teams knew they'd never *be* the Yankees, and would never have a history like the Yankees. But they could take pride in the rare trouncing, in occasional revenge against the Yankees for being everything they were not: the best, the richest, the most powerful, the most confident. Yankee Killers punished the Yankees for preventing everyone else from *being* the Yankees, from being winners, from having a fair chance.

Dominant Dogs

Baseball ownership and management continued to wear mustaches even while players were shorn. Yankees business manager Ed Barrow joined the team at the start of the Babe Ruth era. He reflected on his old life in Pittsburgh: "I got to be a bit of a sport myself, and raised a mustache, a big fine soup strainer." Jacob Ruppert, dominant dog, wore a mustache too.

The arrangement was akin to the relationship of a queen bee to worker drones, and it earned the Yankees honey. They took third in the American League with ninety-five wins in 1920 but won six pennants and three World Series during the next decade.

Defeat at Black Bob Park

I was on the pitcher's mound, fourteen years old. But I was not a pitcher. My right arm was thin and frail, my hands too small. No curve, no slider, no knuckler, no fastball, no change, no mustache. It was my only appearance on the mound in my short baseball career—I was the relief for the real pitchers. It had been a bad inning; several runs had already scored. No outs, bases loaded again. It was dusk, the sky the color of marigolds. Sparrows sat atop the chain-link backstop, and girls from my junior high school preened in the bleachers. A mile down the road was the 7-Eleven, and I wanted a Slurpee. I could barely focus on the batter waiting for my pitch. I was thinking about sunflower seeds. I was thinking about *tits*.

After giving up seven runs and retiring only one batter, I was yanked from the game.

Back on the bench, where I started the inning, I chewed sunflower seeds until my cheeks and tongue were lacerated and sore. I used my calculator watch to figure my earned run average. It was 189.19. I pondered this embarrassment, and consoled myself by noting it would be a little lower if I took into account that at least one of the runs scored on an error. Other people's mistakes do not count against you in baseball's ghostly math, though they count against you in the actual game. And in life.

My arm hurt. My mouth hurt. I switched to bubble gum. I crammed in a pink wad of Big League Chew and chomped and drooled and blew bubbles until the sugar coated and sealed the cuts made by the sunflower seeds. My teeth glowed.

Finally my teammates joined me on the bench. The inning was over, and the other team had scored twenty-one runs. We lost thanks to the slaughter rule, which mercifully terminated the game if one team dominated the other. The floodlights at Black Bob Park shut down for the night, the asphalt dark and depopulated as we trudged to our cars for the drive home.

Mr. Bob

As a kid playing baseball at Black Bob Park, I never heard anyone explain how our field got its strange name. It seemed normal. Invisible history. Turns out Black Bob was a man. He led a breakaway group of Shawnee resisting control and removal by the government. His people tried to live and work communally. Black Bob's Shawnee resisted accepting the allotments of land the government set aside for individuals. He knew that private ownership caused infighting and property loss due to back taxes. Removal was made "legal" by President Andrew Jackson, and it was enforced with laws and federal troops. Apart from wholesale slaughter, removal was the most violent way the United States took land from Native Americans. The Black Bob Shawnee had settled in Kansas after being pushed from their homes farther east in Ohio and Missouri. They were tired of the pressure to relocate and wanted to stay in northeast Kansas, but in 1862 Confederate General William Quantrill's men attacked the Black Bob Shawnee, killing one man and raping several women. The raid pushed the Black Bob Shawnee still farther west.

These events took place near the park later named for Black Bob. I never had a sense of history when I played baseball there. At the time, the greatest tragedy about Black Bob Park was not the past it obscured, but the evening I gave up seven runs in a third of an inning.

An Errant Pitch

Ray Chapman played for the Cleveland Indians when he was killed by Yankees pitcher Carl Mays. The submariner had a reputation as a beanballer, and a pitch got away from him and drilled Chapman in the head. Mays initially thought the ball hit the handle of Chapman's bat. He scooped and threw to first, but the umpire was already calling to the stands for a doctor. Chapman died the next day. The ball had knocked loose a piece of skull and shoved the gray matter against the other side of his cranium. Chapman had set a major-league record for sacrifices in 1917 with sixty-seven, and led the league in sacrifices in 1919.

The Indians had previously been known as the Blues, Broncos, and Naps. Their star player and manager had been Napoleon Lajoie, and when Lajoie left for Philadelphia after the

1914 season, the fans chose to name their team the Indians. The Indians, the ballplayers, played in a state home to many Native American groups, including the Wyandot, Mingo, and Shawnee. In the midst of government pressure to cede their land, a Shawnee leader named Tecumseh rose and led the militant resistance in defense of his homeland. In 1814, the village of Cleveland was incorporated. Progress steamrolled west. Baseball soon replaced the horror of what had taken place on the land.

Referring to Ray Chapman, Carl Mays told the press: "It is the most regrettable incident of my baseball career, and I would give anything if I could undo what happened. Chapman was a game, splendid fellow."

A NEW HOME

Success led to expansion. The Yankees had improved under Ruppert and Babe Ruth and the Giants grew weary of their upstart guests. A new stadium was finished in time for the 1923 season. During preparations the Yankees bought a lumberyard from the Astor family, who had become fabulously wealthy buying furs from Native Americans and selling them on the luxury market in the eighteenth and nineteenth centuries. Their business helped yank Native Americans away from subsistence living into the cash economy, and when fur-bearing animals declined, Native Americans went into debt. They paid with their land. The Astor lumberyard became the site of the first Yankee Stadium.

The Yankees also bought two smaller lots of land for their stadium grounds. They were at 161st Street and River Avenue. A man named Peter Braschoss received $5,000 cash and $10,000 through installments for the land.

I wonder what became of him, whether he was glad for the windfall, or if he'd planned to make a home there and resented the intrusion. I wonder whether he became a Yankees fan, if he rooted for the Giants, or if he wanted to entirely ignore the national pastime.

ENTRAPMENT

The Yankees took a train west to Chicago, and a man traveling with the team suggested the players go to a nightclub in nearby Joliet. It was 1922, during Prohibition, and the team had forbidden the players from drinking. Jacob Ruppert's brewery had begun producing the legal "near beer," but he didn't want his players drinking anything stronger.

Manager Miller Huggins had hired a private detective named Kelly to watch the players, and co-owner Tillinghast Huston sent Kelly on the trip. Kelly was to report back if the players caused any trouble. They raised hell at the nightclub in Joliet, and posed for a group picture there: Bob Meusel, Whitey Witt, and Lefty O'Doul were in it. Busted. Babe Ruth, too.

But detective Kelly was the one who invited them out to drink in the first place.

RUTH'S LOGIC, OR THE EVENING REDNESS IN THE WEST

Babe Ruth barnstormed across the United States during off-seasons, playing baseball in small towns that lacked major-league clubs. For strength, Ruth's diet was buffalo meat.

For white Americans in the nineteenth century, buffalo had been a symbol of wildness and strength. William Cody, aka Buffalo Bill, had been viewed as wild and strong because he shot thousands. The buffalo he killed made him wealthy and famous, and their absence helped force western Native Americans to change their ways of life, join the margins of an industrial economy that did not want them, and move to reservations.

During his trip, a paper said of Ruth, "Boarding a train means returning to his diet of the past four days, wild buffalo, wild duck and wild rice."

Ruth said, "I'm going to get me a flock of buffalo when I get back to my New England farm. . . . I ought to hit 100 home runs next year on a buffalo diet."

Icon
Babe Ruth spent a night carousing in a brothel with a blonde, a brunette, and plenty of champagne. He left behind a half-smoked stogie. Like a phalange from a long-dead saint, the cigar now rests in a California reliquary. Joe Dugan, Ruth's teammate, recalled, "He was an animal."

The Importance of Etymology
Babe Ruth's maternal grandfather was named Pius Schamberger.
Pius is a name that suggests religious duties. Popes use it.
Scham means: genitals, vulva, and shame.
Berger means: mountain dweller or townsperson.
Babe Ruth was a modern, living god in his time. He hit more home runs than any other player. He had more fun. More hot dogs. More women. More cigars. More beer. Sometimes all at once. He was the king of New York City.

Participation
Newspapers offered free Babe Ruth Baseball Scorers to fans who mailed in six consecutively numbered coupons clipped from the paper, along with five cents for postage. The scorers were small handheld devices with round windows on the front through which numbers could be seen. The fan could now keep track of runs, hits, and errors for the visiting and home clubs,

as well as innings and outs. These little machines helped fans believe they were collecting facts.

HIPPODROMING

On a rainy day in Chicago, the Yankees were losing 5–1 in the fourth inning when manager Miller Huggins made a pitching change. They had already retired two batters, and the bases were empty, so the change was unusual.

The move caught the attention of Ban Johnson, the president of the American League, who chastised Huggins for deliberately slowing the game. The contest was rained out before it became an official Yankees loss. The crafty Yankees manager said, "I am not going to deny that we tried to slow up the game until the rain could wash out the defeat that stared us in the face."

THE SANDLOTS

George Uhle rose from the sandlots of Cleveland and became a star pitcher for the Indians. His specialty was beating the Yankees. Uhle held down legendary Yankees teams like the 1927 club, nicknamed the Murderers' Row.

The route to the big leagues in the 1920s, as today, was through the minor-league system, but Uhle was the best sandlot star in town and the Indians noticed. He joined the club in 1919 when he was twenty years old. Uhle and another pitcher, Slim Caldwell, beat the Yankees in both games of a doubleheader in September 1919. Caldwell pitched a no-hitter against the Yankees in the first game, which the paper attributed to his recently being hit by lightning. Uhle won the second game, initiating a habit he kept for the rest of his time with the Indians. He beat the Yankees six straight times in 1923 and five straight times in 1926.

In the middle of the 1926 season, the paper described Uhle's dominance of the Yankees:

> George Uhle, the quondam sandlot hurler of
> Cleveland, was the lad who twirled the lariat
> around the necks of the hapless New Yorkers.
> He roped and threw them with a fast curve and
> a faster straight one. Last Thursday, in the first
> game of the series, he hauled the Yanks back
> with one run and eight hits. Yesterday he
> improved on this performance by making the
> Yanks look like a troop of Indian club swingers
> out for a drill.

CHERRY BLOSSOMS DO NOT LINGER

In April 1927, a team sponsored by the Fresno Athletic Club traveled to Japan at the invitation of Meiji University. Most of the players on the American team were nisei, the first generation of their families born in the United States. One player, a right-fielder named Harvey S. Iwata, kept scrapbooks of his trip. He saved newspaper clippings in English and Japanese, ticket stubs from the ocean liner Korea Maru, brochures from the Park Hotel in Matsushima, details of social events at the Parisienne Ballroom in Osaka, and pictures of his teammates. Iwata had a poetic sensibility. It was cherry blossom season when they arrived in Japan, and Iwata included an essay he found about the flowers:

> The splendor of the cherry blossoms is feudal in
> nature. It represented the samurai's readiness to
> die for the State. Cherry blossoms do not linger
> like other blossoms in falling when the appointed
> hour has arrived, but before that hour they
> bloom in glory and splendor, as if they were
> absolutely oblivious of what a night wind might
> bring upon them. . . . The fact was the samurai
> was an unproductive class and its disintegration,

like the scattering of cherry blossoms, was only
a matter of time.

Iwata was not an average ballplayer. He seemed to value not
just the sport, but also the world around the sport. His teammates included Kenichiro Zenimura, the manager; Fred
Yoshikawa; Johnny Nakagawa; and Ty Miyahara. Miyahara had
once been a guest of Calvin Coolidge at the White House.

The Fresno Athletic Club dominated the Japanese baseball
teams. One headline read, "American Invaders Beat Local
Teams: Fresno Hits Hosei." Another headline described them
as "Conquerors of All Japan."

Westerners living in Japan attended the games, including
political and cultural luminaries: the British ambassador, the
military attaché at the American embassy, the American charge
d'affairs at the embassy, and a medical doctor. The physician
was an American who later raised funds to rebuild St. Luke
International Hospital, which had been destroyed by a devastating earthquake. He was in Japan to spread Christianity and
American sports.

After their tour, the Fresno Athletic Club sailed to the U.S.
territory of Hawaii for eight more games. Harvey Iwata hit .346
on the islands and was the star of the Hawaiian series.
Newspapers proclaimed him the best hitter on the team. A
headline read, "Smallest Player Makes Best Showing." The
Fresno Athletic Club returned to the United States in mid-July
1927. Harvey Iwata listed everyone's batting averages in a typed
sheet he affixed to the back of a scrapbook. He had 61 hits in
183 at bats, for a .333 average.

After they returned to California, news of their success
spread. That fall, the Larrupin' Lous and the Bustin' Babes, two
barnstorming teams headed by Lou Gehrig and Babe Ruth,
traveled across the West Coast. When they stopped in Fresno,

Kenichiro Zenimura, Johnny Nakagawa, Fred Yoshikawa, and
Harvey Iwata were invited to play with Ruth's and Gehrig's
teams. Ruth and Gehrig even attended a dinner held in honor
of the Japanese team at the Hotel Fresno.

The Biggest Chew

Art Shires claimed he learned how to play first base in Douglas,
Arizona, in the midtwenties. Several Black Sox festered there in
a league of exiled ballplayers. Shires bragged his instructor had
been Hal Chase, the crooked old Yankee. Shires said a lot of
things, and many of them were outrageous boasts and lies. He
was a different sort of ballplayer, a throwback to the days before
money and propriety became gods. He was the baseball equiv-
alent of Arthur Cravan, who had talked his way into the
Amateur Light-Heavyweight Championship of France in 1910
and later became a Dada poet. Shires called himself "What-a-
Man," "Great Shires," and "Arthur the Great."

The skin of his cheek was engorged with a giant wad of
tobacco, and he spit streams of gritty sluice onto the infield
dirt. Shires said of himself, "If they cannot remember me as a
ballplayer, they will remember me as the man who had the
biggest chew any man ever put in his mouth." Though he had
talent, his career was doomed.

Art Shires played in the Ruppert era, the period of increasing professionalization and domestication of ballplayers, the
period when owners began to approach their teams like they
were a complex piece of industrial machinery. And because he
was the *anti*-Ruppert, the *anti*-Yankee, the untamed spirit, the
country was fascinated with him. People read about his follies,
and for a few months he rivaled Babe Ruth for attention.

Nobody could control Art Shires—not even Art Shires. He
was a beast. All he lacked was a tail. The White Sox acquired

him in 1928 from the Waco Cubs. Earlier that summer Waco had visited Shreveport, where Shires fired a ball into the stands. Walter Lawson, a Shreveport fan, was hit in the head. He suffered severe injuries to his brain, and, after lingering several months, died in December. He was fifty-three. The paper noted, "The ball was thrown in the Negro section of the grand-stand by Art Shires, Waco, Texas, first baseman, after consider-able ragging by the colored fans." Petty revenge seemed the motive, but a grand jury exonerated Shires of any criminal wrongdoing.

Though he had yet to accomplish anything in baseball, Shires wrote poems about his ability.

> They is a Ball player
> He is the Great Shires
> Which he can paste that old apple
> Anytime he tries

Shires had a solid season in 1929, with a .312 batting average across a hundred games. But he made his name with his fists and teeth. In September the team traveled to Philadelphia to play the Athletics. Shires returned to his hotel from what he called "addressing my public" and drank a few shots of Prohibition gin. He ordered ginger ale to wash it down, and two policemen arrived with it. Shires claimed the next day that Lena Blackburne, the manager, charged him. Shires, who was only twenty-three and had played less than a full season, promptly beat up Lena Blackburne and team secretary Lou Barbour. During the brawl, somebody bit Barbour's finger. Shires blamed it on the manager: "There was nothing left for me to do. I had to give the pair of them a good trimming. The only thing I'm sorry about is Lena biting Lou's finger. The poor fellow had to go to a doctor to have it dressed. . . . I'm not so sorry about Blackburne's eye. I don't believe I ever gave a man such a sweet shiner. It was a masterpiece."

Art Shires wanted to make extra money to supplement his contract and earn back his fines, and so during the 1929–1930 post-season he began to stage boxing matches around the country. He wrote a poem to announce his decision:

> Great Arthur's been a chump
> And now he's lived to rue it
> Fought fights gratis
> It cost him bucks to do it

> Henceforth when Arthur blacks an eye
> Folks'll pay to see it happen.
> The kid's a pugilist now
> And soon he'll be a scrappin'

He smacked the hell out of a man named Dan Daly, but Daly later admitted he had taken a dive. Shires believed his own hype and arranged a match against Chicago Bears player George Trafton, who flattened the Texan but failed to shut his mouth. The Trafton fight was ridiculed in the paper, which published its own mock poetry slam between the men:

> Mr. Shires to Mr. Trafton
> I'd love to take a sock at you
> And knock you for a base.
> But if I swing and missed I fear
> I'd fall right on my face.

> Mr. Trafton to Mr. Shires
> You have the chin I'd love to smack,
> The nose on which I'd land.
> I'd hit you, too—ah, yes I would—
> If I could raise my hand.

Shires was banned from boxing by the Michigan State Boxing Commission due to the stench around the Daly fight. Commissioner Landis grew sick of Shires's antics, and told him to stay out of the ring. When he demanded a raise from the White Sox, the team grew sick of the young man who talked big but hadn't accomplished anything. They traded him to Washington, where he fit in better as a Senator.

Clean-Cut Boys

Philadelphia has the honor of having hosted John Titus, the player who retired the mustache from baseball in 1913. It was also home to the Athletics, one of the most hair-conscious teams in the history of the sport. Just as the World Series was beginning in 1930, a group of mug shots appeared in newspaper ads. They were the Philadelphia Athletics, every one of whom agreed to shave their faces with Probak Blades, a competitor with Gillette for the baseball player whisker market. Clean men: Jimmie Foxx, James Dykes, Joe Boley, Jack Quinn, Al Simmons, Mule Haas, Bing Miller, Mickey Cochrane, Max Bishop, Dib Williams, Cy Perkins, E. McNair, Bill Shores, Jim Moore, Kid Gleason, Lefty Grove, Rube Walberg, Wally Schang, Geo. Earnshaw, H. Summa, and Ed Rommel.

Their jowls, cheeks, and stubble belonged to the Auto Strop Safety Razor Company. Connie Mack's club won a hundred and two games during the regular season and beat the St. Louis Cardinals in the World Series. The razor company proclaimed, "Here's what every member of Connie Mack's hard-slugging Athletics says about the revolutionary Probak blade: 'Next to the crack of a clean four-bagger there's nothing sweeter than the music of a Probak gliding through your beard.'"

Champions of the World

Colonel Ruppert hired Joe McCarthy to manage the Yankees in 1931. McCarthy beat out Babe Ruth for the job. The new manager fit well with Ruppert's system: he was a fanatic about hygiene, insisted his players wear clean uniforms, and when they were at their hotel before or after games they had to look sharp. Ed Barrow, the business manager, remembered what McCarthy said: "'You're supposed to be champions of the world,' he growled. 'Well, go out there and look like champions of the world—and act like champions.'"

Babe Ruth himself had been an anti-Yankee like Art Shires. He was the id for the entire team, the unruly spirit on a platoon of pawns in white woolen suits. Such a man could not be put in charge of others.

The Conveyor Belt

By 1932 the Yankees had dominated baseball for a decade. They had spent money on the best players: Babe Ruth, Lou Gehrig, Tony Lazzeri, and Waite Hoyt were just a few of them. That year, Alva Johnson described Ruppert's strategy in the *New Yorker:* "He gathers in his raw materials like crops or ore. The coming baseball star practically rides on a conveyor belt from the cradle to Yankee Stadium." Once they arrived, Yankees players were expected to be neat, shaved, presentable, and sober. They were to behave as widgets in Ruppert's factory.

Reversal

There was one team the razor companies never got near. They were the House of David, and were part of a religious group called the Christian Israelites. The House of David was based in Michigan and raised money by sending a team of ballplayers barnstorming around the country. They played against Negro-league, major-league, and minor-league teams in the early and mid-twentieth century. They reveled in spectacle. Members of the House of David traveling team were forbidden from cutting their hair or shaving their faces. They took the field with beards, mustaches, and long hair. It flowed in the breeze.

Jackie Mitchell Strikes Out the Yankees

Jackie Mitchell was one of the stars of the House of David in its later years. She signed based on her fame as a female member of the minor-league Chattanooga Lookouts. As a kid, her neighbor Dazzy Vance taught her to pitch. Vance hurled for the Dodgers and was eventually elected to the Hall of Fame.

She signed with the Lookouts in 1931, and struck out Babe Ruth and Lou Gehrig. Ruth swung at and missed her first two pitches, and then took a called third strike. Gehrig swung hard at all three pitches Mitchell threw, and missed all three. After botching a bunt on the first pitch, Tony Lazzeri neglected to swing, and Mitchell walked him. She was removed from the game. The national press gave her a rough time. The *Washington Post* said that after Jackie Mitchell walked Tony Lazerri, "Jackie probably remembered by that time that she was a woman, and after all the excitement she undoubtedly wanted to go off and have a good cry."

At least in myth, she was another Yankee Killer, another David against Goliath. Her power came from the theater of everyday life. Ruth and Gehrig were playacting. They could have hit Jackie Mitchell. They were two of the greatest hitters in baseball. Lazerri was a Hall of Famer and could have hit her too, but chose the middle ground. The Yankees let her strike

them out because it was good for publicity. It brought people
to the ballpark. It generated money. Sometimes you have to for-
feit a battle to win the war.

MOE BERG

Art Shires was an oddity, a coyote in a league of dogs, but his
eccentricities were trumped by his teammate on the White Sox,
catcher Moe Berg. The two men were nothing alike. Shires was
self-educated; Berg graduated from Princeton. Shires was a
loudmouth; Berg was retiring. Shires was limited by his Texas
roots; Berg had an appreciation for other cultures and lan-
guages. And it was Berg's willingness to interact with the rest of
the world that made his life more interesting than the average
workaday ballplayer's.

In the early 1930s Berg joined the great hitter Lefty O'Doul
and other players for off-season tours of Japan. In 1931 they
destroyed their Japanese competition. The next year, Berg, Ted
Lyons, and O'Doul traveled to Japan to teach players about
catching, fielding, and pitching. Afterwards, Berg meandered
alone throughout Japan, China, the Middle East, and arrived in
Berlin as the Nazis took power.

In 1934, Berg joined another all-star team—this one featur-
ing Babe Ruth—on its tour of Japan. Berg brought along a
16mm movie camera. One day, while his teammates played a
game in Omiya, Berg slipped away to Tokyo. There he donned
a kimono, bought flowers, and went to St. Luke's Hospital, one
of the tallest buildings in the city. Visiting a patient was his
cover, but it was a ruse. Instead he made his way to the top
floor, withdrew his movie camera from his kimono, and
panned across the city. The catcher was on his way to becoming a spy.

MR. NAGASAKI

When Babe Ruth brought the all-stars to Japan, they were sponsored by Tokyo publisher Matsutaro Shoriki. Ruth was revered as a hero throughout Japan, and the tour was hugely popular. Like the U.S., the country was in an economic depression. Nationalist elements resented the visit by the American ballplayers, and specifically Babe Ruth, because they believed that paying them was sending cash out of the country during a time of need.

In late February 1935, a man named Katsuke Nagasaki stabbed Matsutaro Shoriki in an act of revenge for bringing Babe Ruth to Japan. The assassin believed Shoriki was insufficiently patriotic, and his association with the American ballplayers proved it. Nagasaki was a member of a group called the Warlike Gods Society. Upon hearing of the attack, Babe Ruth told the newspapers: "Yes, I knew Mr. Shoriki well and liked him. He was a fine host and full of energy and hustle. He wasn't in the game for money, but because he believed that baseball would be a good thing for Japan."

A Japanese businessman traveling in the United States at the time sent Ruth an open letter in response to the stabbing, saying that Ruth's visit to Japan was "one of the best means of promoting the Japanese nation's understanding of true Yankee spirit."

FRENCHY'S REBELLION

John Titus nearly lost the distinction of being the last man to wear facial hair on the field. In 1934, the paper reported, "One of Bill Terry's Giants recently started a lip hedge, but a vigilance committee overpowered him and dispatched the adornment." Titus's crown of shame lasted two more seasons.

Frenchy Bordagaray broke the hair barrier in 1936. The young Brooklyn Dodger arrived at spring training with a "narrow streamline type" of mustache. There hadn't been hair on a player's face since 1913, and Bordagaray's sprouts delighted the press. He had spent the winter in Hollywood, where he said, "The boys out my way wear 'em—helps you get jobs as extras in the movies." He had a bit role in the John Ford film *The Prisoner of Shark Island.* Frenchy said, "I did the best flag-waving since George M. Cohan in 'Yankee Doodle'—it was a masterpiece in flag-waving—and they cut it all out."

The movie told the story of Dr. Samuel Mudd, a physician who treated John Wilkes Booth's broken leg after Booth slaughtered President Lincoln. Mudd was convicted of conspiracy to murder the president and sentenced to life in prison. He was pardoned in 1869 by Andrew Johnson.

Bordagaray retained his bristles when the Dodgers traveled north to start the regular season in 1936. He wore them until a slump in May, when he was benched and his position with the club was jeopardized. If he'd hit .400, things might have been different. But the game remained bound by chaetophobia. It would be decades before players were able to wear mustaches and beards with pride.

THE PURITANS

After a long career in New York, Babe Ruth returned to Boston to play for the Braves in 1935. The National League club had been the "Braves" since at least 1913, but before that they were the Beaneaters and the Red Stockings.

Puritans founded the city of Boston in 1630. After thousands of years of Native American settlement in the area, colonists codified their control of the land. The baseball Braves were named for a word white Americans used to refer to Native American men they had battled. The word evoked men their grandparents defeated, humiliated, and expelled.

WHAT REMAINED OF RUPPERT

When Yankees owner Jacob Ruppert died in 1939, his sculpture collection was donated to local institutions. The Metropolitan Museum of Art accessioned the bronzes, which included several with frontier themes: *The Fallen Rider, The Snake in the Path, The Head of an Indian Brave,* and *The Scalp Lock.* That year the Yankees fielded one of the best teams in baseball, and won 106 games. The Red Sox came in second. Though the Indians finished twenty games over .500, they were suppressed by the Yankees and held to third place.

THEY SAY PIGEONS ARE INBRED DOVES

The great Ted Williams, arguably the best hitter to ever live, wasn't known for being friendly. But early in his career he did a favor for the Fenway Park grounds crew. The place was infested with pigeons, a bird viewed by many as no better than a rat with feathers. During the worst of the pigeon infestation, Williams arrived at the stadium in the early morning with his gun. Watched by Donald Davidson, the clubhouse boy, Williams shot the birds one by one. Then Williams blasted the lights on the scoreboard that tracked balls and strikes.

CHAPTER 3

War

The News at the Ballpark

*I*t was the start of the season, and I was struggling at the plate. At nine years old, I didn't understand that the goal was to win, or that to win you have to try, and that to try you have to *want*.

I was sitting under a tree after practice, overheated, tired, thirsty. It was a mulberry, one of many along the fence behind the field. By the end of most games, my hands were stained purple.

When my dad arrived to pick me up he gave the news. "We bombed Libya," he said. I leaned back in the passenger seat and savored the Buick's cooled air. Ronald Reagan had bombed Libya and its leader, Muammar Gaddafi, known pejoratively as "the Mad Dog of the Middle East." There was worry in my dad's voice. Should America be the policeman for the world? Can we bomb whomever we want, whenever we want? It was 1986. I listened carefully, but my highest aspiration was to see *Teen Wolf.*

The Oddity of the Everyday

Lou Gehrig's career ended when amyotrophic lateral sclerosis weakened his body. Early in the Yankees' 1939 season he removed himself from the lineup, and when, on July 4, the Yankees held a day of appreciation for their ailing star, he made his famous speech about being "the luckiest man on the face of the earth." Two years later he died.

Gary Cooper played Lou Gehrig in the 1942 film *The Pride of the Yankees*. It portrays the great ballplayer's skills fading and his strength waning. It is terrifying, and sad. Damon Runyon wrote an epigraph for Gehrig that appears on screen before the film: "He faced death with that same valor and fortitude that has been displayed by thousands of young Americans on far-flung fields of battle."

The film made me wonder what lay underneath Runyon's pairing of war and baseball. There is nothing unusual about what he wrote, which is precisely why I wonder how it came to be that way. The illusion of normality renders meanings invisible. A Yankee became a symbol for America in a time of war.

YANKEE DOODLE, DO OR DIE

That same year, 1942, the movie *Yankee Doodle Dandy* was a hit. It tells the story of theatrical producer George M. Cohan's life and career. Cohan, played by Jimmy Cagney, sits in Franklin Roosevelt's office and receives the Medal of Honor for his contributions to the country through patriotic songs and musicals.

Little Johnny Jones had been one of Cohan's biggest hits. The jockey rides a horse called Yankee Doodle for the English Derby Cup. After Johnny is suspected of throwing the race, he sings slowly, his voice full of melancholy: "I'm a Yankee doodle dandy. Yankee doodle, do or die."

In one of the major scenes of *Yankee Doodle Dandy*, a group of average American citizens marches along—a police officer, a blacksmith, a chef, a priest—and they chant, "We're one for all and all for one, behind the band behind the gun, and now that we're in it we're going to win it, there's work to be done." The crowd breaks into "My Country 'Tis of Thee" while they salute the flag. Uncle Sam and Lady Liberty walk into the song-and-dance number, and the song shifts to "You're a Grand Old Flag" while the capitol building looms. Another of Cohan's famous songs featured the refrain "the Yanks are coming, the Yanks are coming over there!"

DIRT IN THE SKIRT

In the early forties, professional baseball teams for "girls" were created to help the home front during the war. Decades later, Penny Marshall made a film about them called *A League of Their Own*. Comely sister milkmaids, skilled with their hands, try out for the league in a scene filmed at Wrigley Field. As the women walk through a dark tunnel toward the light, toward the glowing field, the scout who recruited them—a slick, mustachioed huckster—sneers, "Hey cowgirls, see the grass? Don't eat it."

After enduring obedience school, in which they are trained to walk properly; eat properly; wear their hair properly; cross their legs properly; and to avoid improper, though exhilarating, things like roadhouses, dancing, whiskey, and, by implication, sex, the Rockford Peaches finally win their way to their very own World Series. Before the first game, their poorly shaved, partially sober manager, Jimmy Dugan, bends his rickety knee and leads them in a clubhouse prayer.

Penny Marshall inverts the sport's bewildering piety by directing Dugan to pray, "Uh, Lord? Hallowed be thy name? May our feet be swift, may our bats be mighty, may our balls be plentiful. And Lord I'd just like to thank you for that waitress in South Bend. You know who she is, she kept calling your name."

One of the former milkmaids is traded to Racine and becomes the World Series heroine for her team, the Belles,

whose motto glows with a human touch Billy Sunday never
had the balls to savor: "Dirt in the Skirt."

MOTIVATION
New Britain is an island in the Bismarck Archipelago near
Papua New Guinea. It was a strategic location for the American
military during World War II, and marines were sent to try to
wrench control from the Japanese occupiers. Some Japanese
were still angry about Babe Ruth's tour of Japan in 1934, and the
"heroics" of blade-wielding Mr. Nagasaki were even more
meaningful in the midst of a war. Men charged American
troops, yelling, "To Hell with Babe Ruth!"

The events in New Britain inspired the *New York Times* editorial page to spin fantasies of revenge: "When the peace treaty
with Japan is signed it will be well for our envoys to remember
'To hell with Babe Ruth!' and not overlook the vital importance
of bringing about the elimination of the samurai, the Black
Dragon, the Warlike Gods and other secret societies in that
country."

STANDARD OPERATING PROCEDURE
In January 1942, not long after the Japanese attacks on Pearl
Harbor, baseball commissioner Kenesaw Mountain Landis
wrote President Roosevelt asking whether the sport should
take a hiatus during the war. Roosevelt famously responded:
"I honestly feel that it would be best for the country to keep
baseball going. There will be fewer people unemployed and
everybody will work longer hours and harder than ever
before. And that means that they ought to have a chance for
recreation and for taking their minds off their work even more
than before." Baseball, as a means of escape, was essential for
victory.

Near the end of the war, Del Webb purchased a stake in the Yankees. He partnered with Captain Dan Topping and Colonel Larry MacPhail to buy the team for $2.8 million. Over the course of Webb's long career as a construction contractor, he built shopping malls, air force bases, a Las Vegas casino called the Flamingo, and the first operational Intercontinental Ballistic Missile facility, from which the atomic Minuteman would launch in the event of nuclear war. Webb became famous for creating the Sun City retirement communities, where "oldsters" live with convenient shopping and entertainment options near their self-contained clusters of homes.

As in the corporate world, Webb was successful in baseball. He maintained a businesslike mindset while owning the Yankees. Webb standardized procedures, and his staff called it "Webberization": extreme pressure toward uniformity applied to people to make work more efficient and more profitable.

Within a month of Roosevelt's suggestion that baseball continue during the war, he issued Executive Order 9066, which forced people of Japanese descent out of their homes in portions of the West Coast without being accused or convicted of a crime. Japanese Americans were rounded up, imprisoned, and their properties confiscated. Roosevelt acted on precedent: it had been done to Native Americans many times in the past.

Roosevelt's order created an urgent need for housing. Del Webb's company won the contract to build camps near Parker, Arizona, named Poston. Most Americans at the time didn't know what happened to Japanese Americans during the war. The massive construction projects near Parker brought jobs, workers, and an influx of business to an otherwise sleepy region of Arizona, and the few white Americans who knew why did not protest. Webb chose to build Poston's three concentration camps on Native American land, despite arguments from the Colorado River Indian Reservation Tribal Council.

A map of Poston Unit I from November of 1942 makes the camp look like one of the Sun City retirement communities Webb would create decades later. The map shows a woodcraft shop, a drama center, a library, a hospital, a center for adult education, a barber, and a beauty parlor. The perimeter is clearly marked, but the fence is not labeled as a fence. Apart from the police department, there is no evidence of the fact that residents were not allowed to leave. Webb was a former semi-pro baseball player, and his camp included America's favorite pastime: the map shows a baseball field between the hospital and the Buddhist headquarters.

Harvey Iwata, the young ballplayer who had kept the scrapbook of the Fresno Athletic Club's tour of Japan, and Kenichiro Zenimura, his manager, were both sent to camps. Iwata went to Poston. Zenimura, who'd been born in Hiroshima, was in the Gila River Relocation Center, where he organized a baseball league. There were camps in seven states, and all of them had baseball teams. An anonymous prisoner in Poston wrote a now-famous poem entitled "That Damned Fence." Two lines fleetingly evoke a ballpark at night before the meaning becomes much darker.

> We seek the softness of the midnight air,
> But THAT DAMED FENCE in the floodlight glare
> Awakens unrest in our nocturnal guest,
> And mockingly laughs with vicious jest.
>
> With nowhere to go and nothing to do,
> We feel terrible, lonesome and blue:
> THAT DAMNED FENCE is driving us crazy,
> Destroying our youth and making us lazy.
> Imprisoned in here for a long, long time,

> We know we're punished—though we've committed
> no crime,
>
> Our thoughts are gloomy and enthusiasm damp,
> To be locked up in a concentration camp.
> Loyalty we know, and patriotism we feel,
> To sacrifice is our utmost ideal,
> To fight for our country, and die perhaps;
> But we're here because we happen to be Japs.

Units ii and iii of Poston closed permanently on September 29, 1945, as Del Webb was finishing his first season as co-owner of the Yankees. That day, as the camps closed and Japanese Americans regained a measure of their freedom, Del Webb's Yankees blanked the Boston Red Sox five to nothing. Spud Chandler, recently back from fighting in the war, pitched the shutout. President Roosevelt had been right. Baseball had proved valuable as a way to keep Americans in a state of distraction.

Years later, *Sports Illustrated* said of the concentration camps, "Both the wisdom and the morality of this project have since been seriously questioned, but at the time it was a job to be done, and Webb did it remarkably well."

BILLY GOAT BATTLE

In 1945 the owner of the Billy Goat Tavern, William Sianis, wanted to take his pet goat to Wrigley Field. The Cubs closed their doors to the goat. Sianis cursed the Cubs, and they languished for decades without winning a World Series. After a generation or two, winning was beside the point to the Cubs and many of their fans. Beer took on greater importance, along with hot dogs and the emotional buzz that comes from being perennial losers. The Cubs became the best team in the contest of who can be the worst team, proving true the old cliché: it is better to feel despair than to feel nothing.

ON THE TRAIL OF HEISENBERG

During World War II, Moe Berg, long retired from baseball, joined the Office of Strategic Services (OSS), the wartime intelligence agency later replaced by the CIA. Berg's code name was Remus, in honor of one of the mythological twins suckled by a she-wolf before founding Rome.

In late 1943, Berg was assigned to project AZUSA, and an important objective was to learn whether Werner Heisenberg, the German physicist, had made progress toward developing the atom bomb under Hitler. If Heisenberg was close, Berg would turn assassin. But German atomic science lagged behind the Manhattan Project, and Berg's gun remained cold.

BASEBALL AT LOS ALAMOS

When the United States was testing its first atomic bomb in the summer of 1945, a code system was created so its success or failure could be communicated back to Washington without worry of the news leaking.

"Cincinnati Reds" would mean the test had failed.

"Brooklyn Dodgers" would mean the test had gone as planned.

After scientists tested the first nuclear weapon, and knew the war in the Pacific would end, and that all life on Earth *could* end, the signal of unimagined triumph went back to Washington.

The message read: "New York Yankees."

ALL FOR ONE

It was only the third inning; the sun was still sinking, and we were ahead by eleven runs. The other team only managed to field eight players and there was a gap in right centerfield where we kept hitting the ball. Younger leagues had a slaughter rule, but not ours. We were too old for blowouts. Somehow, in my final season as a player, I had been chosen for the best team in the city league. Our coaches were in their early twenties. One had a belly like he was hiding a soccer ball under his shirt, and had short, black, greasy hair. He bragged he would go to medical school someday.

We were at bat, and the talk on the bench was about how terrible the other team was. We'd all gotten hits. The enemy coach, an older man, a father, called time, walked onto the infield, and motioned for the umpire and our third-base coach. We couldn't tell what was happening.

When the inning was over, our coach trotted back to the dugout. "They wanted to quit. I said no." He was angry. He looked at us, trying to gauge our reactions. I glanced at the other dugout. A kid was putting on a red batting helmet. I had been on the losing side and always welcomed the reprieve of the slaughter rule. But we thought we had outgrown it.

"Take the field," he said. I was taking my turn on the bench, but everyone else picked up their gloves and straightened their caps and jogged out to their positions. I felt no sympathy for the other team. I knew the quitter's son. We all did. He was a nice enough kid. We went to the same high school. Instead of empathy I felt disgust. Even though we were already killing them, I wanted them to suffer.

THE JOKE

In the documentary *The Atomic Café,* the screen shows images of jubilant crowds at the end of the war. Parades, confetti, kissing. It shifts. There's a black-and-white image of a radio. A hand tunes the dial and finds an old comedy routine.

Man 1: "Say, did you see that city where the first atomic bomb was dropped?"

Man 2: "We flew over Hiroshima for about half an hour."

Man 1: "It was a shambles, huh?"

Scorched vacant land fills the screen.

Man 2: "A shambles? It looked like Ebbets Field after a double-header with the Giants."

The audience laughs. The laughter hangs in the air as the screen shows blocks of the leveled city. The camera lingers on a charred baby.

Good Will Should Be Exploited

Twenty years after Moe Berg and Lefty O'Doul toured Japan, O'Doul was still invested. Friends, enemies, and now friends again following the firebombing of Tokyo and the slaughter in Nagasaki and Hiroshima, Japan and the United States both viewed baseball as a national pastime. O'Doul wanted to bring Major League Baseball back to Japan, and have a Japanese team visit the United States.

O'Doul met with the Department of Defense and the head of the Psychological Strategy Board (PSB), a unit of government charged with coordinating American propaganda during the Cold War. It was October 1952, a week after the Yankees beat the Dodgers in seven games for another World Series title. In a memo for the record, the PSB noted of Lefty O'Doul, "He apparently has met with some opposition in his efforts to take the New York Giants to Japan, due to certain major league regulations, and also to the attitude of the baseball commissioner."

But O'Doul was persuasive, and Dr. Raymond Allen, interim head of the PSB, agreed to call on Commissioner Frick to press the case for sending a team across the Pacific. In 1955 the Yankees made a postseason tour of Japan.

A colonel present at the PSB meeting between the ballplayer and the propagandists noted that, "Mr. O'Doul's activities have resulted in a great area of good will which should be exploited for the mutual benefit of all concerned."

MEA CULPA

Sometimes the gods have a sense of humor. During game four of the 1955 World Series, Yankees pitcher Don Larsen hit a foul tip into the stands, where it bonked owner Del Webb in the head. The Yankees lost the series to the Dodgers that year and then toured Japan. Webb's skull healed, and he went along. Only ten years had passed since the war in the Pacific ended: ten years since the domestic internment camps were closed, ten years since the United States detonated nuclear bombs over Hiroshima and Nagasaki, and fourteen years since the Japanese bombed Pearl Harbor. The trip fulfilled the aims Lefty O'Doul and the PSB had discussed. Baseball gave the Japanese and Americans something to talk about besides radioactive fallout.

Elston Howard, the first African American to play for the Yankees, had just completed his rookie season as a backup catcher and outfielder. He brought along a 16mm movie camera and shared it with Andy Carey, the young third baseman. Afterwards, Carey edited the footage into a silent color film, which they distributed to their teammates.

First stop: Hawaii. A young man, a Yankee, dances with two Hawaiian women. He's got palm fronds on his head and a lei around his neck. They move together. It looks like Billy Martin, the second baseman. The entire team, just off the plane, still in suits and leis, poses for a photograph. Down in front, the balding man, the one with glasses, the one too old to be a player and too distinguished to be a coach, there in the middle—that's Del Webb.

The Yankees are on a boat and gradually approach a small memorial. A dock appears. A sailor clad in white watches the players as they step onto his dock. They linger on the memorial, their faces blank. Solemn. Japanese fighter pilots killed 2,402 Americans here. Casey Stengel, the aging manager, wears a black shirt decorated with bright flowers. It is out of harmony with the mood. His mouth moves and words are formed, released, and carried away by the wind. Back on the boat, they pull away, and the American flag shrinks into the water.

The Yankees and their wives are crowded around a pool. Behind them is a thatched roof. They mill about, uncertain. Nobody swims. One player in front sports trunks, but the rest wear street clothes. Maybe Yankees are too dignified to swim, or not allowed. Suddenly a shirtless man rises above the group, in the back, sitting on another's shoulders. He is happy. He flexes both arms, fists downward, then flexes his right arm alone in a funny S shape, which looks like a cobra in a coil. It's Billy Martin, laughing, a moment before he's tossed into the water. The rest scatter, expecting reprisal.

Next stop: Japan. The team walks down the long steps from the plane to the tarmac. A sign says, "Well Come Yankees." The ballplayers wear suits, their wives wear dresses. Del Webb waves to the camera. During a motorcade through Tokyo, signs in English and Japanese welcome them, thousands smile and wave in the streets, and confetti floats in the air.

There is a large building with a grass lawn. Inside, Japanese men talk to reporters. An older man wearing glasses with thick black frames answers questions, and the five microphones arranged around his face look like rays of a setting sun. Several Yankees and their wives shake the older Japanese man's hand. The camera angle changes. It is Prime Minister Ichirō Hatoyama seated at a table with Casey Stengel, Del Webb, and their wives.

Everywhere the Yankees go in Japan, they are greeted by crowds eager to see Americans. The Yankees ride around in open-topped cars, waving to fans. The stadiums are packed, the Japanese media omnipresent. The Yankees visit Osaka, Nagoya, Sapporo. Locals give flowers to the players before the games. Red balloons are released and float toward heaven. The mood is light. Everyone, players and fans alike, seems happy. Baseball is a softer kind of violence than war.

The pleasant mood falls away. They are in Hiroshima. There are no fans, no convoys of waving Yankees, no welcome signs, no games. It could not have been a stop on the official itinerary. The cameraman focuses on a shrine. Shot from the side, it has the shape and look of a covered wagon, though it's built of cement or stone and emits a dull gray color, like nothingness extruded from the sky on a cloudy day and used as paint. A patch of sunlight illuminates its center. The light catches the cameraman from behind, and his shadow wavers. Several other shadows are there, too. They seem to reach for the shrine and almost touch it. Ephemeral as ghosts, their faces are never shown.

The cameraman has stepped around the shrine and moved closer to the building for greater impact. The dome, which had looked blue, is more visible now. It is not blue. It was a trick of perception. The dome is nothing but naked, skeletal framing for the cupola of a ruined building. The blue came from the bleeding sky. The bottom floors are intact, the top ones are collapsing. The same golden light that struck the shrine now makes the building glow. The clouds behind are dark, and the contrast gives the building an otherworldly feeling. Its broken walls make it look like the edge of a key. The building vibrates. The cameraman is trembling.

The front of the building is now visible. Locals pass on bicycles as though nothing had happened. They live with the memory every day. They survived. They are rebuilding their lives. The cameraman continues to shake. The image flickers. The ruined edge of the building becomes clear, revealing broken walls singed black. The camera pans to the right, lingering over the damage. Andy Carey, the editor of the film, devotes more time to this building than to any other image in the tour of Japan. Finally the camera reaches the far right of the crumbling edifice, then pans up to the dome. The camera is wobbling. It shows the crown, the empty, burned-out crown. It cuts.

A Japanese man stands in front of the building. He wears a dark blue coat and a white shirt, and has longish black hair. He looks grim. The camera focuses on him, then shifts to reveal his English-language sign.

THE ATOMIC BOMB CASUALTY SHOP

BOMB VICTIM NO. I K. KIKKAWA

I am introduced in the LIFE TIME

and other magazines as the Atom Bomb

Victim No. 1. Over half of my body was

burned by the Atom Bomb on Aug. 6

1945. I was taken into the Hiroshima

Red Cross Hospital stayed there for

6 years and during the period I had 16

operations. Miraculously I was saved

and now I want to support myself

Thank you for your kind attention

BOMB SOUVENIR MATERIALS

The camera cuts away, back to the building. But this time it starts with the pool of water beneath, where its image is imperfectly reflected. In the water, the building has come apart. Its pieces have eerie spaces separated by water. This aquatic vision of the building ripples and shimmers, looking like a memory, looking like buildings American scientists filmed during atomic bomb tests as they trembled, shook, dissolved, and blew away in a single overwhelming gust of burning, radioactive wind.

The cameramen rejoin their team and document the final game in Tokyo. The crowd is huge and people look happy. The players assemble on the field before the game, and one by one they walk to home plate to receive gifts. In a long line of Yankees in sober uniforms, there is Elston Howard, wearing a new orange kimono. The final scene in Japan is at the Imperial Palace. The camera shows the palace with a drooping tree branch in the foreground. The image seems styled after nineteenth-century woodblock prints, the kind Vincent van Gogh was inspired by after Japan was opened to the West by Commodore Perry.

Third stop: Manila. The Yankees play at a stadium named after José Rizal, the Filipino man who inspired a revolution against the Spanish, their colonial occupiers. After the Spanish were kicked out, the Americans remained.

The camera doesn't dwell on baseball in Manila. It shows a sign on the outfield wall that says, "1st Home Run, Dec. 9, 1934, Lou Gehrig" and another that says, "2nd Home Run, Dec. 9, 1934, Babe Ruth." It shows the scoreboard, which lists the Yankees lineup for the game: Bauer, Martin, McDougald, Berra, Skowron, Cerv, Howard, Carey, Turley.

Mostly the camera reveals life on Manila's streets. Clothes hang from lines in the space between apartment buildings, a woman washes her child in a bucket, kids and young men play basketball. Two men crouch in the road. One, wearing a straw hat with a broad brim and a blue shirt, holds a white cock by its frilly tail. Another wears a yellow shirt and holds a black one. The men's faces are turned down, toward the birds, away from the camera. The birds jump toward each other, and their feet collide in the air before their owners pull them down. The men whisper to the birds, and one touches its leg as though to encourage it to kick. Their neck feathers flare exactly the way a dog's hair bristles before a fight. Children gather.

Billy Martin and other Yankees loiter in the street with two Filipino men. They go inside a cockfight pit. It is dark, but the birds are visible. They attack. Feathers tear loose and float above a blur of feet and legs affixed with spikes.

After the fight the camera shows a field of grass. There, beyond a green hill, at the dawn of a neocolonial era, filmed by a pawn in the neocolonial game, stands a replica of the Statue of Liberty.

WARRIOR

Decades later, former Yankees owner Del Webb died of complications from cancer surgery. Before his death, he'd been asked to reflect on his long, successful career: "'I think the greatest thing our company ever did was move the Japs out of California. We did it in ninety days back in the war.'"

MAJOR

Ralph Houk played for the Yankees in the forties and fifties. He'd been a hero fighting Germany during World War II. He later managed the Yankees. When he died, his teammate Tony Kubek remembered him. "Ralph learned leadership the hardest way possible—seeing his friends and comrades die around him in the Battle of the Bulge," said Kubek. "Ralph had a few more difficult times in a leadership position, leading the remnant of a platoon in Europe, than managing a team in a pennant race."

INTERNATIONAL UNDERSTANDING

We were in the dugout, lined up against the chain-link fence, shouting for Klaus to swing. It was the short fall season in the county league. Klaus was a German exchange student living with our baseball coach. At school he wore black clothes and black bracelets. He was thin, pale, and had black hair. He looked frightened and awkward wearing his uniform, like a priest without his collar.

Klaus stood at home plate holding his bat with loose fingers. He was in a crouch, but looked like a poodle lowering its backside to defecate. His body trembled. I could see his fear from twenty feet away.

A miracle. Klaus drew a walk. He stood near first base with a six-inch lead, and we shouted that he should get ready to run. He looked back at us, nodded, and raised a fist with devil's horns. We cheered. The next batter hit the ball, and Klaus galloped directly across the infield, hurtled the pitcher's mound, and arrived safely at third base. He smiled and waved, not realizing he skipped second.

POLITICS

Art Shires was long out of baseball and back in Texas running a shrimp shack when he decided to run for the Texas state legislature. It was May 1948. "I'm going to fight the battle of the little man," he said. "The little man really gets pushed around in Texas." But instead of joining the Texas state legislature that year, Shires was charged with murder. He had killed again. On October 3, he got into a fight with his friend of twenty-five years, former baseball player W. H. Erwin. On the night of the fight, Shires had delivered Erwin a steak, but Erwin had responded by walloping Shires with a telephone.

Shires told the police, "I had to rough him up a good deal because he grabbed a knife and started whittling on my legs."

The police report described the fight and levied the charges. It said Shires had "willfully and with malice aforethought killed William Hiram Erwin by beating him with his, the defendant's, fists and stomping him with his, the defendant's, feet."

BLACK AND WHITE

My younger sister posed a question to my dad and me that showed she was thinking deeply even at the age of five, even during the late eighties, even with a Hollywood has-been for a president. She wore large glasses with translucent pink-and-blue frames. Her hair was long, and blonde, and she was smart.

She asked, "Why is Bud Black white, and Frank White black?"

Both men played for the Royals. Black was a Caucasian pitcher, and White was an African American second baseman.

42

Other players had passed as white before him, but when Jackie Robinson joined the Brooklyn Dodgers for the 1947 season, he became the first openly African American player in the major leagues during the modern era. Around the country, National League fans taunted and yelled at Robinson, but he endured. His aggressive base running and solid hitting won him Rookie of the Year. Larry Doby integrated the American League that same season for the Cleveland Indians. Their example put pressure on institutionalized racism in other realms of American society, like schools, restaurants, and the military. It also opened a lucrative new market for Major League Baseball: African Americans. Within a few years, the Negro leagues folded.

PUBLIC RELATIONS

During the Cold War, President Eisenhower encouraged widespread propaganda campaigns around the world to counter Soviet influence. The Soviets were outrageous liars but sometimes spoke the truth: they claimed minorities in the United States were discriminated against and had a lower standard of living than whites. To counter the negativity of Soviet portrayals of American life, and to reach the world's youth, the United States Information Agency shared stories about American athletes. The successes of Jim Thorpe and Willie Mays proved that minorities enjoyed equality.

BUSINESS AS USUAL

Hank Aaron stands at the plate, captured in frames of black-and-white film, a television commercial from the sixties. A disembodied white male narrates. Aaron is ready for the hit-and-run. He swings and the ball flies toward right field.

The commercial cuts, and the announcer stands against a wall in the locker room. Aaron walks in wearing a white T-shirt. His face and shoulders are reflected in a mirror. The announcer shifts from talking baseball to Hank Aaron's slick, clean-feeling shave.

The frame cuts to Aaron's face caked with shaving cream, a black man painted white. He pulls the Gillette razor across his cheek, removing hair and lather. Gillette—momentarily, publicly, unwittingly—whitened Henry Aaron to sell its razors.

He speaks, praising washing, lathering, and his Gillette Super Speed Razor.

The commercial shows fans mobbed outside a stadium, as if to imply what ought to be done with a black man who does not make himself white. There is a close-up of the Gillette razor as it sits on a shelf. Only one dollar, and if you buy it soon, it comes with a booklet, "The Secret Language of Baseball."

A TESTAMENT BETRAYED

Clark Griffith had managed the Yankees as a younger man during the grim years when they were owned by Big Bill Devery and Frank Farrell. Unfortunately, the biggest success Clark Griffith had in New York was at the racetrack in the guise of the horse the gambler Farrell named after him. After leaving New York, Griffith managed and then owned the Senators, whose main rival was the Yankees.

Griffith had paltry success with the Senators. Although they won the World Series in 1924 and made it back in 1925, they never won it again. They earned the pennant in '33 but lost the Series. By 1951 the Senators and Griffith had been squashed by the Yankees for seventeen straight seasons. That year, while living in Cuba, Ernest Hemingway wrote *The Old Man and the Sea.* By then Clark Griffith's glory was in the past. He was the old man who had gone eighty-four days without taking a fish. Baseball and the Yankees are a theme throughout the novel. Santiago, the old man, tells young Manolin to play baseball. The old man reads the papers to get the latest scores, and tells the boy to have faith in the Yankees and the great DiMaggio. When Santiago learns the Yankees are ahead in the American League, he tells the boy he'd like to take DiMaggio fishing. When Santiago notes that anyone can be a fisherman in May, but larger fish are out in September and the biggest caught in October, he's talking about marlin. But Hemingway is also talking about the postseason and the World Series.

Hemingway pairs Santiago and Clark Griffith in subtle ways. Once Santiago hooks his marlin, he compares its bill to a baseball bat. The marlin Santiago battles for so long and finally catches is analogous to Griffith's illusive American League pennant. When the battle with the fish is over, before the sharks eat it, Santiago says he believes the great DiMaggio would be proud of him. The sharks come because Santiago dips his bleeding hand, which has been cut by his line, into the sea. They smell the wound, the weakness, and attack the marlin as though they were the mighty Yankees facing the horrid Senators in late September. When the sharks arrive, Santiago reflects that he would have killed the first one if he'd had a baseball bat and could swing it with both hands. Hemingway imagines Griffith trying hard, coming close to victory, and killing several of the sharks that bite and tear at his prize, but in the end the sharks, the Yankees, take everything.

The old man is left with a skeleton, with nothing but his memories of having once been a winner. He constantly thinks of the Yankees, praises the Yankees, wants their approval. Santiago idolizes winners without being one himself. That is his tragedy. Mako, Tiger, Hammerhead: DiMaggio, Martin, Berra.

INTELLIGENCE

Allen Dulles, the director of the CIA during the fifties, was a fan of the hapless Washington Senators. Maybe he read his national security briefs while staring at a boxy new television set in the corner of his office, straining his eyes at the static as his team failed to fend off the Yankees. Maybe his radio was tuned in to ballgames while he and his brother, Secretary of State John Foster Dulles, went about their task of making the world safe for capitalists.

What becomes of a man whose favorite baseball team is a perennial loser? Cubs fans drink and blame others; Royals fans remember the glory of years past. After his long spell without a catch, Santiago ventured farther from shore in search of a monstrous fish, a fish that could earn him back his pride. His losing streak forced him to take risks. A giant marlin was the prize for his daring, but Santiago was soon reduced to muttering about the great DiMaggio as sharks devoured his catch.

The Dulles brothers had their own sharks, but they were not always Yankees, and they were not always Communists. Their sharks were an intense fear of a world in which foreign countries determined their own destiny, and the damage true autonomy could do to moneyed interests in the West. So Allen Dulles, playing the game of nations and working behind a veil of secrecy, battled his fears by venturing into foreign lands in search of a trophy.

Between August 15 and 19, 1953, Allen Dulles's beloved Senators played grueling double-headers two days in a row in Boston, followed by a series in New York. They went four and two while the CIA sparked a coup in Iran, overthrowing its prime minister, who had recently nationalized the country's oil supply. The Iranians wanted to benefit from their own natural resources, but Western oil companies stood to lose money. Using fear of Soviet influence in Iran as one justification, the CIA installed the Shah as the new leader. President Eisenhower was fond of the fresh government, and relations improved. Within a few years, on the occasion of the opening of an American atomic energy exhibit in Iran, Ike issued a proclamation:

> To the people of Iran, I send friendly greetings from the people of America. The Atoms-for-Peace exhibit is a visible sign of the Iranian-American atomic energy agreement, another bond of friendship between your land and ours. It is fitting that Iran and her able scientists join us in the development of this great energy for the benefit of all mankind. To the betterment of human life, the science of the atom will play an increasingly important part. It is good to have

> Iran and America working together in this
> promising field.

The coup in Iran was a stunning victory for Allen Dulles in a year his Senators equivocated for a record of 76–76.

The next season, the Dulles brothers did it again, this time in Guatemala, whose president had the nerve to nationalize banana fields controlled by United Fruit Company. Between the eighteenth and the twenty-seventh of June 1954, as the Guatemalan president was overthrown by a CIA-trained cluster of propagandists, troops, and bombers, the Senators were on an extended road trip, during which they won six games and lost four in Baltimore, Chicago, and Detroit.

Sports fans are known to enact peculiar rituals in order to help their teams win.

PARASITE AND HOST

A man named Arnold Johnson bought Yankee Stadium in 1953, leased it back to the Yankees, and then bought the Athletics and moved them to Kansas City. When the Kansas City stadium needed renovation, he hired Del Webb's company for the job. Though Johnson sold Yankee Stadium in 1955, his friendship and business dealings with Del Webb and other Yankees owners persisted. There were murmurs of collusion.

Throughout the fifties, until Johnson died, the Yankees and A's made twenty trades involving sixty-four players, and people noticed the A's lost more talent than the Yankees. The most infamous trade sent young slugger Roger Maris to the Yankees for the 1960 season. In his first two years in New York, Maris won two MVP awards, and in 1961 he broke Babe Ruth's single-season home run record.

Kansas City fans complained their team was little more than a farm club for the Yankees, that wealthy New Yorkers were preying on struggling Midwesterners. Yankees general manager George Weiss summed up the partnership: "The Yankees and the A's have faith in each other."

The A's owner died suddenly of a cerebral hemorrhage, although fans in Kansas City joked about how a man couldn't die from the failure of an organ he lacked. The new owner, Charles O. Finley, obtained a bus, painted its side with the words "Shuttle Bus to Yankee Stadium," and set it on fire. Smoke spiraled into the air and flames whipped through the bus to cleanse the A's of their Yankee infestation. But the A's soon traded their best pitcher, Bud Daley, to the Yankees for a whiff of Yogi Berra's jockstrap.

STEALING THIRD

I slid into second base. Safe! I called time, stood, and caught my breath. Dust drifted away. A double down the left field line. Not bad. I wiped my hands but left my pants coated with brown dirt like I was George Brett. As play resumed and I took a lead off second base, I heard a voice behind me. The infield umpire.

"Nice hit," he said.

"Thanks."

"What school do you go to?"

"Indian Trail."

"Do you know Mrs. Glenham?"

"She's my English teacher," I said.

"She's my ex-wife."

"Oh. She's nice."

"She's a bitch," the umpire said, but then added, "How's she doing?"

I focused on the pitcher's mound. He wound, and I sprinted for third.

LOYALTY

The Day the Earth Stood Still tells the story of a spacecraft landing on a baseball diamond in the National Mall in Washington, DC. An alien named Klaatu emerges, is apprehended by the government, but eventually escapes into the city. His only friend, and one of the only good guys in the movie, is a little boy named Bobby.

Klaatu warns earthlings that the other planets in the universe have become worried that humans will destroy everything with their atomic weapons. He is shot, revived, and tells a group of scientists who have assembled outside his ship that the choice is theirs: people can begin to live and work in peace, or they will be slaughtered. Though Bobby lives in DC, he shuns his hometown Senators and wears a New York Yankees cap.

THE RESCUE

The movie *Ace in the Hole* tells the story of a man buried alive in a collapsed mine. Chuck Tatum is the reporter covering the accident. He was a big-time newspaper reporter, but lost his job and wound up at a small paper in New Mexico. Albuquerque is abhorrent to him, and he's determined to get back to New York. As the mine disaster unfolds, with each passing day his

news stories become more dramatic and reach thousands of
readers around the country, so he obstructs the rescue to keep
his name in print. Meanwhile, Tatum rants about New Mexico
to Ms. Deverich, a secretary in his newspaper office.

"When the history of this sun-baked Siberia is written,
these shameful words will live in infamy: No chopped chicken
liver. No garlic pickles. No Lindy's. No Madison Square
Garden. No Yogi Berra."

Tatum pauses. "What do you know about Yogi Berra, Ms.
Deverich?"

"I beg your pardon?"

"YOGI BERRA!?"

"Yogi, why, it's a sort of religion, isn't it?"

"You bet it is. A belief in the New York Yankees!"

BILLY SUNDAY'S CHILDREN
Beginning in the fifties, Little League Baseball players were
taught a pledge:

> I trust in God
> I love my country
> and will respect its laws.
> I will play fair
> and strive to win
> but win or lose
> I will always do my best.

LA RUSSA
In 1954, Cuba was a friend of the United States. Communists
would not take control until later in the decade. President
Batista was in power and the island nation had casinos, luxury hotels, and fancy restaurants patronized by wealthy
tourists. A youth team from Ybor City, Florida, traveled to
Cuba to play baseball. One of the children was Tony La

Russa, who later became one of the best major-league managers of all time.

BILLY MARTIN

Billy Martin had a reputation for being wild. He liked to argue. To fight. To drink. Martin had the passion of Babe Ruth, the craftiness of Frank Farrell, and the temper of Art Shires. These traits caused him trouble with the Calvinist Yankees across the next four decades. Management believed he led other Yankees astray. The team dominated the sport, but found Billy Martin impossible to control.

While his idol, Billy Martin, played in the 1953 World Series, a young kid from the Bronx named Johnny Durkin was stuck in the hospital with polio. Johnny lay in bed dejected and depressed. During the middle of the series, Johnny's dad, Lawrence Durkin, told a friend who knew Billy Martin about Johnny's plight. Soon a gift arrived at the hospital. It was an autographed baseball and a photograph of Billy Martin sitting in the locker room signing the ball to Johnny. It made Johnny happy, and his dad wrote Martin a letter: "He never dreamed that you could find time during the big World Series to send him a ball. Some day, with God's help, he will be able to run again." Johnny's family sent Martin a photograph of the sick boy posing with Martin's baseball, smiling. The Yankees beat the Brooklyn Dodgers to win their fifth World Series in a row. Billy Martin, never a great hitter, had twelve hits and was named the World Series MVP.

THEM RUSSIANS, THEM RUSSIANS

It was a sunny Saturday afternoon during the late eighties. I had been moping around the house all day, bored, though I avoided saying so because my parents had declared it forbidden. My dad suggested I go to the park and see if any kids were there. I could organize a game of pickup baseball. When he was a kid, neighborhood friends would meet and play baseball for hours. He made it sound wonderful. As I stood in the kitchen listening, I imagined my friends down at Arrowhead Park, roughly a mile from my house. I didn't wonder how the park got its name. Instead I pictured hitting ball after ball into the outfield. I pictured striking out my friends. I was excited. I didn't understand why I'd never done this before. Pickup games!

I ran to my bedroom and grabbed my glove, bat, and a couple of baseballs. I bolted out the front door, down the street for several blocks, and cut through someone's yard. The infield was hard and sandy, and the outfield grass was yellow and burned crisp under the August sun. An old turquoise Johnny-on-the-Spot lay on its side fifty feet off the first base line, a victim of older kids goofing around. But nobody was there. The air was humid, thick, and still. No kids were in sight, though we dominated the neighborhood. The sound of cicadas echoed through the early evening, eeeeeh-ooooh, eeeeeh-ooooh, eeeeeh-ooooh.

I walked to the pitcher's mound, dropped my bat, and threw toward home plate. The pitch was high. I picked up my second ball, wound, and tossed another pitch. Inside. I would've hit the batter—if there were a batter. I walked slowly to the backstop, bent down, and picked up the balls. I walked slowly back to the mound. After a few more pitches, I quit.

Under the grove of trees behind the backstop I found several large light-green hedge apples. I practiced my golf swing using the bat, and blasted two of them across the dead grass. I grew bored, and swung my bat like an ax at one. It split, and its pulp was white with hints of yellow. I imagined I had broken the skull of a Communist. I beat the brains of several more Russians then walked home.

I had not given up on playing baseball. I called a friend down the street. His mom would not let him play outside. Too hot. I called another friend. He and his brother wanted to stay inside and watch *Mad Max*. With that, I gave up. I trudged from the kitchen down the stairs to the family room. I opened a can of fruit punch, a rare treat, and sat on the brown carpet. I turned on the television and flipped through the channels until I found *Mad Max Beyond Thunderdome*. I watched, listless and blank in the chilly air. Tina Turner sang "We Don't Need Another Hero." My sweaty hair dried in clumps. The punch stained my upper lip red.

WILLARD NIXON'S MONKEYS

Willard Nixon was never great. Over the course of his career as a Red Sox pitcher he lost more games than he won. His main talent was his ability to forge Ted Williams's signature. When a box of baseballs arrived in the clubhouse for Williams to sign, he would send them over to Nixon.

His other talent, oddly, was beating the Yankees. He did not lose to the Yankees between 1951 and 1954, when they were otherwise nearly unbeatable. He stopped them four times in 1954, four in 1955, and held them scoreless for nineteen consecutive innings in 1956. By this time Nixon was well known and feared by Yankees fans. In May of that year, the Red Sox played the Yankees in New York and Nixon was perfect against them until he walked Mickey

Mantle with two out in the seventh. He lost his chance at a no-hitter when Billy Martin hit a triple in the eighth, and Yankees fans booed. They booed *Billy Martin* for stopping Willard Nixon, their enemy. Nixon had earned their respect.

Nixon said, "I have no earthly way of explaining my mastery over them."

During the final month of the 1956 season, Casey Stengel offered his perspective: "I can't understand it. . . . That guy just makes monkeys out of our guys."

GOOFS

The writer Jack Kerouac loved baseball. In the forties, fifties, and sixties he played a private fantasy baseball game that involved a marble and either a toothpick or a nail. The game could also be played using cards. Kerouac created teams, players, and entire leagues. He played full seasons and postseasons and recorded them in detail. He wrote fictional news stories of who won and lost, and described fictional contract disputes. But he never told his friends William S. Burroughs and Allen Ginsberg about his fantasy baseball game. Like Mark Twain, Kerouac discovered the seepage between the culture and the sport. He created the New York Chevvies, the Philadelphia Pontiacs, and the Boston Fords, who starred Pancho Villa in centerfield.

HOLINESS

In the Robert Frank film *Pull My Daisy*, young Beats seem confused, intrigued, or both. They have brought a bishop to their apartment for a conversation. He is drinking tea at the kitchen table, surrounded by self-conscious writers drinking beer. They all look about the same age, twenties or early thirties.

Kerouac narrates in a whimsical, ironic tone and speaks the parts for those present.

"'Yes, uh, kind of strange and interesting evening,' says the bishop."

The camera shows an older woman who had come with the bishop. His mother. She looks dour. Kerouac's narration makes the bishop seem confused. The frame freezes on his face, too young to shave. The frames of his glasses are clear plastic. His expression is dull. He knows he's outnumbered. The camera cuts to his hands and his cigarette, whose ash is nearly half its length. Kerouac narrates:

"Peter says, uh, had you ever played baseball and seen girls with tight dresses? The bishop says, uh, well, I've seen, uh yes I suppose so.' He says, 'Is baseball holy?'"

The screen shows young poet Peter Orlovsky pulling a cigarette from behind his ear and swinging it like a bat, and the bishop blinks and repeats to Peter, and to himself, "Is baseball holy?"

The film cuts to an outdoor scene, and the women from the party and others are standing and listening to the bishop preach. It's windy. A woman holds an American flag next to the bishop, the wind blowing and tearing at the flag. It snaps into the bishop's face as he speaks. Kerouac's narration is silent as melancholy music plays. The bishop continues speaking, but the flag keeps whipping and fluttering into his eyes, and soon the bishop's visage is completely obscured. He turns, shakes the flag away, and resumes preaching. The crowd below recites a prayer or sings a song, and the flag again smacks him in the face.

STERN ADVICE

Casey Stengel sits in the Yankees dugout. It's the midfifties, and he's nearing the end of his career. His face is wrinkled. He is uncomfortable, like a man who knows he's being looked at. It's a television commercial for Gillette razors. A disembodied male voice says the Yankee wizard figures *all* the angles.

The film cuts to Stengel in his office. He still wears his uniform, legs crossed. There are books on his shelves. Mel Allen, the famous baseball announcer, stands next to Stengel looking dapper, clean, smooth, safe. Like a pile of money.

Stengel says, "There's something special about being a Yankee. We want our boys to be a credit to the club anywhere. Know what we tell 'em? Especially the youngsters. To act and look like champions, to dress neat, and keep clean shaved."

Lew Burdette's Blarney Stone

The Yankees were easily the best team of the fifties, but they were stopped by Braves pitcher Lew Burdette during the 1957 World Series. The Braves were good, even great. They had Hank Aaron, who remains the all-time home run king of Major League Baseball*, Eddie Mathews, and Warren Spahn. Pitcher Bob Buhl had eighteen wins that year. But the Yankees were better. Don Larsen had pitched a perfect game in the World Series the year before. The Yankees were used to winning in the postseason.

Burdette had once been a Yankee himself, but was traded to the Braves in 1951 after being given just one inning to prove himself. It was humiliating for Burdette, because the Yankees sent him away in exchange for aging pitcher Johnny Sain, who'd already lost thirteen games at the time of the trade. Burdette had a reputation for throwing spitballs.

An article appeared in the paper after Burdette won the first game of the series. He was listed as the author, and attributed his victory to a good luck charm: "I had a little something extra going for me today that the Yankees didn't know about—a piece of Blarney stone I stuck in my jacket pocket before I came out to the park."

Whether it was the lucky Blarney stone, the spitballs, or the need to avenge his humiliation, Burdette beat them twice more. He shut them out in game seven in the Bronx, and the Braves manager was so happy he told the papers, "Oh, that Burdette, if he could cook I'd marry him."

NEXUS

In 1957 a hundred thousand people crammed into Yankee Stadium to hear Reverend Billy Graham preach during his latest "crusade." That was the term he chose to describe the popular meetings in which he converted nonbelievers in huge numbers. Unlike the actual crusades, Graham declined to use swords. Among the guests of honor on the stage was Vice President Richard Nixon. Graham introduced Nixon, describing him as an "ambassador of good will, a young man with vision, integrity and courage." In his remarks, Nixon told the crowd he bore greetings from President Eisenhower, and assumed a pious air: "We as a people can be only as great as the faith we have in God."

In his Yankee Stadium sermon, Billy Graham fused religion and politics: "The principles of Christ form the only ideology hot enough to stop communism."

The paper noted, "There were no similarities in his delivery to that of the late Billy Sunday, who never missed an opportunity to 'slug it out with the devil,' in a dramatic pantomime of a baseball game."

THE MILWAUKEE EFFECT

After the Soviet Union launched Sputnik, the world's first satellite, in the fall of 1957, the United States tried and failed to launch its own. The Soviets were suddenly ahead in the Space Race. In November the Communists launched Sputnik II, and their little dog Laika became the first animal to orbit the earth. A month later, Vanguard, the American rocket designed to launch a satellite, exploded just four feet off the launch pad. The American government was embarrassed, the public was furious and afraid, but the Canadians enjoyed the spectacle. Toronto audiences watching newsreel footage of the Vanguard explosion cheered. It was about time the United States got a dose of humility.

The next fall the Yankees played the Milwaukee Braves again in the World Series. United States Information Agency director George V. Allen—a man charged with implementing psychological warfare and propaganda programs overseas—briefed the National Security Council on what he called the "Milwaukee Effect." He noted that in the ongoing World Series, the Braves drew "many friends whose only interest in the contest is to see the leading team brought down to size." The Yankees, along with the United States itself, had "dominated the big leagues for a number of years." And that was why the residents of Toronto, and so many other people around the world, took such delight when the Soviets beat the Americans to space. Allen continued: "Our chief problem is to grow up psychologically. We boast about our richness, our bigness, and our strength. We talk about our tall buildings, our motorcars, and our income. Nations, like people, who boast can expect others to cheer when they fail."

Everyone loves a Yankee Killer. Except a Yankee.

MENTAL TOUGHNESS

It was my last year playing ball on a real team, the best in the city league. Our first baseman took a stick of eye black before a game and painted his face with jagged lightning bolts like Gene Simmons from KISS. He was rumored to have once shaved his head, eyebrows, legs, arms, and any other place that held patches of hair. Before and after games my teammates stood around hot-boxing cigarettes.

I had lost the ability to swing a bat. It was my Mackey Sasser moment, my Chuck Knoblauch syndrome. Those guys, Sasser for the Mets, Knoblauch for the Yankees, suddenly, inexplicably, lost the ability to throw. Their arms were fine, but their minds weren't. I wanted to swing, my body was healthy, but I couldn't. I hadn't swung since the first game of the season, when I doubled. Afterwards, I had begun reading Ted Williams's autobiography. Williams said he was great because he always waited for the perfect pitch. So I began waiting for *my* perfect pitch. I kept waiting. I stood there and either walked or struck out looking every time, a victim of my own psychological warfare.

One game, near the end of the season, I stood at the plate. The bases were empty, two outs, and I was looking down the third base line at my coach. He flashed signs. At first I failed to understand. He gave me the hit and run. I stepped out of the box and raised the palm of one hand to ask what he was doing. He slapped his thigh, wiped his brow and clapped twice. No question: hit and run.

It's a play usually enacted with a runner on first base and fewer than two outs. In fact, it's *only* enacted with runners on base and fewer than two outs. Suddenly I realized our team lacked a sign for "swing no matter what," which was why he gave me the hit and run. Because I had not swung my bat in five weeks. I nodded, stepped in, and swung. The ball dribbled down the third base line, which I beat out for a hit, one of the last of my career.

FRANK STRONG LARY

Frank Lary was the most effective Yankee Killer of the late fifties and early sixties. He pitched mostly for the Tigers, and had a solid overall record of 128–116. For most of his career he was an average pitcher, but against the Yankees he was a *great* pitcher. Lary beat them twenty-eight times over the years. Remove his wins against the Yankees, and Lary would have a lifetime losing record.

Like some who did well against the Yankees, Lary claimed not to know why. "Better pitchers than I have had little success against them. They've been tough for me, too, but I've managed to beat them fairly consistently. Don't ask me why. I really don't know unless I unconsciously bear down a little harder against them because of their reputation."

During 1958, the year he won seven games against them, the paper described the pattern: "Frank Lary, the Detroit right-hander whose middle name is Strong, was precisely that sort of pitcher—as usual—against the Yankees yesterday at the Stadium."

OBSESSION

Baseball Nut! Vanilla ice cream with nuts and a dark raspberry vein. Throughout my childhood, it was my dad's favorite flavor at Baskin-Robbins. It was created to commemorate the Brooklyn Dodgers' move to Los Angeles, one of the most infamous events in baseball history. My dad had been a Dodgers fan as a kid because their AM signal somehow traveled halfway across the country to find his radio in rural Minnesota. Duke Snider, Brooklyn's slugger, was never the same after the team journeyed west. The market's invisible hand had taken a good thing, ruined it, memorialized it, and convinced the public to celebrate the change. Baseball Nut!

GASOLINE

A group of Yankees went to the Copacabana nightclub to celebrate Billy Martin's twenty-ninth birthday in 1957. While Sammy Davis Jr. performed, they got into a fight with a bowling team. The Yankees fined Yogi Berra, Whitey Ford, Johnny Kucks, Hank Bauer, and Martin for their roles in the fight. A few weeks after the fight, Martin was exiled to Kansas City as part of a seven-player trade. Martin had recently said, "What makes me a 'bad boy'? All I know is that I'll play my heart out for Stengel at all times. I am 100 percent loyal to him." The Yankees had decided Billy Martin made Mickey Mantle drink and was leading Johnny Kucks astray. Mantle was their best asset. Martin was too passionate for the Yankees. He wasn't docile.

Bobby Richardson replaced Martin at second base. Richardson had majored in accounting in college. He was a good player, had better statistics than Martin. He also wasn't the type to dance with Hawaiian ladies wearing palm fronds or parade about on someone's shoulder and get dumped into the pool. He didn't fight. Richardson was a manageable asset, a piston in the engine. Billy Martin was the gasoline.

INFIDEL

Widespread rumors that Fidel Castro once tried out for the Washington Senators or the New York Yankees are false, but it's true he liked baseball. After he seized control of Cuba in 1959, Fidel played exhibition games with a team called *Barbudos,* which in English means "Bearded Ones." It was almost as if he were challenging the norms of American baseball by flaunting his beard.

In January 1961, a Cuban employee at the American military base in Guantanamo Bay claimed the Americans there had tortured him. Fidel spoke at a rally for thirty thousand people after the party's paper, *Revolution,* ran the provocative headline "Yankees Torture a Cuban Worker." It was ironic. Cuba itself was known to torture its enemies, and it was decades before the Americans themselves sanctioned the use of torture. Fidel's regime suppressed dissent, freedom of speech, and other rights Americans took for granted.

In early 1961 Allen Dulles was the victim of a coup performed by Major League Baseball. His Senators began their season not in Washington, but in Minnesota. Back in DC, a team called the Senators played its games, but they were the Senators in name only. It was an expansion team inserted by the league. The real Senators had been exiled to the hinterlands, where, in a gesture akin to a deposed and exiled ruler entering the Witness Protection Program, they changed their name to the Twins to obscure an unpleasant past.

As the major-league season was getting underway and these depressing facts were doubtless weighing upon Mr. Dulles, a CIA-trained paramilitary group sailed toward Cuba. This time the issue wasn't oil, or bananas, but the real thing—a genuine bearded Communist ninety miles from Florida with an interest in missiles. American aircraft and ships provided inadequate support for the botched attack. A man named Manuel Perez Salvador operated a machine gun on the prow of a ship called the *Houston.* Salvador had been a catcher for the Class C Fort Lauderdale Braves of the Florida International League. In five hours during the invasion he fired five thousand bullets. When the attack failed to wrest Castro from power, the American public learned the invasion had been secretly planned and carried out by the CIA. The Bay of Pigs was the end of Allen Dulles. The newly installed Senators of Washington lost a hundred games that season, and each of the next three seasons.

Far from the sordid drama of Washington, Billy Martin, by then a journeyman on the Twins, played his final season at second base. He then began his long metamorphosis into a manager.

Exports

John F. Kennedy's administration did not always have an easy relationship with Japan. In 1962, to remain in good standing, Kennedy refused a recommendation that he raise tariffs for the export of baseball gloves.

Psyche-Outs

Gaylord Perry is a member of the Hall of Fame, as he should be. But he deserves it partly for being one of the best practitioners of psychological warfare the sport has ever known. Toward the middle of his career, even when he wasn't throwing his sinking spitter or devastating greaser, he touched his throwing hand to his "decoys." These were spots the umpires and batters assumed he'd smeared with grease. Before each pitch, he ritually touched his hat, wrist, hair, ear, neck, belt, armpit, and sundry other places just to scare the batter. Then he'd throw a regular fastball and catch the hitter off guard. "I just want to lead the league every year in psyche-outs," Perry said.

To Be Owned

The Hustler is a movie about pool, but you can also apply it to the Yankees and professional baseball as a whole. The film was released in 1961, the pinnacle of the Yankees' domination of the American League and the year Roger Maris broke the single-season home run record. Paul Newman stars as the undisciplined but skilled Fast Eddie Felson, and Jackie Gleason as the less talented but more successful older player, Minnesota Fats. Burt Gordon, who manages Fats and later Felson, is played by George C. Scott.

Fast Eddie is a stand-in for Billy Martin, albeit one with more natural ability. Eddie tells his girlfriend, Sarah, played by Piper Laurie, why he showed up a group of two-bit hustlers and got his own thumbs broken.

> I just had to show those creeps and those punks what the game is like when it's great when it's *really* great. Anything can be great, anything can be great. I don't care, bricklaying can be great. If a guy *knows*. If he knows what he's doing and why and he can make it come off.

Sarah pauses, and responds, "You're not a loser, Eddie, you're a winner. Some men never get to feel that way about anything."

At the end of the movie, Fast Eddie easily beats Fats. What nobody notices is that Fast Eddie Felson and Minnesota Fats are on the *same team*. They are the players, the ones who *do*. I understand what Sarah was saying about people like Burt Gordon. They are the losers. They never know what it's like to be good at something. They get their strength by controlling players with talent, guys like Felson and Fats. And Billy Martin.

Burt Gordon barks, "Where do you think you're going? Eddie!? You owe me MONEY!" As Eddie's owner he had extracted much of his winnings on their tour through Kentucky. Fats had his routine to make himself focus, Fast Eddie had his "fast and loose" style, and they both had talent and the admiration of the crowd. But all Burt Gordon had was a nice car, his dark sunglasses, and a need to dominate people. He arranged the matches he wanted, created the rules, controlled his players, and treated anyone who seemed an impediment to victory like a horse with a broken leg. Burt Gordon is the Yankee in this movie. And not merely a Yankee, but an owner. Burt Gordon is Del Webb, whose riches came from manufacturing

the maze that people ran within: shopping malls, baseball
games, retirement communities, casinos, and internment
camps, with a hefty cut for his purse and the consummation
of his American dream.

CHAPTER 4

Animals

THE CYCLE

*W*hile living in Chicago I visited Wrigley Field one sunny afternoon. It was another sellout, and the stands were littered with blue and red. Vendors sold hot dogs, pretzels, cotton candy, beer. Three innings in, the Reds were winning. We went down in order again, and I stood, stretched, and walked to the restroom. I took my place at the long silver trough, wedged between forty or fifty other Cubs fans. Beer, piss, beer, piss. It is a familiar routine at every sports stadium. For many in Wrigleyville, it is beer, piss, beer, piss, beer, piss, lose. Bar, beer, beer, home, puke, piss.

Mine was clear and splattered against the back of the trough. As I felt relief I wondered whether it came from a hidden meaning in the beer-piss cycle. The park was crowded. Although I was surrounded on all sides by my fellow Cubs fans, I saw some Reds jerseys. I thought nothing of it. I drank, walked to the bathroom, and pissed into a trough as though on autopilot. Rather than mere relief, I was marking my territory like a dog lifting its leg. It was like the scene from the movie *Never Cry Wolf,* where the biologist drinks cup after cup of tea and then hops around his tent, marking his territory to keep the wolves at bay. There at Wrigley, I claimed a space among the other dogs.

HUNTING THE COW

One fall after the season ended, Billy Martin and Mickey Mantle went deer hunting near Kansas City. They stopped at a farmer's house to ask if they could hunt on his land. Martin got out of the car, walked to the door, and talked to the old farmer, who proposed a deal. The Yankees could hunt on his property if they would shoot his ailing cow. The animal was ill but the farmer didn't have the heart to shoot it himself. He loved the cow. Martin agreed and walked back to their car.

Bastard won't let us hunt, he told Mantle. Martin slowly drove the car along the edge of the property. Soon they came to a field, and Martin spotted the sick cow in the herd of healthy animals.

I'll show him, Martin said. He stopped the car, grabbed his rifle, and got out. He aimed and shot the cow in the head, killing it. Mantle fell for the trick. He opened his door and raised his rifle. Before Martin could stop him, Mantle fired three times. Three cows down. That'll teach the bastard, said Mantle. They drove back to the farmer's house and sheepishly paid for the extra cows Mantle had killed.

HAIR (OF THE MULE)

The Yankees, with their emphasis on order, cleanliness, and the removal of whiskers, had a natural opposite in the American League—the Kansas City Athletics, the little team whose stars they loved to poach.

The Athletics had evolved from their days as clean-shaven lads in Philadelphia. Charlie O. Finley, the Athletics' eccentric owner, had a feeling for the game's taboos and how to break them. Sheep grazed deep in the outfield at Kansas City Municipal Stadium. Finley wanted to draw more people to see his awful team. He also wanted short grass, and the sheep obliged.

In 1963 the Yankees opened their season in Kansas City. The A's wore new gold and kelly green uniforms, and the sheep in the outfield wore gold and kelly green blankets. Finley discussed his strategy: "If we get enough gold and green color in the stands, the Yankees will be so dazzled they won't have a chance." The sheep were a popular attraction, though not universally. They baaahed, they pooped, they smelled like sheep. They made the team seem less serious than, say, the Yankees.

Legend has it that one day someone hit a long home run that arched high in the air and smacked a sheep in the head. The sheep died, and early in the 1965 season, Charlie O. Finley replaced the sheep with a mule. Its name was Charlie O. The mule traveled with the Athletics, but trouble ensued when they reached Chicago. The White Sox refused to let the mule into Comiskey, so Finley protested in the parking lot. A band played music, and six lovely models mingled near the mule wearing signs. They read:

1. Unfair to Charlie O., the Mule
2. Unfair to Charlie O., the Man
3. Unfair to Baseball
4. Unfair to Sox Fans
5. Unfair to Animals
6. Unfair to Muledom

THE HALF-PENNANT PORCH

Finley was obsessed with the Yankees and attributed their success to the short distance to the right field fence in Yankee Stadium. He believed sluggers who batted left-handed, like Babe Ruth, Mickey Mantle, and Roger Maris, had an unfair advantage. The fence was the sole reason the Yankees were winners. Before the 1964 season, Finley sought to create his own advantage. He moved his right field fence so that it was 296 feet from home plate and called it his "Pennant Porch." The commissioner forced Finley to change it to 325 feet.

The A's were still terrible that year, but their head groundskeeper, George Toma, was watching and learning. Some factors that influence the game remain beyond the grasp of its players.

THE BULL GOOSE LOONY

Set in the fall of 1963, the film *One Flew Over the Cuckoo's Nest* follows R. P. McMurphy, a thirty-eight-year-old prisoner who has faked insanity to avoid hard labor, only to be committed to a mental hospital. Jack Nicholson plays the starring role.

In a key scene, McMurphy motivates his fellow patients to vote to watch the World Series, but Nurse Ratched terminates the election before the winning vote is counted. Defeated, McMurphy sits and fumes in front of a blank TV. But then light enters his eyes. He glances toward the nurses station, then the dark TV, and begins calling an imaginary play-by-play.

"Koufax, Koufax kicks, he delivers, *it's up the middle it's a base hit, Richardson is rounding first he's going for second.*" The other patients creep around the corner toward McMurphy and look at his blank TV, which now reflects their own faces. They crowd in, uneasy but giddy, because they know something wonderful is happening. McMurphy, encouraged, calls a home run by Yankee Tom Tresh, and the men jump and holler for the first time in ages. They are transcending their status as mere patients. "Someone get me a fucking wiener before I die," McMurphy yells, overcome with mirth.

The camera cuts to Nurse Ratched at her station. She glowers behind glass, angry but expressionless. McMurphy's imaginary ballgame has weakened the institution's control over the men and given them a taste of what they needed, but what scared them most: freedom. The camera stays on Nurse Ratched's face, and slowly inches closer to her cold eyes.

Meanwhile, the imaginary game continues. McMurphy calls Mickey Mantle to the plate and screams, "It's a fuckin' home run!" The men cheer and scramble around the room in ecstasy.

Finally, Nurse Ratched, the voice of the institution, speaks through the intercom:

"Gentlemen, stop this."

But Mantle has homered!

"Stop this immediately."

McMurphy has helped the patients transform, ever so briefly, into participants in a complex game—that of their own fate within a country that loves freedom but often demands uniformity.

CHANCE DAMNS THE YANKEES

In 1964, Dean Chance, a young pitcher for the Los Angeles Angels, had a phenomenal year, leading the league with twenty wins and a minuscule ERA of 1.65. Chance was just twenty-three years old, from Ohio, and owned an eighty-acre farm, sixty head of cattle, and one hundred hogs.

Chance was talented, had endurance, and was focused. In one game against the Yankees in May, he pitched fourteen scoreless innings before he was pulled to save his arm. The Angels lost. The only run Chance gave up to the Yankees in 1964 was a home run to Mickey Mantle in late July. This was a good Yankees team, a club that made it to the World Series and lost in seven games to the Cardinals.

It was the peak of Chance's baseball career. By August of 1966, two seasons later, he had lost his magic against the Yankees and his overall performance was down. Though he was a pitcher, Chance even tinkered with his batting stance and experimented with hitting left-handed. Of the switch, an unimpressed sportswriter noted, "Over 20,000 guinea pigs have already died in the experiment."

That year Chance tossed a three-hit shutout against the Yankees in New York. The former phenom yelled to his aging teammate and fellow Yankee Killer Lew Burdette, "That's how I used to do it. . . . Honest. I know you never believe me."

THE INVASION OF THE LONG-HAIRED BEATLES

Shea Stadium opened in 1964, at which time the Yankees and Yankee Stadium were well past middle age. The Yankees had invited popes and protestant ministers to preach. Shea Stadium hosted the Beatles. They arrived August 15, 1965, and played to a crowd of more than fifty-five thousand. They were free-spirited, goofy, rebellious enough to seem cool, and their hair covered their ears and reached below their eyebrows.

The fans screamed so loudly they couldn't hear which songs the Beatles played, and neither could the band. The meaning of the songs collapsed, and new meanings emerged. During the concert, spectacle and celebrity became ends in themselves. People howled for them, and the Beatles saw the future.

SOLUTIONS

In October 1965 Billy Martin made it back to the World Series, but as third-base coach for the Twins, who opened the contest at Metropolitan Stadium in Minnesota.

Two days earlier, Pope Paul VI spoke to ninety thousand parishioners at Yankee Stadium. The Yankees were terrible that year, and lost eighty-five games. If not for the Pope, the stadium would have been empty. He welcomed those who were present from other faiths, and said, "Politics do not suffice to sustain a durable peace."

STEINBRENNER SAVES THE YANKEES

Columbia Broadcasting System, Inc. (CBS) bought a stake of the Yankees in 1964. They won the pennant that season with Yogi Berra managing. It was their last year as a great ball club for nearly a decade. In 1965 CBS bought Del Webb's final 10 percent of the team, and the next year they were terrible. They finished the season in last place, nineteen games under .500, playing as though they were merely a division of a giant corporation. Their corrosion roughly corresponded to the worst years of the Vietnam War: 1967–1973. It was as if the Yankees, as a symbol of America, had also lost their way.

A man who was a shipbuilder and an investor in theatrical productions bought a stake in the Yankees in time for the 1973 baseball season. His name was George Steinbrenner and he was born on the Fourth of July. The Yankees improved by 1974 and remained contenders for much of the rest of the decade. Steinbrenner represented the opposite of corporate ownership. He had passion, wanted to win, and gambled millions for the chance.

CHARLIE FINLEY'S REVENGE

Steinbrenner was a showman, but Charlie O. Finley was even more inclined to spectacle. Finley continued to be a trickster in Oakland after moving the A's there from Kansas City for the 1968 season. As the team rambled west from Philadelphia to Kansas City to California, it had worried less and less about propriety, but despite his fondness for fur-bearing mammals, Finley still enforced vestigial rules against facial hair. Or he tried to, until the great slugger Reggie Jackson challenged the owner's power in 1972 by refusing to shave his vigorous mustache. Rather than risk losing a public showdown with Jackson, Finley decreed "Mustache Day" and offered his players bonuses if they grew one. He may have thought that by having the entire team look like Reggie Jackson it would tame the star's spirit and make the group conform, but the opposite happened. The hirsute Oakland A's of the early seventies, the hairiest bunch of baseball players in major-league history*, dominated the game. They won five division titles and three World Series in a row, raising the question of whether testosterone levels rise when razors are left on shelves and facial hair is allowed to bloom. Frenchy Bordagaray would have been thrilled to play alongside Jackson, Catfish Hunter, and the other A's.

Charlie Finley was eccentric in ways that make him seem alternately fool and genius. He seemed to understand the power of the animal locked within his players, though it was not an immediate discovery. The strange relationship between domesticated ballplayers, domesticated animals, and domesticated fans leaked into his ownership style. He was a secular priest, performing rituals to challenge taboos and gain power from their destruction. The curved mustache worn by Rollie Fingers made him look like Salvador Dalí. The A's had one thing in common with the surrealists: by revealing normal routines imposed by society as bizarre, they challenged, weakened, and tried to destroy them in the hope that something better would arise. For the A's, the "something better" was a baseball dynasty.

ROYALTY

After the A's left for California, Kansas City was awarded an expansion team for the 1969 season. Their name, the Royals, made it seem as if the cow town with a crappy major-league

---

*See also the 2013 Boston Red Sox, who weaponized their beards after this book was written.

history was desperately clinging to outdated notions of inher-
ited nobility, the proper entitlement of the rich, and endorsing
the subjugation of the common person by a class structure that
once served the monarchies of Europe. The team's logo was a
blue-and-gold crown, as if by pretending their roots stretched
to some vague ancestral title, Kansas City could trump the
Yankees simply through the power of a name. But in calling
themselves the Royals, they forgot what happened in 1776.

It was no worse than naming a baseball team after a group
of people subjected to organized repression, expulsion, and
genocide (the Indians, the Braves), or after a garment that tends
to stink (socks). In retrospect, the Royals should have named
themselves the Masses, because their economic plight in recent
decades is mirrored by the vast majority of us.

THE MASTER

Gaylord Perry was a spitballer and a greaser at a time when
hurling the moist pitch was against the rules. His success
attracted Richard Nixon, who asked Perry how he got away
with it. Perry told the president, "There are some things you
just can't tell the people for their own good."

Billy Martin, by then manager of the Tigers, thought he'd
found a foolproof way to catch Perry tossing a greaser. Martin
demanded that the umpire smell Perry's ball: "Smell it. Go on,
smell it . . . well, do you smell it?" Another time, Martin supposedly brought a bloodhound to the stadium in a failed effort
to track down Perry's grease.

As his pitching style earned him wins, awards, and infamy,
Perry opined, "I think the spitter has added controversy and
excitement. It has livened up more ballgames than wearing
double-knit uniforms and letting hair and whiskers grow."

Tradition

When George Steinbrenner bought the Yankees in 1973, he claimed he would not interfere with the day-to-day operations of the team. Then he noticed many Yankees had long hair. It bothered Steinbrenner, and he imposed grooming rules to retain order and control his club.

He later explained: "I feel very strongly that we have to set an example and I like self-discipline and neatness to be a part of that example. I believe it reflects in the way a team performs. I really do. . . . I'm not waging a one-man war against long hair. I'm just saying if you want to be a Yankee, this is the way it's got to be."

Tigers Try Samson Approach

In the spring of 1973, Billy Martin was still exiled from his Yankees. The Oakland Athletics had won the World Series the year before while wearing mustaches, and people were joking it had helped them win. The Tigers manager was unimpressed: "(Bleep) the A's and Mr. Finley. . . . I left my mustache in my razor blade," Martin said. It was an attitude he had internalized in New York.

"A lot of guys, including me, had big mustaches when we came to camp but they made us shave them off," said Tiger Norm Cash.

Billy Martin Could Be a Pretty Good Guy

Billy Martin and outfielder Isaiah "Ike" Blessitt were drinking at a Florida bar that spring when Blessitt got into an argument with another patron. Martin led Blessitt outside to talk, and a police car slowed and stopped. Martin recounted his version of the events.

"One of the cops said to Blessitt, 'O.K., black boy, you're under arrest.'"

Racial prejudice was normal in the South, but Martin refused to let it pass without comment. He pointed out that Blessitt had not done anything, and asked why he was being picked up. The officer responded that Martin was now *also* under arrest.

They were charged with "uttering profanity in public," a thirty-two-dollar fine.

The officer claimed Martin started the problem by observing, "This is the way southern police treat black people."

Blessitt had made it to the big leagues the previous fall, when he played in four Tigers games but had zero hits in five at bats. Neither he nor Martin knew it when they were arrested, but Blessitt was to never play another game in the majors. He finished his career with a batting average of zero zero zero.

LeFlore

Ron LeFlore was locked up in the State Prison of Southern Michigan after being convicted of armed robbery. He had grown up in a rough part of Detroit and never played sports in high school, but when he got to prison he played basketball, football, and baseball. Word got around that he was fast, had decent power at the plate, and could throw.

An acquaintance gave Billy Martin a tip on LeFlore, so the manager made a trip to the prison to see him play. When LeFlore was paroled in 1973, Martin gave him a tryout at Tiger Stadium. The independent spirit that made Billy Martin troublesome to his owners also propelled him to give others a chance. The Tigers signed LeFlore to a minor-league contract. He made the big leagues in 1974, and the All-Star team in 1976. Overall, he played eight seasons with the Tigers, the Montréal Expos, and the White Sox.

FIRST BLOOD

If George Steinbrenner had been tried by a jury and found
guilty of all fourteen felony counts the Watergate special prosecutor filed against him for illegal activity related to the financ-
ing of the 1972 presidential campaign, he could have been fined
$100,000 and sentenced to fifty-five years in prison.

Instead, Steinbrenner pled guilty to two counts: one of conspiracy to violate campaign finance laws, and another of being an
accessory after the laws were violated. Once he confessed, the government dropped the other charges. Steinbrenner had been
involved in a complex scheme that funneled money to Nixon.
The president shared Steinbrenner's hatred of long hair, stylish
among the antiwar Left. The Yankees owner paid a $15,000 fine
and avoided prison, but baseball commissioner Bowie Kuhn suspended Steinbrenner for fifteen months. Effectively, Steinbrenner
sat out the 1975 season. Upon learning of the suspension, he was
sarcastic: "Naturally, we are shocked beyond belief by Mr. Kuhn's
decision. It is certainly a wonderful Thanksgiving present."

Steinbrenner eventually became a secret FBI informant, and
was later pardoned by Ronald Reagan.

BEYOND THE SPORTS PAGES

Commissioner Bowie Kuhn wanted to work with the Cuban
Government Sports Agency and have major-league players
travel to Cuba. The U.S. State Department became involved.
Sources within the government observed, "The match would
be seen as a shrewd Yankee political move" and "Picking a game
we are likely to win would go well with Americans."

In a memo classified "secret," Henry Kissinger was
informed of Kuhn's view that "U.S. Major League Baseball has
a 'magic value in projecting a positive image of the U.S.' wherever the sport is played."

Kissinger's underling added: "In the United States, the announcement that a major league squad was to play in Cuba in late March would have a symbolic significance not limited to the sports pages. In the event that we go forward, we should contemplate whether the president or you might make the announcement."

The games never happened. Kissinger was against the idea. Communists were more useful as Cold War enemies.

MOSES

Marvin Miller, the labor negotiator, led the Major League Players Association and pressured owners to grant free agency to their serfs. When he died, Miller was remembered as "a silver-haired man with a mustache he had cultivated since he was 17.

"There was something about Miller, a wariness one would find in an abused animal. It precluded trust or affection.

"His legacy is that through his work, ballplayers for the first time attained dignity from owners."

UAW

We were too young to shave and too old to be seen in public with Kool-Aid mustaches, but Bruce, the son of our coach, appeared at every practice and every game with his mouth stained purple. The United Auto Workers sponsored our team, and our caps read "UAW." Coach was a mechanic, I guess. Bruce and I spent the season on the bench together. As he drooled and picked his nose, I watched my team play and silently critiqued his dad's managerial choices. The best hitter should bat third and the slugger fourth—that's what I had learned from Royals radio broadcasts. But Coach never got the message, and I thought he was a moron. Children are tyrants.

My dad was a doctor, and his dad a doctor before him. Not knowing my own future, I took it for granted that anyone who wasn't a doctor was an idiot. Especially autoworkers and their stupid union. I failed to understand that doctors and mechanics have more in common than it seems: the ability to comprehend complex systems, the arts of diagnosis and repair. And now I wonder what else I was blind to because of the prejudices I held in a suburb that pretended social class didn't exist. Could this have been the season my teammate wore jeans to games and always said "like butter"? Could it have been the *norm* for my teammates to come from "blue-collar" backgrounds, but I never noticed because they didn't matter? Decades later, I would love to have the job security of a union member. I would love to have an organization fighting for my quality of life: a living wage, health care, sick days, paid vacation, protection from exploitation by the ownership class.

Coach stood at third base giving me signs I ignored. I wasn't a great hitter, but I'd learned to "go with the pitch," and in revenge for being benched, in misplaced disgust at my coach's profession and his union, I was determined to smack an inside ball down the line and drill him in the head. And I did, missing by inches.

FREE AGENCY

With the advent of free agency in 1976, ballplayers were no longer bound to a single team for their career. They were no longer subject to total control. Players tested the market and went to teams that paid the most. Mustaches and beards sprouted. Hair crept past collars. The animals had broken free, and owners allowed it. They were forced to. The power dynamics had shifted. The exception was George Steinbrenner, who held to his insistence that Yankees be well groomed.

HOME-FIELD ADVANTAGE

In keeping with their policy, the Yankees bought what they could not beat. They acquired Catfish Hunter, the star A's pitcher. Hunter hated facing the Royals in Kansas City. When he played for the A's in the sixties, he had come to know George Toma, the local groundskeeper, very well. Toma had been good to Catfish. The pitcher liked the dirt on the mound soft and loose. On days he pitched, Toma had made sure to sculpt the mound the way Catfish liked it.

Catfish Hunter moved with the Athletics to Oakland and later became a Yankee—the enemy. When the Yankees visited Kansas City, Toma, still the groundskeeper, would put two inches of mud on the mound when Catfish was scheduled to pitch. As it dried it became as hard as George Steinbrenner's heart. During the 1976 playoffs, Catfish said, "He really knows how to make it tough. When you combine that artificial surface with that wet mound, it's almost impossible to pitch there." He was one of the best pitchers of the early seventies, but between 1972 and 1976 he lost six of seven decisions in Kansas City. George Toma was a Yankee Killer who never played a game. He knew: curate the field on which the game is played and you control the game, its players, its outcomes.

PRIDE

During spring training in 1976, George Steinbrenner ordered his Yankees to cut their hair. Oscar Gamble had to cut his ten-inch afro before the team would issue him a uniform. Lou Piniella chopped his locks, but was asked to get a closer trim. The owner roamed the field gawking at scalps. Steinbrenner personally told Catfish Hunter to exert control over his follicles.

The Boss defended his edict:

> I have nothing against long hair per se. . . . But I'm trying to instill a sense of order and discipline in the ball club because I think discipline is important in an athlete. They can joke about it as long as they do it. If they don't do it, we'll try to find a way to accommodate them somewhere else. I want to develop pride in the players as Yankees. . . . I like to see a player look neat. Maybe I'm wrong, but we'll see. I'll try to explain it to them at a meeting. They'll joke about it, but sooner or later we'll get it ingrained in them.

One by one, the players complied. They played shorn and clean. Later that summer, Yankees catcher Thurman Munson— a scruffy character in his own right—described the Boss: "George wants some kind of regimentation. He knows you need that in a business. He loves baseball and he wants to win in the worst way."

CACHING THE KILL

In 1976, a rookie pitcher for the Detroit Tigers became the biggest star in baseball. His name was Mark Fidrych. He was tall and lanky. His hair was curly and wild. He reminded someone of Big Bird, and the name stuck. The Bird won nineteen games that first year, and six in a row in 1977 before a shoulder injury destroyed his career.

Decades later, baseball fans still remember his pitching. They also remember his bizarre behavior on the mound. He talked to himself between pitches and during his windup. To sportswriters, fans, and people watching at home, it looked like he was whispering to the ball. He compulsively knelt to sculpt the mound. He took excess dirt from one part of the mound and used it to fill in the hole other pitchers' feet had dug. From the stands, it looked like he was burying something. Fidrych said he never realized he was doing it until someone told him. It was an instinct. He did not want to step into a hole dug by another pitcher. The Bird made the mound his territory. It was like something out of the *Journal of Mammalogy*.

Leopards, spotted hyenas, wolverines, and mountain lions all kill their prey and then cache the meat under dirt. So do brown bears. Although brown bears enjoy grazing on blueberries, they also kill and eat things closer to their own size, like moose and sheep. The *Journal of Mammalogy* reports many bears cache their prey by scratching the ground around the victim vigorously, and at length, until the corpse is covered with dirt, herbs, grasses, mosses, and blueberries. Then they eat at their leisure. They usually cache their victim when competitive animals like wolves or ravens are in the vicinity.

TRANSUBSTANTIATION

The Yankees were terrified of Reggie Jackson, so they acquired him. The slugger became a huge star in New York City. He hit home runs, bragged about hitting home runs, and was a clutch hitter in the World Series. In 1978 the Reggie Bar was named after him. Fans enjoyed its mix of caramel, peanuts, and chocolate. It was like spectators decades before eating the first "hot dogs," and Babe Ruth's buffalo-meat diet, but for fans who adored Mr. October.

PROXY WAR

Billy Martin returned to his beloved New York Yankees as a manager in 1975, though his tenure was marked by repeated firings by George Steinbrenner. As manager, Martin held a key to a private liquor cabinet in the pressroom at the stadium. In the summer of 1978, he announced that doctors had told him to stop drinking because he had "a spot on [his] liver." Although Steinbrenner offered to let Martin voluntarily resign for "health reasons," Martin didn't take him up on the offer: "I'm not a quitter. I want to try to win this thing. I owe it to the Yankee fans. . . . I still got my key. . . . As long as I got my key, I'm all right."

The Yankees had won the World Series in 1977, but by July of 1978 they were barely in contention in the American League East and everyone knew that Martin's job was at risk. He refused to go to the hospital to get his liver tested because he knew it would give Steinbrenner a reason to fire him. But after the owner threatened to send Martin's pitching coach to the minor leagues, Martin also used the possibility of his getting tests on his liver as a threat to Steinbrenner. If Martin got the tests, was proven ill, and Steinbrenner chose to replace him, Steinbrenner would have been stuck with the rest of Martin's contract. The only way out for Steinbrenner was to have Martin choose on his own to resign.

It was a proxy war, like Korea or Vietnam. The battlefield was Billy Martin's liver.

That same summer, Martin and Steinbrenner taped a Miller Lite beer commercial. The legendary ad shows them sitting at a table in an upscale pub. They were probably the only people in history to drink Miller Lite out of heavy glass goblets. Martin says it's less filling, Steinbrenner insists it tastes great. They argue back and forth and finally Steinbrenner exclaims, "You're hired!"

Martin did finally resign at the end of July, after making his infamous comments about Reggie Jackson and George Steinbrenner: "The two of them deserve each other. One's a born liar, the other's convicted."

Similar to Martin's replacement at second base by Bobby Richardson two decades before, the Yankees promptly hired manager Bob Lemon, a far more palatable personality.

BEAST

In August 1979, the Twins manhandled Yankees pitcher Ron Davis. Martin, by then rehired, visited the mound. Umpire Dallas Parks told Martin that if Davis was still on the mound, Martin couldn't talk to him. The Yankees manager knew he was within the rules, and exploded. Parks stood still, his hands at his sides, his mouth slightly open. Martin kicked the infield dirt, dust coated the ump's pants, and a cloud rose. According to the *Journal of Mammalogy*, this is called ground-scratching behavior. When trying to mark or protect their territory from a real or imagined threat, dogs will stop, pee, and scratch. Most dog owners understand. The interesting thing about ground scratching is that dogs do it even when they *don't* pee. They raise their legs and dig in the dirt even when nothing much comes out of their bodies. Marking your territory is about more than laying down your scent. It is a performance. If a dog sees another dog a hundred yards away, it will put on a ground-scratching display in order to show the other dog who is boss. The marks in the dirt are an additional warning. Any dog who walks by will know the land has been claimed. It backfired for Billy Martin, who was ejected from the game and left the field.

PEACE

In October of 1979, Pope John Paul II visited Yankee Stadium.
The Yankees had finished fourth in the American League East,
so the stadium was free. He spoke in English, though it was not
his first language. Among the words that gave him trouble:
hegemony.

Before going to the stadium, he had addressed the United
Nations. He spoke on behalf of human rights, voiced concern
about the nuclear arms race, and pleaded for equality for the
Palestinian people. He voiced support for all people "abused by
nations in the name of 'internal security.'"

Later, at the stadium, he gave an evening mass to eighty
thousand people:

> We must find a simple way of living. For it is
> not right that the standard of living of the rich
> countries should seek to maintain itself by
> draining off a great part of the reserves of energy
> and raw materials that are meant to serve the
> whole of humanity. For readiness to create a
> greater and more equitable solidarity between
> peoples is the first condition for peace.

The rich countries were behaving like the Yankees, taking
everything for themselves.

WHAT'S GOOD FOR THE HORSE

Kenny Clay was a pitcher for the Yankees who, in September of 1979, gave up four runs to the Royals. Two scored on a home run by George Brett. Clay had spoiled a 5–0 Yankees lead. Steinbrenner trashed him in the press, saying: "In horse racing we have what we call a morning glory. This horse works great three or four furlongs in the morning workout and looks sensational. Then when the race comes he starts sweating during the parade to the post, and when he gets in the gate and the race starts he stinks the place out. He spits the bit. Kenny Clay is a morning glory. He spit the bit. He doesn't have the courage."

What Steinbrenner did not say is that when a horse spits the bit, it's bad for the owner, but the horse is liberated.

CUD

In 1980 Wrigley began selling Big League Chew. Two pitchers dreamed it up while sitting bored in a bullpen. One of them was Rob Nelson, a lefty for the Portland Mavericks. His friend and teammate Jim Bouton helped him attract the company's interest. Bouton had been a Yankee in the mid- to late sixties, and had written *Ball Four,* a book that deflated the myth of baseball players as gods. It was considered outrageous during its time, even scandalous.

Players chew tobacco and bubble gum as often as cows, sheep, and other ruminants chew cud. The sugary gum was intended to provide an alternative to tobacco. Baseball players have fewer stomachs than cows and sheep, but they constantly chew, spit, and blow bubbles. Big League Chew forms a bulbous wad that would have weakened the knees of Art Shires. Sometimes players wrap their tobacco in slippery blobs of Big League Chew, "a fun gum that keeps your mouth from getting dry when the game is on the line."

Ornithology

We were in my backyard playing baseball, my friend and I. We were eleven, maybe twelve. My dog, Lillian Goodrin, watched from the shade of a yellow forsythia. Her tongue lolled. My friend had never played baseball. He stayed inside all summer to play video games. Colecovision Smurfs. "Ghost man on second," I shouted, pointing my bat. He wound, threw the pitch underhand, straight up. I swung, but the huge red tomato we'd stolen from my mom's garden dropped at my feet and split. "Look at the birdies up in the sky," he shouted. He lobbed another four feet over my head. It splattered against the top of the wooden fence a full second after I swung. A seed stuck to my neck. "Ghost man on second!" This suburban Saberhagen was thin, pale, addicted to Smarties, and should not have been able to entice me with his Eephus pitch. "Swing at the birdies," he shouted. I was ready to fling my bat at his knees. I steadied myself, focused on restraint, but as the next tomato entered its orbit I felt my lead foot stepping forward and my hands beginning to swing.

Bugs

Billy Martin claimed George Steinbrenner had tapped his phones while he was manager. Martin asserted this in his 1980 autobiography. By then he was managing the Oakland A's. Yankee Stadium manager Pat Kelly, who coincidentally shared his name with the private detective who trailed Yankees players during the early twenties, denied that any stadium phones had been bugged. Kelly attributed Martin's claim to an effort to increase book sales, saying, "Our system does not provide for anyone to possibly bug the phones—and we are very careful about that—because Mr. Steinbrenner is very paranoid about bugs and tapping." Steinbrenner said, "I can't believe he said those things. . . . Billy and I are getting along fine now. If he said it in bitterness when he left, that's fine. We're still friends."

ANOTHER TAKE ON HAIR
Roy White played for the Yankees between 1965 and 1979, then went to Japan to play for the Yomiuri Giants, that nation's winningest franchise. He famously remarked, "Rooting for the Yankees was like rooting for General Motors. You didn't love them, but you respected them."

Wa is a concept that connotes group harmony, and it is the motto of huge Japanese corporations like Hitachi. It was also the motto of Yomiuri Giants manager Tetsuharu Kawakami, who won nine league championships in a row in the sixties and seventies. The concept of wa begs a question: is there a difference between harmony and conformity? The Giants forbade players from wearing beards, mustaches, and long hair.

One American who played in Japan, Crazy Wright, said that a teammate would run past him, reach inside Wright's uniform, yank out chest hair, and put it down his own shirt—good luck.

OCTOBER SURPRISE
In 1979 radical Islamists in Iran overthrew the puppet government the CIA had created in the early fifties, and turned the nation into a theocracy antagonistic toward the West. Mobs broke into the U.S. embassy and took Americans hostage until they were finally released in early 1981. Baseball commissioner Bowie Kuhn gave them each a free life pass to any ballpark in America.

THIRD BECOMES FIRST
Tension with owners led players to strike in June 1981. At issue was compensation for clubs who lost players to free agency. The

owners wanted to increase compensation because they feared losing their best players and the escalation of salaries. The players revolted. After ballgames had been canceled for two months, an agreement was finally reached. A team that lost a player to free agency would be entitled to compensation by picking from a pool of players left "unprotected" from each team. The team obtaining the free agent would have to leave two additional players unprotected.

The heart of the 1981 season was lost to meetings between lawyers. The strike turned fans away from baseball—many believed it had been overtaken by greed. One fan declared his intent to boycott products sponsored by Major League Baseball: "Even though it'll be like spitting in the ocean, I'm going to have my personal vendetta against sports; I've eaten my last Farmer John hot dog, bought my last tank of Union Oil, and I'm going to boycott whatever else these guys are selling."

Baseball fan David Cartier of New Britain, Connecticut, was so disgusted by the strike that he publicly burned his collection of baseball cards. He joined twenty other people who burned their collections. Cartier himself burned twenty-five thousand, including a 1952 Mickey Mantle. As he set fire to the tiny effigy, he said, "I represent all the fans who aren't ready to welcome baseball back with open arms—the fans who aren't ready to kiss and make up, because we know we've been had."

In Los Angeles, a group of disgruntled fans created the Cosmic Baseball Association. The group is akin to Jack Kerouac's old fictional baseball leagues. Their activities are a mix of poetry, philosophy, social criticism, and baseball. They describe themselves as a "league of the imagination," which "emerged from the rising dissatisfaction with reality baseball. Major League Baseball was corrupt and ubiquitous greed had soured the sport; but not its myths."

Major League Baseball announced that for the second half of the 1981 season, teams would start over with a record of zero wins, zero losses. It was not true in reality; three months of baseball had already been played. But it became true when the officials decided it would be true. They created the new reality and imposed it onto the season. For many people, reality isn't what *is,* but what the system says it is. Two plus two equals five.

Reggie Jackson saw through the gimmick. When the season resumed in August of 1981, Jackson saw a sign at Yankee Stadium that read "Opening Night." Jackson said, "It's not opening night. . . . It's the resumption of the season. There are 52 games left, we're playing for all the marbles. But it's not opening night." The postseason was ultimately determined by pitting the teams with the best records from the first half of the season against the teams with the best records from the second half, within each division. The White Sox, Orioles, Rangers, Cardinals, and Reds all failed to reach the postseason, despite having better overall records than the teams that actually made it. The Yankees, who had the *third*-best overall record in the American League East, made it to the World Series, eventually losing to the Dodgers.

Thrash-Urination

When the Yankees played lackluster ball during the World Series that year, Steinbrenner appeared before the press with a black eye and his left arm in a cast. He had supposedly brawled with two Dodgers fans in an elevator. They had mocked his Yankees, and he slugged it out. "I clocked them," he told the press. "There are two guys in this town looking for their teeth."

The black eye may have been makeup, the cast a prop. If the fight had merely been Steinbrenner's bluster designed to

motivate the Yankees, it didn't work: the Dodgers won. When
the conditions are right, Roosevelt elk thrash-urinate. It's like
fighting, and threatening to fight, and involves making a big
scene to intimidate rivals. They use hooves and antlers to make
dirt and pee fly everywhere. Master bulls do this much more
frequently than bachelor bulls. The *Journal of Mammalogy*
found that "a bull which did not thrash-urinate would be
advertising its weakness, and the absence of this display might
precipitate serious challenges by other males." Steinbrenner
was behaving like a bull elk. So was Gaylord Perry when he
touched the decoys on his uniform before each pitch.
Presidents do this too. Roosevelt signaled to the Japanese community by sending many to internment camps during World
War II. Nixon waved the peace sign, smiled, and bombed
Cambodia. George W. Bush wore his flight suit and declared
victory. Master bulls.

SUCCESS NEVER COMES

In an eight-month period in 1983 and 1984, the Yankee Bandit
robbed sixty-four banks. In November he robbed six in a single
day. He earned the name because every time he wore a Yankees
cap. Eddie Chambers Dodson was an antiques dealer in Los
Angeles who liked to party with John Belushi, but when he got
addicted to cocaine and heroin and needed nearly a thousand
dollars a day to support his habit, he began robbing banks.

He was the Don Mattingly of bank robbery. Victims
recalled the Yankees hat, a smile, and a starter pistol. Later, after
a stint in prison, a straight life as a landscaper, and a return to
drugs and robbing banks, the police closed in on the Yankee
Bandit at a cheap motel. He'd jacked a Mercedes. To the cops,
he said, "Kill me! Kill me!"

SUBLIMATION

It is considered un-American to question the morality of capitalism, but the same people who reflexively defend it in a conversation will not hesitate to express hatred for the New York Yankees. The Yankees have all the money, so they buy the best players and win the most games, keeping the rest of the league weak, ensuring they will earn more money. Teams like the Royals remain terrible for generations and are unable to keep good players, who leave for wealthier and better teams. The rich get richer, the poor get poorer. People praise the profit-sharing system in professional football and observe how it has led to better teams across the league and a healthier overall game. And though some critique the lack of equity in baseball, few make the connection to the larger world, in which America operates like the Yankees and most other countries are like the Royals. This anxiety about capitalism and the many decades of success by the Yankees is evident in how fans react when the Yankees are beaten. They love it. Yankee Killers leave people trying to figure out how in the world they beat the unbeatable team. Religion, good luck charms, extreme focus, and other forces have been used to describe Yankee Killers' success. They reveal how fans see the Yankees, but also hint at how the rest of the world sees the United States.

HUEVOS

Whenever his Royals played the Yankees, George Brett was John Brown against the unjust law. The third baseman arrived in Kansas City from Southern California in 1973, with longish hair popular among surfers on the West Coast. His mullet was a warning to George Steinbrenner of the battles to come. He played loose like a surfer, but he was fierce like Billy Martin. Brett and Martin became enemies because nobody wanted to win as badly as they did. Brett was the only player to win batting titles in three decades, and he helped the Royals win their division in 1976, '77, '78, and '80. He led them to the World Series in 1980, losing to the Phillies, but they won the championship over the Cardinals in 1985.

During the summer of 1980, Brett hit better than anyone since Ted Williams in 1941. Brett kept his average near .400, and hit .390 for the season. Umpire Steve Palermo said, "The way George Brett is hitting right now, God could have him down no balls and two strikes and he'd get a hit." Teammate Hal McRae countered, "I wouldn't go that far. If the Lord was up 0–2, He might get George out . . . but God better hit the black." A Royals coach named Charlie Lau had taught Brett to perfect the mechanics of his batting stance, but by the summer of 1980, Lau was coaching for the Yankees. When the teams met, Lau watched Brett with both horror and pride, and observed in July: "I'm in a Yankee uniform now. I have mixed feelings. I know the little S.O.B. loves to hit in front of me. God, he's played eight games against us this year and he's got 17 RBI (and a .500 average). I feel like Dr. Frankenstein watching his monster on the loose."

After a game that summer, Brett joined a golf outing that included Royals announcer Fred White. Brett had a sore ankle, so instead of playing he zoomed ahead in a cart to await the group near the green. Someone teed off and the ball flew toward Brett. As the tiny white sphere rocketed toward him, Brett raised a golf club, steadied himself on his good foot, and smacked the ball back down the fairway.

Brett's most dramatic moments were usually against the Yankees. He was clutch. He had *huevos*. At a time when he was not considered a home run hitter, he hit one in a key playoff game against the Yankees in 1976. The next year, Brett hit .300 against the Yankees in the Royals' eventual playoff loss. The Yankees were afraid of Brett because he stretched singles into doubles, believed the Royals could win, and made them win. In the final game of the 1977 ALCS, Brett hit a triple off Ron Guidry. As Brett slid into third base, Yankees third baseman Graig Nettles kicked him in the chest. Brett tore to his feet, punched Nettles, and the benches cleared. Billy Martin put Royal Freddie Patek in a headlock. At a time when Yankees ace Ron Guidry was nearly unhittable, Brett insisted, "Guidry ain't God."

They were afraid of Brett's passion. "George is hot-blooded," Hal McRae noted. The only Yankee who came close was Billy Martin. If Billy Martin had had Brett's ability, he might've been the greatest player ever. The same could be said of Brett if he'd had Martin's wicked, conniving, plotting, scheming, dastardly, lawyer-like baseball intelligence.

DISTANCE FACTORS

My sisters and I were in the backseat of my parents' station wagon, rambling south through Iowa in the summer of 1983. We were on our way back to Kansas from our annual trip to Minnesota. We had spent a week in a tiny cabin on Pelican

Lake, where every night we had campfires on the beach. By day I had stalked the weed lines with a butterfly net, looking for schools of bullhead fry. Now in the car we scanned the fields, counting horses to pass the time. My dad drove and listened to the radio. We had just entered the range of the Royals AM broadcast. I could hear the static fizz, and my dad fiddled with the dial. The Royals were playing the Yankees in New York.

Suddenly my dad shouted, "All right Brett!" and he slipped his hand into the backseat for me to slap him five. I did it, but I didn't understand. I didn't know who George Brett was or what the Yankees were, but Brett had hit a home run to give the Royals a 5–4 lead. It was the top of the ninth. They had been down by a run, and there were two outs. Goose Gossage was on the mound for the Yankees, an old rival of Brett's dating back several years. Suddenly my dad turned up the radio, and the static crackled. The radio announcers sounded puzzled. I didn't understand what they were saying. Something about Brett's home run. I heard the name Billy Martin. Home run. Martin. Pine tar. Brett. Martin. Brett. Martin. Out.

"No!" my dad grunted.

"Rats!" he barked, and slapped the steering wheel.

It was the most vile curse he could muster, a curse I later associated with the role of the lowly rat in the pivotal scene in *1984* when Big Brother breaks Winston by forcing him to wear a rat cage as a mask. It was directed at Martin, the Yankees manager, who had scampered onto the field and argued that Brett had applied too much pine tar to his bat and therefore should be called out. Pine tar is a sticky resin made from sap that players rub on their bats to help them get a better grip. The umpires measured Brett's bat and its thick coating of dark, sticky pine tar against the length of home plate.

They agreed with Martin. Everyone knew Brett used too much pine tar. The sap stained his blue helmet brown. "Doggonit!" My dad slapped his knee and the station wagon swerved a few inches to the right. I heard the rough patch on the side of the highway rumble as our wheels vibrated. He corrected the car. Suddenly the announcers on the radio raised their voices. My dad squawked. George Brett had charged onto the field to tackle the umpire! He was being restrained! The announcers had never seen such a thing before! Chaos loose on the field!

I looked up at the front of the car. I asked my dad what happened.

"Billy Martin," he said. "The Yankees."

The Royals lodged a formal protest. Ancient spitballer Gaylord Perry, by then a Royals pitcher, stole the suspect bat and hid it. Dick Howser, the Royals manager, later said, "I didn't know what was going on. I saw guys in sport coats and ties trying to intercept the bat. It was like a Brink's robbery. Who's got the gold? Our players had it, the umpires had it. I don't know who has it—the CIA, a think tank at the Pentagon."

THE RULES BEHIND THE RULES

George Brett never wore batting gloves. He was one of the last holdouts, claiming that he could feel the bat and its contact with the ball with greater precision barehanded. For players without batting gloves, pine tar was essential. Brett smeared it everywhere, taped his fingers, and the wad of tobacco in his cheek rivaled Art Shires's. Brett, like Mark Twain, played by his own rules.

Earlier in the summer, Yankees infielder Graig Nettles told Martin that Brett was using too much of the goop. Nettles was keyed in to the rules regarding baseball bats because a few years before he had been caught corking his own against the Tigers. Martin developed a plan. The rule was that a bat may not have any foreign substance beyond eighteen inches up the handle. It was the kind of rule that went along with bans against corking bats, throwing spitballs, and, in recent years, taking steroids. The difference is that pine tar only helps a player *grip* the bat, it doesn't make the ball fly any farther. The rule was therefore rarely enforced. The room for interpretation comes in because although pine tar and all other substances are banned from being more than eighteen inches up the bat's handle (rule 1.10 b), the batter can be called out for using a bat that has been manipulated to improve its "distance factor" (rule 6.06 d).

Martin had realized his opportunity to use the rules to the Yankees' advantage. He had waited patiently. When Goose Gossage gave up the ninth-inning home run to Brett, seemingly losing the game, Martin protested and Brett was called out. Martin said, "It's a terrible rule, but if it had happened to me I would have accepted it. It turned out to be a lovely Sunday afternoon."

The Royals protested. Since pine tar does not make the bat propel the ball farther, but merely helps the batter gain a better grip on the wood, Martin and the umpires were overturned by the league, which decreed Brett did not violate the "spirit" of the rule. Brett's home run stood. When the inning resumed weeks later in mid-August, Martin stood near a black baseball bat that lay on the dugout steps. It was covered in shaving cream, and Martin insisted it was legal. After mocking the league's decision, Martin tried to win on another technicality by having his pitcher throw the ball to first to claim Brett had missed the bag while circling the bases in July. The plot failed because the Royals had obtained a signed affidavit from the original umpires stating that Brett and U. L. Washington, who'd been on base, indeed touched them all before scoring. The Yankees made three outs quickly in the bottom of the ninth and officially lost the game.

The Yankees had never been liked in Kansas City. But after the pine tar incident, the disgust turned to hatred, which has stayed with locals ever since. Brett, who technically broke the rules, is regarded as a hero, while Martin, who enforced them, remains a villain.

KNOW YOUR ENEMY

When shown a web page with a photograph of George Brett as part of a study, men and women reacted differently. Women only looked at George Brett's face, but men also looked at his crotch. An author of the study said, "Survival can be eating the right berries in the woods, not getting hit by a bus or not clicking on a blinking mortgage ad. I think the body part study is the same [evolutionary] idea: the behavior is hardwired into us and we're checking people out to see if we can mate with that thing."

When instructed to browse the American Kennel Club website as part of the study, men looked at the *dogs'* junk, too. One interpretation is the men were checking out the armature of critters they perceived as potential rivals, Brett included. They were sizing up the competition.

The Kiss

George Brett was playing his last home game in his final season, and my dad and I were there. He beat out an infield hit, a final hustle befitting his long career. After the game, Brett circled the stadium in a golf cart and waved at the fans. We cheered, Brett waved, and everyone was overcome with emotion. For nearly two decades Brett had made the Royals great. He had led by example. He had beaten back the Yankees when it mattered. He was clutch.

The golf cart circled the field and approached home plate. It stopped. Brett got out, knelt down, and kissed it. I didn't cry, but I felt I should *want* to cry.

Years later I learned the story behind the kiss. Hank Bauer, who had played for the Yankees during the fifties, had retired to a suburb of Kansas City to operate a liquor store. He told Brett to kiss home plate during his final home game, and Brett took the old Yankee's advice. When Bauer died, Brett recalled, "Hank Bauer was my all-time favorite Yankee . . . the only Yankee I like." The funeral for the old Yankee was held at Prince of Peace, a church a mile or so from Black Bob Park, where I had given up seven runs in a third of an inning a few years before.

Inputs, Putouts

Major-league players gradually began to internalize the mechanisms of control. Precisely because they could move from team to team to collect ever-increasing amounts of money, some began to soften their style of play in order to reduce the risk of injury. George Brett stretched singles into doubles, and Pete Rose arrived at first base on his belly, but they were considered throwbacks to an earlier era. Many played more conservatively. Why risk millions? Their attempt to control their own fate as players depended on their ability to control their own bodies in a game with inevitable injury, fatigue, and aging. Jogging, weights, batting practice, and shagging fly balls were no longer enough. They began to ingest anabolic steroids and growth hormones, which gave them muscles, speed, and endurance: a temporary but real advantage over fate.

Reading between the Pixels

As a kid I was obsessed with playing RBI Baseball, a game for the original Nintendo. I was always the American League All-Star team because it had Bret Saberhagen and George Brett. All the digital ballplayers on the field were fat, bulky, inflated. Little humanoid balloons. Even their faces were bloated. The only players with realistic bodies were Tony Gwynn, John Kruk, and Fernando Valenzuela, who were portlier than others in the sport.

I was nestled under an afghan in the family room, nestled within a suburb, nestled within the state of Kansas, nestled within the United States, which considered itself distinct from much of the world. Exceptional. There were Communists out there. It was the late eighties.

RBI Baseball had a slaughter rule. No matter what inning it was, if one team got ahead by ten runs and the other team failed to score, the game was over. I was about to score that tenth run. Valenzuela tossed an undulating wobbler, and Brett and I swung. It was a long drive to left; the outfielders moved slowly toward the wall, but it was gone. Electronic fireworks exploded beyond the electronic fence. I wiggled and stretched my thumbs to keep them limber for the next game.

The designer who created the imagery for Nintendo, the Japanese company based in Kyoto, was a prophet, the first person to predict how ballplayers would look during the steroid era: Jose Canseco, Roger Clemens, Mark McGwire—bloated, bloated, bloated.

It Was Fun, for a While

Mark McGwire and Sammy Sosa were hitting home runs faster than any ballplayer in the history of baseball. It was the summer of 1998, and I was finally paying attention to baseball again after the last strike had left me bored. Earlier in the summer a friend bought tickets to a Cubs–Cardinals game in St. Louis scheduled for Labor Day weekend, and as the season progressed, we realized we might see the fall of Roger Maris's single-season home run record.

We drove from Chicago to St. Louis. It was several hours before the game, but fans were everywhere. Mark McGwire entered the game with sixty home runs. The record, held for decades, was sixty-one.

As we walked toward Busch Stadium, a middle-aged man approached wanting to buy my ticket. We had outfield seats, and my friends and I planned to catch the record-tying and -breaking home runs. That was what everyone at the game wanted. Even us Cubs fans. We were stepping through the turnstiles as I stopped to chat with the man. How much do you want, he asked me. I wanted a ridiculous amount of money.

"How much?"

"A thousand dollars."

"Two hundred," he countered.

"A thousand."

He shook his head. "You're crazy." I walked through the turnstiles not considering myself greedy.

I had never been to a game with such a charged feeling. We crowded into the outfield seats and joked about how we'd kill each other when the ball came our way. Even from five hundred feet, McGwire and Sosa were huge, imposing, menacing at the plate. The giants of the game. The leaders of their sport.

We didn't wait long. McGwire batted in the first and flashbulbs popped all around the stadium. The ball smacked the Plexiglas in left field. Number sixty-one tied the record. It was the most exciting thing I had ever seen at a game. The most fun. We were part of history, of something tangible and real. The excitement built as we waited for another home run, and we booed every outside pitch.

YOU FUCKED UP

A few weeks later, I drove with a different group to Milwaukee County Stadium to watch McGwire break his own home run record. It was my first exposure to Milwaukee baseball. The team was named after the process of feeding sugar to yeast, collecting and bottling their poo, and selling it to people to drink. Brewing. County Stadium was the park where Bud Selig got his start in baseball. He retired from peddling used cars and parlayed his fortune into a job lording over the integrity of the game.

The evening was clear, crisp, and the park filled to capacity. Everyone wanted to see McGwire swat another home run. We were sitting in the outfield with rowdy fans, who were drunk and starting fights. During one scuffle a security guard waded through the crowd toward the belligerents. First one fan, and then hundreds, shouted, "Use your gun! Use your gun!"

During the seventh-inning stretch, there was a footrace between giant encased meats: a hot dog, bratwurst, and Polish and Italian sausages galloped around the field. McGwire hit his sixty-fourth home run, setting a new record he would break a couple days later. Fans began to fight, and this time, as the security guard led a staggering, slobbering gentleman up the stairs and out of the stadium, hundreds chanted, in unison, "You fucked up! You fucked up!"

MONOLITH

Rampant steroid abuse made it clear that humans are not just enlightened beings capable of higher reasoning, compassion, and incredible athletic feats, but are also members of the animal kingdom. When baseball players inject steroids and improve their skills, they look more muscular, more threatening, more like apes. It's difficult to hide when you're on the juice. They behave more like beasts, too. When Roger Clemens chucked a broken bat at Mike Piazza during the 2000 World Series, I couldn't help but see the ape-man at the beginning of Stanley Kubrick's *2001*. Agitated by the appearance of a mysterious black monolith, the ape-man bangs a long bone against the ground in a kind of frustrated rage before tossing it into the sky. For Clemens, the monolith was his own awareness of the limitations of his natural ability.

Maybe this ape-ness is why the public objects to steroids more than other forms of cheating, like scuffing, spitballs, corking the bat, and stealing signs. Steroids create a visual image that looks a lot more like our forest-dwelling cousins than people would like.

SIDE EFFECTS

Tetrahydrogestrinone is a designer steroid created for the Bay Area Laboratory Cooperative. It is also called "the clear" and THG. Barry Bonds used the clear during a time when it was illegal to take anabolic steroids without a prescription. He was a great hitter *before* using the clear, and became the best hitter *while* using the clear.

THG and other, natural, anabolic steroids have serious side effects. One of them is hirsuteness, in which hair grows wildly and abundantly on a person's arms, legs, chest, pubic regions, face, or back. Sometimes a shaggy, luxuriant mane grows everywhere, all at once.

SCAPEGOAT

Blaming the Curse of the Billy Goat, rather than the ownership and players, is therapy for some Cubs fans. The notion of a scapegoat comes from the Old Testament of the Bible and probably a bunch of other religious texts that did not survive the corrosive effects of sand, wind, sun, and human chicanery to find a place in contemporary libraries and houses of worship. When a person was known to have sinned, to have transgressed against God, self, or another person, a goat would be selected from the herd and the sin symbolically transferred to the animal's head. The goat would then be released into the wilderness, which meant death from dehydration, starvation, or between the fangs of a carnivore. The goat took the blame for human folly, which was better than having your neighbors pelt you with stones. It was also a way of helping people feel better about their bad behavior, and of drawing a sharper distinction—where perhaps none was deserved—between themselves and other domesticated mammals.

Sometimes a Cubs fan takes desperate measures to try to win. There is a statue of fabled broadcaster Harry Caray outside Wrigley Field. One year, after the Cubs frustrated their fans yet again, someone killed and skinned a goat. The anonymous penitent placed the carcass onto the statue as a sacrifice.

WHALING

It was game seven of the 2003 National League Championship Series. Game six, which ended the day before, was already infamous because the Cubs lost to the Marlins after a fan at Wrigley

Field was falsely blamed for interfering with a ball. The Curse of the Billy Goat. I sat at a table in the famous tavern, waiting to see if the Cubs could outpace their hapless past.

The bar filled with tourists, business people, and local folks I had seen there before, including a man with a beard and a Cubs shirt who looked like Bruce Sutter. The cooks standing at the flat metal grill shouted the usual: "No fries, chips!" "No Pepsi, Coke!" and customers lined up for their food and teased each other: "He wants a fry!" and "He wants a Pepsi!"

The game was about to begin, and the television showed the fan who had been blamed for the team's collapse. The young man apologized. A thin man with long brown hair was bellied up to the bar. He said loudly, "They're showing his name? He's a dead man. If the Cubs don't win tonight, he's a dead man." Another barfly with white hair and a tumbler of brown liquid in his hand said, "They call him a 'lifelong Cubs fan'? Well, he sure as hell ain't a long-*life* Cubs fan. It's going to say that on his tombstone."

The Marlins scored first, a three-run homer by Miguel Cabrera. The Goat fell silent. In the silence, a man at the bar shouted, "Shoot 'em!" Looking around, everyone I saw was a Cubs fan, or at least a fan of Chicago. Nobody wanted them to lose. And if they did, they were keeping it to themselves. A man of immense girth ambled down the steps into the bar and parked himself at the cheeseburger stand. He was followed by fifty wide-eyed suburbanites on a tour. The Goat was noisy and chaotic. Another man slipped past me and ducked into the women's restroom. "Emergency," he said meekly. The tourists shouted about Coke, Pepsi, chips, and fries. Someone ordered a triple cheeseburger and the cook at the grill was finally impressed. "Triple cheese?" he asked. He was incredulous.

"Triple cheese!" he shouted and slapped the beef onto the silver grill.

A line drive up the middle nearly killed pitcher Kerry Wood. The catcher recovered it but threw it away. It was a classic self-defeating mistake for the Cubs. It began to feel as though the game was over. But the bar remained electric, and when the television showed another replay of the innocent Cubs fan, the chorus around the Goat was, "Stone him!"

Moises Alou hit a two-run homer and the Cubs took a 5–3 lead. I still felt like the Cubs were destined to lose. Out of the corner of my eye, I spotted a Marlins hat. The enemy fan was standing just inside the door, as though he wanted to stay and watch but was afraid. He took his hat off and held it close. He watched the television for a minute. The Marlins took the lead, 6–5. He caught my malignant gaze and left the bar. The Cubs lost the momentum. Sammy Sosa dropped a ball, another bounced off Farnsworth's glove. Somehow the Marlins led 9–5. Someone at the bar shouted, "It's déjà vu all over again!" Which of course was first uttered by Yankees legend Yogi Berra. The noise tickled the inside of my ears. Beer flowed.

Behind me, I heard one of the cheeseburger chefs say curtly, "You need to put down the harpoon." I kept my eyes on the game for a minute, thinking I had heard wrong. Then I turned around and saw a man standing near the grill. On the floor next to his feet I saw a twelve-foot harpoon, sturdy and sharp. I glanced around, but nobody else in the bar seemed to have noticed that a man had entered the Billy Goat Tavern with a harpoon fit to kill a whale.

"I'm an Eskimo," he said to the cooks and to me by way of explanation. He smiled. He used that term, *Eskimo,* for our benefit. Then he continued. "I'm an Alaska native." He wore jeans and fit in perfectly, apart from his harpoon. Cheeseburgers sizzled.

"My wife is at a conference in Hammond, Indiana. This is my first time to a big city. I heard this is the place to get a good cheeseburger."

Troy O'Leary hit a home run. The man from Alaska finished his cheeseburger, picked up his harpoon, and left the Goat. Nobody had noticed—every eye was on the televisions. Sosa struck out. The game ended a few minutes later. The Marlins had won three straight and would go on to win their second World Series in six years. The Cubs had not won since 1908. Someone in the tavern chanted, "The Goat! The Goat! The Goat!"

CHAPTER 5

Nationalism

SOMETHING DEAD IN THE WOODS

One summer evening during a visit to Cooperstown I stood in the pink dusk facing the sunset. Something in the sky beyond the town's buildings and trees caught my eye. A large bird, its wings spread in patient soar, circled miles above. Must be a bald eagle, I thought.

I lingered on the sidewalk and watched its slow pattern around the perimeter of town and then walked to the shore of what James Fenimore Cooper called Glimmerglass Lake. Its surface was flat and reflected white light like a tub of newly set grape Jell-O. The open stretch of calm water, flanked by hills and woods in the distance, gave a clear view of a pale orange horizon dotted with large, dark birds. It was beautiful—the gentle eagles, the serene lake, the spiritual home of baseball. I had never seen so many eagles flying together. It was like a squadron. As I strained my eyes to make out the birds' features, the majestic soaring turned menacing. They were vultures, not eagles. They were waiting for something weak to die.

I walked back to my motel, the Mohican. My mood was grim. I wondered whether baseball itself was the dead thing. I began to see not just what is gaining on us, but what overtook us from the beginning.

MILITIA

George W. Bush became the managing general partner of the Texas Rangers in 1989, when he joined a group of businessmen to buy the team. The Senators had moved from Washington to Texas for the 1972 season, where they became the Rangers. Bush retained his position until he became governor.

The team was named for a law enforcement organization formed in 1823, which became a formal part of the Department of Public Safety in 1935. The Rangers were known in the Old West for fighting Native Americans and for helping the United States win the Mexican-American War. The "war" was an act of conquest in which the U.S. grabbed about forty percent of Mexico's land, which later became New Mexico, California, and Arizona. The Mexicans who lived on the land were suddenly on American soil due to the simple change in the map.

When Bush was an owner and managing partner of the Rangers, the city of Arlington built a new stadium and leased it to the team. After urging by the Bush conglomerate, the city raised taxes to pay for the stadium, and also used eminent domain to take thirteen acres from the Curtis Mathes family. It was socialized baseball. The Rangers played their games on this conquered territory. When the team was sold to Tom Hicks a few years later, George W. Bush personally made $14.9 million from the deal.

Ironically, when he ran for governor, he said, "I understand full well the value of private property and its importance not only in our state but in capitalism in general, and I will do everything I can to defend the power of private property and property rights when I am the governor of this state."

THE IMPORTANCE OF CHARACTER

A special award hanging in the Hall of Fame honors players who are not only good at the sport, but whose lives are honorable and worthy of emulation. It's called the Lou Gehrig Memorial Award, and is "presented annually to the Major League Baseball player who both on and off the field best exemplifies the character of Lou Gehrig, Columbia University '25, who played in 2,164 games as a member of the New York American Baseball Club."

Past winners include Pete Rose in 1969, and Mark McGwire in 1999. Not only are they already "in" the Hall of Fame, they are there precisely because of their personal character.

PROGRESS STEAMROLLED WEST

TERRY MANN: People will come, Ray.

MARK: You're broke, Ray. You sell now, or you'll lose everything.

TERRY MANN: The one constant through all the years, Ray, has been baseball. America has rolled by like an army of steamrollers. It's been erased like a blackboard, rebuilt, and erased again. But baseball has marked the time. This field, this game, it's part of our past, Ray. It reminds us of all that once was good, and could be again. Oh, people will come, Ray, people will most definitely come.

WHIMSY

Billy Martin, the Yankees manager, and Nicolae Ceausescu, the Communist Romanian dictator, both died on Christmas Day, 1989. For Communists, it was the latest in a series of misfortunes that would culminate with the collapse of the Soviet Union. For the Yankees, it was a similar tragedy. Billy Martin had been the guts of the team for nearly forty years.

By 1989 the Yankees had won twenty-two championships across the eighty-eight years of their existence, while the

Bolsheviks had only managed to conquer roughly sixteen countries during their seventy-two years. The Bolsheviks were coming to their end with capitalism still intact. At least the Yankees still had the Joe Torre era on the horizon and another two decades of George Steinbrenner. The United States, in contrast with the once-feared Soviet Empire, had been in existence for over two hundred years and had conquered countless nations, though not Vietnam. If its tally included sovereign Native American nations, it approached seven hundred conquests.

Richard Nixon attended Billy Martin's funeral. He had been a friend of the Yankees ever since George Steinbrenner helped him get reelected in 1972.

FANATICS

George Steinbrenner paid forty thousand dollars to a young gambler for dirty information on Dave Winfield. The news leaked in 1990. It was a bad time to be caught with gamblers if you were part of Major League Baseball. Pete Rose had been banned for life a few months prior for betting on the game. Commissioner Fay Vincent investigated Steinbrenner and banned him from baseball.

A few days after Vincent's decree, the Yankees owner's son, Hank Steinbrenner, said:

> I'd hate to be the son of a great president or world leader. But you have the ability to put things in perspective. Dad is known because he's the owner of a baseball team, and for the way he's gone about owning it. Somewhat flamboyant. He's not Churchill, or Roosevelt or Einstein. . . . I learned from my father that you have to outhustle people if you're going to succeed, that there's always a time when you can

take a good business risk. And if you're the boss,
you have to be a benevolent dictator.

Commissioners have tremendous power through a rule that
enables them to act in the vague "best interests of baseball." It's
up to the commissioner to decide what that means. It's like the
Patriot Act, the Military Commissions Act, and the National
Defense Authorization Act all rolled into one, but for baseball.
Steinbrenner was reinstated in time for the 1993 season. During
his time away, fans wrote Commissioner Vincent letters with
passionate and contradictory opinions about what should happen to him.

An inmate at Fishkill Correctional Facility in Beacon, New
York, wrote Vincent a letter on October 16, 1991. The inmate,
a self-described "rabid" Yankees fan, supported George
Steinbrenner. He wrote with dismay that some Yankees fans
cheered when Steinbrenner's ban was announced, and said in
defense of the owner, "I would've liked to crack each and every
one of there [sic] skulls with a Louisville Slugger to put some
sense into their heads!" The prisoner was a former convenience
store cashier and said that because of his own unjust prison sen-
tence—three to ten years for gun possession—he knew a bad
deal when he saw it. Steinbrenner had gotten a bad deal. The
prisoner urged forgiveness: "This is a decent guy that deserves
to be back at the helm of the ship."

A few weeks later, a missive was written on the letterhead of
the Episcopal Mission Society in Manhattan. The author, a reverend, was a passionate Yankees fan with strong opinions about
George Steinbrenner. The reverend was direct: "I write to plead
with you to ban George Steinbrenner permanently from Major
League Baseball."

The reverend described his love for the sport's "artfulness
and drama." The reverend complained that Steinbrenner,

though a convicted felon, was allowed to run the team. The reverend said, "I believe in giving people a second chance and have worked with prison inmates most of my professional career." But the reverend's forgiveness had limits: "It is time to end the Steinbrenner story."

Some letters imbued Yankee Stadium with religious qualities. A man in New Jersey told the commissioner, "To us Yankee fans in particular and most baseball fans in general the name 'New York Yankees' is virtually another name for baseball itself. Yankee Stadium is not just a ballpark, but rather the most hallowed arena in all of sport. A 'shrine,' if you will. The place where a veritable 'who's who' of immortals has plied their craft. Yet, if he gets his way, Steinbrenner will move the team to New Jersey and this 'Cathedral' of the baseball world will never be the same."

Other fans were insane. A man from Clifton, New Jersey—the home of Rupert Pupkin, the psychopath in Scorsese's *King of Comedy*—sent the commissioner a paranoid letter about Steinbrenner. After saying he had been a Yankees fan since DiMaggio, he wrote:

> J. Edgar Hoover, the CIA, the Military, the Kennedy Family, JFK as President, RFK as Attorney General, LBJ, who appointed the Warren Comm. the Justice Dept., big Business Corporations, Government Agencies, all and those not mentioned, and the "Mob" as has been said, in one way or another represent Power!!! And that is precisely what Mr. Steinbrenner wants back, POWER!!! I, if I had a say, he'd have to sell out his complete interests and go back to shipbuilding. Was he not found in bad light in his contribution to the Nixon campaign? Who repealed him? Do not think for one minute it will not happen again, it will. In one way or another.

All of Commissioner Vincent's responses to the fans included an identical paragraph: "As I have expressed on many occasions, I believe that baseball occupies a special place in American life. Consequently, I am always interested in knowing the views of the fans whose devotion to the game has made it a national institution."

IMPEACHED

In August 1991 George Steinbrenner was in the middle of his suspension and things were not going well for management or the players. The Yankees were on their way to a last-place finish when Steve Farr, Matt Nokes, Pascual Perez, and Don Mattingly were asked to get haircuts. Team captain Don Mattingly refused to cut his, which was "just above his collar."

Stump Merrill issued the orders, but Mattingly blamed general manager Gene Michael. Mattingly was benched for refusing to submit to the scissors and missed a game against the Royals. He said of Gene "Stick" Michael, "It's kind of silly to me, but we're not winning and this is Stick's club. . . . He wants an organization that will be puppets for him and do what he wants." Mattingly noted his status as team captain meant little after the order. "They should take that away. It doesn't mean anything. Take it. It's been stripped. I've been impeached."

The next day Mattingly was back in the lineup. Michael and Merrill had caved and let Mattingly play. Instead, both men had cut their *own* hair. Mattingly said, "This wasn't any kind of stand for freedom, or anything. . . . It's just that they put me into a corner, and I guess the competitive nature in me came out."

Writer Ira Berkow understood:

> The Mattingly controversy, like the [Oscar] Gamble case, had little to do with grooming,

and much more to do with power. . . . Hair is
an old sheargoat. Control someone's hair and
you control his mind, goes a theory. You manip-
ulate him by sapping his psychological strength,
his sense of identity. That seems the symbolism
in the tale of the clipped Samson. In the same
way, the first thing a private receives in the
Army is a full hedge pruning. He goes into the
barbershop a person and comes out a billiard
ball. Meanwhile, the retaining of one's locks has
often been taken as rebellion.

TRIUMPHALISM

The 1991 World Series was notable because the Braves and the
Twins had been last place teams just the year before. It was the
beginning of a long stretch of the Braves' prowess in the
National League. During rallies their fans pretended they were
chanting Indians and chopped their arms like tomahawks.
Some decorated their faces with war paint. Others wore feath-
ered headdresses.

The American Indian Movement and many other Native
Americans were offended by the appropriation and misrepresen-
tation of Native culture by baseball fans and the businesses that
operated the teams and leagues. Activist Clyde Bellecourt spoke
to the press during protests outside the Metrodome. He said,
"America is scholastically retarded about Indian culture and history, and how the West was really won. . . . It is pure ignorance."

VAYA CON DIOS

The Metrodome allowed baseball to be played inside a balloon
on grass that required a vacuum. For decades the Twins had
toiled at Metropolitan Stadium. When the old park was demol-
ished, the Mall of America, the most extravagant of its kind,
metastasized on its very rubble.

On the day of its grand opening in August of 1992, I visited the Mall of America with an avaricious church youth group. I was fifteen years old, and only three memories remain: a vast asphalt parking lot shimmering in the sun, the false promise of a Hooters restaurant, and a small memorial within the mall showing the precise location of the Met's home plate. Harmon Killebrew, Zoilo Versalles, and Sandy Koufax had played the 1965 World Series in that very space. Billy Martin finished his playing career there, and then worked his way up from third-base coach to manager of the Twins, his first job at the helm. What a hopeful place the old Met must have been for him. I do not believe a just god would send Billy Martin to hell. But if God is a Royals fan, the ghost of Billy Martin haunts the Mall of America in search of an era long since lost. With any luck, his spirit has taken refuge at the Hooters bar, a goblet of Miller Lite quenching his eternal thirst.

WARNING
Several people were arrested during the 1997 World Series in what they viewed as the suppression of their right to free speech. In protest of the Indians' use of the Chief Wahoo logo, which is a caricature of negative stereotypes of Native Americans, the activists burned an effigy of the mascot outside the stadium.

In spring 1998, a judge dismissed the case against the protesters. A few days later, a group of five protesters marked the Indians' season opener by burning effigies of Chief Wahoo and Black Sambo in a gesture that pointed toward the racist and demeaning nature of both images. They were arrested and spent over twenty-four hours in jail. After suing the police for false arrest and for violating their freedom of speech, a judge partially dismissed their case in 2001.

A statement by the American Indian Movement's Grand
Governing Council explained the protesters' beliefs:

> The police and city government have shown a
> double standard as far as the laws are concerned.
> They have decided that it is against the law to
> express our disagreement with racist images like
> Chief Wahoo and the name "Indians." Whereas,
> the fans and Cleveland baseball team can wear
> these racist images and wear headdresses that
> degrade Native culture and identity in a sacrile-
> gious manner. These images have a negative
> effect on the self-esteem of our youth and the
> youth of all nations. It corrupts and pollutes the
> minds of everyone, especially our youth.

They also noted, "Two effigies were burned, one of Chief
Wahoo and the other of Black Sambo, to express outrage at
racist icons being used to promote profit-making businesses."
When the judge in Cleveland dismissed the lawsuit filed by the
five protesters, one of the plaintiffs observed, "The judge's decision in favor of the city and police defendants is a blow to civil
rights and moves the U.S. one step closer to government-
controlled speech and assembly."

How It Happened
During the interim between the November 2000 presidential
election and the Supreme Court ruling that led to George W.
Bush becoming president-elect a month later, the *Observer*
published an article about Bush and baseball.

> "I never dreamed about being president," says
> George W. Bush. "When I was growing up, I
> wanted to be Willie Mays." The legendary out-
> fielder is the man Bush usually names as his
> childhood hero, though he has also mentioned
> Winston Churchill. And if this self-proclaimed
> "baseball nut" is finally named president, he will

owe it in large part to his favorite game. . . . It
fed the notion that this millionaire son of
Washington is a regular guy, and suggested,
falsely, that he had had a hands-on job in a
multi-million-dollar operation. The link with
the ultimate American game has also helped
him seem uniquely American.

Bush commented on the "seemingness" of his career when he
was owner of the Texas Rangers and had not begun positioning
himself for public office: "You know I could run for governor
but I'm basically a media creation. I've never done anything."

HUBRIS

On a freezing, windy afternoon in 2001, I stood shivering outside Wrigley Field, cursing myself. Years before, in high school,
I had a divine revelation that I would play for the Red Sox. I
had failed to make the first cut for my high school team, yet
somehow I felt I would improve my swing and at least play in
the minor leagues. I bet a friend, a former teammate with a
long memory, that by the time I was twenty-four, I would be a
pro.

By 2001, I had not played baseball for several years, but I
had developed a plan to win the bet on a two-pronged technicality. At age twenty-three and eleven months, I had *another*
vision. The Red Sox had not won the World Series since 1918.
The Cubs had not won the World Series since 1908. My argument was that since, from a spiritual perspective, the Cubs and
the Red Sox were the same team, I could win the bet by joining the *Cubs*. I had also come to believe that in the technical
language of the original bet, my friend and I had shaken hands
on the phrase that I would be "in the organization" by the time

I was twenty-four. The meaning of "in" was open to interpretation in the post-Lewinsky era.

I stood outside Wrigley, knocking on a back door that leads inside the park. It was my second interview for a spot on the custodial roster. I would be the guy sweeping up the peanut shells at the end of the game. Being a janitor for the Cubs was the best I could muster, but I figured it was my only chance to win the bet. I knocked on the door again and waited. I knocked again. The wind stung and then numbed my ears and cheeks. My eyes watered. Nothing. I looked at my watch: 2:00 p.m. The interview was at ten. I was four hours late. I had just lost the bet.

UNITED 93

On the morning of September 11, 2001, Vice President Dick Cheney and his chief of staff, Scooter Libby, took shelter in a secure bunker as they received reports of the terrorist attacks in New York and nearby at the smoldering Pentagon.

At two minutes past ten, those in the shelter learned another hijacked aircraft, United Flight 93, was flying toward Washington. Libby recalled Cheney's decision to shoot down the plane if necessary took "about the time it takes a batter to decide to swing."

INTENTIONAL WALK

Two days after Osama Bin Laden attacked the World Trade Center and the Pentagon, members of his extensive family living in the United States secured reservations for a charter plane, pilot, and crew to evacuate them from America. On the nineteenth of September, the Bin Ladens boarded a Boeing 727 that took them to Europe. Among the plane's previous passengers were the Baltimore Orioles.

Baseball Has a Magic Value

George W. Bush walked onto the baseball field, looked around confidently, and waved as people in the stands stood, cheered, and brandished patriotic signs. Cameras flashed around the stadium, and the president strode quickly to the mound. He wound and threw the ceremonial first pitch, a strike down the middle of the plate. The crowd went berserk, shouting, "usa, usa, usa, usa." A man waved a sign, usa fears nobody play ball, its words in huge print above an image of an American flag flanked by two Yankees symbols. Afterwards Bush shook the managers' hands, then walked over to Rudy Giuliani. The New York mayor was sitting close to the field wearing a dark Yankees jacket and cap. Giuliani and Bush clasped hands, and the crowd roared. It was the first World Series after the attacks. A fan held a sign: Home of the Brave.

Rally

In his book *Bush at War*, Bob Woodward describes George W. Bush's appearance at the 2001 World Series. Of the ecstatic reaction to Bush as he gave the crowd the thumbs-up sign, Woodward writes, "Watching from owner George Steinbrenner's box, Karl Rove thought, it's like being at a Nazi rally."

How the Spectacle Played in Kansas

"Such confusing times. Hate the Yanks? Love them? Boo them? Salute them? Can we get a ruling here?"

—Joe Posnanski, *Kansas City Star,* October 26, 2001

What We Talk about When We Talk about the Yankees

A few months after September 11, 2001, I traveled to Istanbul for vacation. It was my first international trip since we'd been attacked. I was tense. While I waited in O'Hare for my flight, an elderly man sitting next to me at the gate leaned his face close to mine and said he was carrying a knife. His breath smelled of coffee and Sen-Sen, his shirt was pressed and neatly tucked into his pale blue jeans, and he wore a mesh ball cap bearing the logo of a seed company. I saw white, hairless skin between the top of his socks and the bottom of his jeans when he stretched his legs. He was on his way to visit his son stationed in Germany. We were sitting twenty feet from the check-in counter. The old man zipped open his brown carry-on bag, reached inside, and pulled out a long maroon summer sausage. It was his cover. If they caught him with the knife he would claim he needed it to slice the meat for a snack. "I'm eighty-seven years old," he said. "I'll go down fighting."

Most people in Turkey are Muslim, and I was curious how I would be treated as an American. Distinctions between secular Islamic states, like Turkey and Ba'athist Iraq, and theocracies built around forms of Islam that critique the West more piously, like Afghanistan, Iran, and Saudi Arabia, had been lost to most Americans after the terrorist attacks.

I had an outsider's view of the beautiful city of Istanbul, and to me the locals seemed kind and generous. One man shouted, "I love Clinton" as I walked past. Over dinner, a Turkish man held one hand up like a tower and positioned his other with thumb and pinkie extended like the wings of a plane. He watched my expression as he crashed the plane into the tower and laughed. Then he said he loved America and wanted to move there and work repairing air-conditioners.

Tourists are drawn to markets, and I was no exception. Vendors sold intrigue: carpets from Turkey, Iran, and several of the 'Stans, spices like ground purple sumac and a special savory mix for aubergine. At one booth that also sold men's dress shirts wrapped in plastic, there were New York Yankees baseball caps.

I began to wonder why Yankees caps were sold in Istanbul. I wondered who they were for: the locals, tourists like me, or both.

PEOPLE WERE COWED

During the weeks leading up to the U.S. invasion of Iraq in 2003, hundreds of thousands of people protested around the country and in cities across the world. Two of them were Tim Robbins and Susan Sarandon, who played Nuke LaLoosh and Annie Savoy in the classic baseball movie *Bull Durham*. The fifteenth anniversary of its release was to be celebrated at the Hall of Fame in Cooperstown, but Dale Petroskey, its president, canceled the event. He sent a letter to Tim Robbins telling him that his political views, and choice to voice them, undermined the war effort. Petroskey had been the assistant press secretary under Ronald Reagan.

Writer Ira Berkow observed, "Baseball in many ways has indeed come to symbolize America. For example, the manager informs the umpire that he's an idiot. That is called dissent, a longstanding institution in this country, but one with which Dale Petroskey, president of the Baseball Hall of Fame, is unfamiliar." Petroskey later gave a half-hearted admission of his blunder on the radio.

A *New York Times* editorial on the Hall of Fame's decision to cancel Robbins and Sarandon remains relevant: "Maybe it's just the stress of war, or maybe it's bad judgment. In any case, people thousands of miles from the front lines are behaving strangely in the name of patriotism."

FATHER AND SON

A bare-chested father-son duo jumped a guardrail, loped onto the field at Comiskey Park, and assaulted Royals first-base coach Tom Gamboa. They flailed their arms and drummed him with their fists, but were captured before they could use their teeth. During the attack one of them dropped a knife, providing evidence of a capacity for tool use. Gamboa suffered hearing loss, the father and son lost their freedom for a short time, and the players lost their sense of invulnerability. Carlos Beltran, the Royals outfielder, said, "We think we're safe at the ballpark. What happened today, that tells us no matter where we are, we're not safe."

FATHER AND SON, PART II

My dad and I had made a trip to Chicago in the early nineties to watch a game in the new Comiskey. We sat behind home plate, miles above the action. I do not remember who played or won, but I saw blood pooled on the concrete as I walked to the bathroom. The maroon lagoon was the size of a catcher's mitt, and it glistened in the artificial light, slowly congealing near a hot dog stand.

Years later I was living in Chicago, and my dad passed through town and insisted we watch the Royals play the White Sox. He wore his Royals hat, but I was too wary to bring mine along. This was during the middle of a string of hundred-loss seasons. There were other Royals fans a dozen rows away, and throughout the game a cluster of Sox fiends berated, harassed, threatened, belittled, and cursed the visitors from Kansas City. My dad and I listened and watched, relieved it wasn't happening to us. After several innings of abuse, security removed the fans. The *Royals* fans.

RAINOUT

Every year, as part of a baseball research conference at the Hall of Fame, attendees play a game of town ball before a picnic. Town ball is an early version of baseball, but the ball is softer and you don't use a glove. I was there in 2006, when it rained heavily and the grass field became saturated. The ground was too muddy for walking, much less running the bases. It would have torn open the field, uprooted the grass, and caused long-lasting damage to land lent to us by a kind area resident. The game was canceled, but the picnic took place under a large open tent on the edge of a hayfield. Conference participants—mostly a group of white men in their forties, fifties, and sixties—huddled under the shelter and feasted on corn on the cob, chicken, and cans of cold American beer. It wasn't entirely homogeneous: there were a few younger men like myself, a few women.

During dinner Tim Wiles from the Hall of Fame's research library stood in front of the group dressed as the Mighty Casey. Wearing a red-and-white uniform and a bristled mustache, he was the master of ceremonies, a shepherd for the flock, a priest for the faithful. We set down our forks and conversations slowed. Wiles led us in a recitation of "Casey at the Bat," and we all joined in a grand call and response, booing and cheering as the crowd does in the poem.

Then Mighty Casey began to sing softly, earnestly. The tent was quiet again. It was a melancholy sound, like a Gregorian chant or the opening to Lou Reed's *Coney Island Baby*, his ode to sports and loneliness.

> Katie Casey was baseball mad.
> Had the fever and had it bad;
> Just to root for the home town crew,
> Ev'ry sou Katie blew

Wiles reached the end of the first verse, and I still had not recognized it. It was quiet, even sad, and despite myself I felt a twinge of the sentimentality the older men seemed to be sharing. I wondered if we had been hypnotized by the music, or if the mood was due to the steroid scandal or larger issues like war and the erosion of the Constitution. I looked around. I was younger than most by twenty years. Baseball's steroid scandal seemed more shocking to these men, who grew up in a time when players like Jackie Robinson, Mickey Mantle, Willie Mays, and Carl Yastrzemski were seen as heroes. When I was a kid, Denny McLain, the last man to win thirty games, had already done time in prison. Several of my hometown Royals had been caught with cocaine. There was a strike, and then another. Pete Rose, Doc Gooden, Steve Howe. I could go on. I never had a hero, and I never felt deprived for it. When it finally broke, the steroid scandal had been almost natural to me, like an extension of everything I had seen so far in sports. I was not disillusioned by athletes using steroids, because I never had an illusion of baseball's purity in the first place. As we sat in the tent listening to the opening of the song, I pinpointed my own feeling of loss as not about baseball, but about America. I had believed so many good things about our nation that had proven untrue once we began to use torture, imprisonment without trial, and domestic spying as tools in the War on Terror. I realized the steroid scandal was just another window into the problems of America: fake home run records, illusory weapons of mass destruction, economic bubbles hyped by Wall Street. All symptoms of the same syndrome. Ballplayers bloated by steroids, fans bloated by corn syrup and sloth. Both rotten with greed and hubris.

Wiles continued his incantation.

> On a Saturday her young beau
> Called to see if she'd like to go,

to see a show but Miss Kate said, "No,
I'll tell you what you can do"

Then, in an instant, we all recognized the song. The tone became jovial. We smiled and chanted along.

Take me out to the ballgame
Take me out to the crowd
Buy me some peanuts and Cracker Jack
I don't care if I never get back

The melancholy burned away. We sang along happily until the end of the song, because it felt how being at the ballpark should feel. Carefree, open, simple. Never mind that it was written by two people who had never been to a professional baseball game. On that day in Cooperstown, it wielded hypnotic power over us as we sat under the tent, our beer cans empty, our plates piled with chicken bones, cartilage, and denuded corncobs.

WAR GAMES
The war in Afghanistan was helped along by baseball. In 2004, the Hall of Fame issued a press release describing a youth-oriented Afghan Baseball League that the American military had started early in the war. Baseball was popular: "Friday is prayer day, but the residents came out for it . . . they are absolutely not supposed to do anything but they came out for baseball."

The army reserve member who commented on the league was stationed in Afghanistan and was soon deploying to Iraq, where he was hopeful baseball would also make a difference.

HORACE WILSON'S SEEDLINGS BEAR FRUIT
The Major League Baseball season opened in Japan in 2004 with a match between the Yankees and Devil Rays. In the days

leading to the official start of the season, the Yankees played exhibition games against the Yomiuri Giants and the Hanshin Tigers. Yogi Berra was there to watch forty-nine years after he, Andy Carey, Elston Howard, and other Yankees from the 1955 team had played around the country. Hideki Matsui, the star Yankees outfielder, hit a home run against his former team, the Giants. The Yankees won 6–2.

The series was designed to capture market share from the large contingent of baseball fans in Japan, just as decades before, Jackie Robinson had opened a new domestic market for the major leagues. As Japanese stars move to the United States to play, the television ratings for the leagues in Japan diminish. Seventy years had passed since Alva Johnson described this process in the *New Yorker*, but his description remains accurate. The conveyor belt to Yankee Stadium was still operating. Now it drew materials from the whole world. Katsuke Nagasaki's worry back in 1934—that the Japanese were sending their money out of the country by paying Babe Ruth and his All-Stars to barnstorm—looks prophetic.

Purity

High school baseball players in Japan wear buzz haircuts. Short hair is said to represent purity, and amateur players are expected to be pure. One high school player who had been taunted by his teammates for letting his hair grow longer than a buzz cut used his baseball bat to beat four of his teammates who mocked him. Then he went home and killed his mother with the bat, so she would not be shunned.

But Really I'm Just as Susceptible as Anyone Else

The old speedball pitcher Bob Feller gave a keynote speech at a research symposium at the Hall of Fame, and I sat in the audience listening closely. He was the prototype for the old cliché of a farm kid throwing a baseball at the side of the barn until he was good enough to make the majors. He joined the Cleveland Indians in 1936 when he was just seventeen years old, and went on to win 266 games even though he spent three years away from baseball in World War II. His speech, about his career and his military service, was one of the few times I have ever been in awe of a baseball player.

After the talk, I left the auditorium and walked along Main Street toward the Mohican Motel. Up ahead I saw Bob Feller ambling along as though he was just a regular guy. I couldn't resist. I walked up to him and said hello and thanked him for his talk. We shook hands, and his grip was strong though he was over eighty years old. In a small way, for a brief moment, Bob Feller cut through all the garbage that has surrounded professional baseball most of my life. I knew enough to understand there were never any "good old days." But it was jarring, in a pleasant way, to shake hands with the old fireballer.

Damon and Ortiz

Johnny Damon and David Ortiz of the Red Sox went from being down three games to none in the 2004 playoffs to beating the Yankees in seven. Damon had dubbed himself and his teammates "the idiots"—Pedro Martinez and Manny Ramirez were goofier than any Yankee, and loosened up the club. Damon had long hair and a full beard. They played like they had nothing to lose. They seemed to be everything the Yankees weren't, though in reality the Red Sox were also a team with a massive payroll, a powerful legacy, and the best players in the sport.

Ortiz, who always hit well against the Yankees, won game four with a walk-off home run, and won game five with a walk-off single. He was MVP of the series. Damon had hit .467 against the Angels in the first round of the playoffs, but then he choked against New York. In game seven, he finally returned to form. Maybe it was the hair and the beard. Maybe he was channeling the ghost of C. A. Sampson, who won the bet against beer baron Jacob Ruppert a hundred years before. Maybe it was the rumored pregame whiskey shots. Damon set the tone immediately in game seven by hitting a single and stealing second base. After Damon got thrown out at the plate, Ortiz hit his third home run of the series. In the second, Damon hit a grand slam against Vasquez and suddenly the Red Sox had a six-run lead. Two innings later, Damon hit another home run, this time reaching the upper deck.

Yankees star Derek Jeter offered a sober analysis: "It's difficult, but we didn't deserve to win. They played better than we did."

Red Sox president Larry Lucchino echoed what many fans believed: "All empires must fall sooner or later."

SUBMISSION

When Johnny Damon left the Red Sox and joined the Yankees, he knew he would have to cut his hair and shave his beard. Unlike Don Mattingly, Damon submitted willingly and even turned his haircut into a publicity stunt for Steinbrenner. The unruly Red Sock chose to submit to the Boss, the symbolic completion of the domestication of major-league ballplayers.

BRAVERY

Bruce Sutter, a 2006 inductee to the Hall of Fame, is the only player in the hall depicted on his plaque with a bushy beard.

SOLOMON

Takeru Kobayashi of Nagano, Japan, is a competitive hot dog eater. He won the Mustard Belt at Nathan's Famous hot dog eating contest every year between 2001 and 2006. Some Americans disliked being beaten by a man from Japan. Kobayashi can eat 110 hot dogs in a sitting. His method is to tear the hot dogs in half and swallow them, and then dip the buns in liquid and gulp them down. Kobayashi reportedly calls this the "Solomon" method. In the Christian practice of communion, it's called intinction.

PROGRESS

November 10, 2005, was declared Kenichiro Zenimura Day by then-governor of Arizona Janet Napolitano. Arizona resident and Zenimura biographer Bill Staples had urged Napolitano to recognize the relatively unknown Japanese ballplayer. He also worked with the city of Chandler to dedicate a new park to the memory of what happened to civil liberties in Arizona during the war. It's called Nozomi Park, after the Japanese word for "hope."

Nagasaki also has a Nozomi Park.

Staples said, "If you think about the relocation camps, it was a loss for the 120,000 nationwide who lost their freedom, but it was also a loss for the country as a whole. He [Zenimura] struck me as being an important figure in baseball history, in American history, and, of course, Arizona history."

In another interview Staples added, "How do you find happiness in a world where we have less freedom? There is a great deal that can be taken from that and applied to the human condition."

MASSIVE RETALIATION

A contest was staged between a grizzly bear from Kodiak Island and Kobayashi from Japan. The bear was eight feet tall and weighed over a thousand pounds. Kobayashi is five feet eight inches tall and weighs less than 140 pounds.

The announcer wore a tuxedo and introduced the bear as the "beast," the "Alaskan Cruncher." When released from its cage, it stood, roared, and ambled up a ramp to where the hot dogs were waiting. The stars and stripes hung on the wall behind the bear, and the Japanese flag hung behind Kobayashi. He wore a cutoff black T-shirt and a bandanna with a Japanese flag on the front. The bear wore its fur. Kobayashi's biceps were much larger than necessary for tearing and eating hot dogs. The same was true of the grizzly bear's teeth and claws.

The bear put his paw on the steel table, lowered his head, and inhaled a hot dog. That was the signal to begin, and Kobayashi began munching hot dogs two by two. Despite lacking hands, failing to understand the nature of the contest, and being placed in a totally foreign environment, the bear had the advantage of having a bigger mouth, esophagus, and stomach. With each nibble it cleared several hot dogs off its plate. Kobayashi's pile of hot dogs steadily and rapidly disappeared, but even with its less determined pace and short attention span the bear clearly had the advantage. The Alaskan Cruncher won. America had achieved overwhelming victory. Again.

An Idea Is the Hardest Thing to Kill
One of the first things Joe Girardi did when he began his managerial career with the Florida Marlins was institute a shaving policy for the team. He had played under George Steinbrenner's rules against hairiness, and when he began his brief sojourn with the Marlins, Girardi told the press, "To me, the idea is to look professional. I understand it's important to players to have their own style, and I don't have a problem with that. But I want players to look neat and clean."

Reminder

The White Sox won the 2005 World Series and in the next season began enforcing their own rules against hair. In mid-April, Freddy Garcia and Neal Cotts, both pitchers, went to the clubhouse and found their orders.

Garcia said, "I don't know what they want, but it will just be a little bit."

Cotts said, "It's part of the rules. It's kind of vague what the rules are."

Strange Animals I Have Known

Ángel Pagán, a wonderfully named rookie for the Chicago Cubs, was thrown out trying to reach third base on a wild pitch. A moment later, manager Lou Piniella waddled out to argue. He threw down his cap and the umpire tossed him from the game. Piniella kept yelling and kicked dirt toward second base. A dust cloud floated across the infield. Piniella scraped dirt toward the ump with his foot, and everyone shouted: "Lou!" He pushed the girth of his enormous stomach against the ump and screamed, then kicked more dirt. The home plate umpire walked up to Piniella and moved him away from the third-base umpire, but Piniella slipped around them and kicked his own hat across the infield. The crowd at Wrigley was thrilled. The home plate umpire tried to hold him back. Another jogged in to assist, and suddenly Piniella was surrounded. He kept barking. His stomach bulged. It quivered. It spoke in sign language. It focused his rage and projected it toward the umps. Piniella walked around the three umpires onto the dirt infield as though he were going to pick up his cap and end the argument. No! He kicked it onto the grass, barely missing the two umpires who were walking away thinking the argument was over. The blue cap lay on the green grass. Piniella rumbled over and kicked it again.

Then, finally, he bent down, picked it up, and walked off the field as cheers sounded across the North Side of Chicago.

Piniella had played for the Yankees when Billy Martin was their manager and cited his mentor as an influence.

THE HATCH

I had done my best to forget the horror of the 9/11 attacks and stay sane during the grim years that followed. Then, toward the end of the decade, I spent time in New York. The tragedy percolated to the surface. One rainy afternoon while walking around Manhattan not far from the financial district, I spied a tall metal cross standing outside St. Peter's. Soldered in shaky writing on a small plaque near the bottom are the words:

> The Cross at Ground Zero
> Founded Sept. 13, 2001
> Blessed Oct. 4, 2001
> Temporarily Relocated
> Oct. 5, 2006
> Will Return to WTC Museum
> A Sign of Comfort for
> ALL

The cross was part of the World Trade Center debris, and in the days following the attacks, workers and mourners alike took comfort in the fact it had survived miraculously intact. It was taken as a sign of the power of American Christianity in the midst of an attack by foreigners of a different religion. It was removed from the rest of the rubble, and served as one of many spontaneous memorials.

I stood on the sidewalk in a light drizzle. The metal cross that survived the crumbling buildings was brown, and the beams were peppered with orange rust. Then I noticed a cement ledge in the middle of the beam, right where Jesus' feet would rest if it were a crucifix. Atop this ledge sat a glass cube, and inside the cube sat two baseballs. I stared at the baseballs, the cross, and wondered what they meant. Instead of ignoring my confusion I let it ferment, and it opened my perspective. On that day, the baseballs perched on the cross looked to me like round white eggs, the eggs of a creature that had made its nest in the rubble.

ON THE USES OF A BASEBALL BAT, ACCORDING TO AN AMERICAN INTELLIGENCE AGENCY

The National Security Archive at George Washington University is devoted to legally obtaining and publishing documents the United States government once kept secret. It released a report called "A Study of Assassination," which defines assassination as "the planned killing of a person who is not under the legal jurisdiction of the killer, who is not physically in the hands of the killer, who has been selected by a resistance organization for death . . . and whose death provides positive advantages to that organization."

It advises that "assassination can seldom be employed with a clear conscience. Persons who are morally squeamish should not attempt it."

Techniques include the use of bare hands, fake accidents, drugs, edge weapons, firearms, the submachine gun, the shotgun, silent firearms, and explosives. The report also discusses blunt weapons: "Their main advantage is their universal availability. . . . Baseball . . . bats are very widely distributed. . . . Blows should be directed to the temple, the area just below and behind the ear, and the lower, rear portion of the skull."

THE TRUTHINESS OF METAPHORS

Marine Lieutenant Colonel Stuart Couch voluntarily returned to active duty after the attacks of September 11. As the Senior

Prosecutor for the Office of Military Commissions, he was assigned to try a man named Mohamedou Ould Slahi, who was accused of helping the Hamburg terrorist cell that planned the attacks. Couch visited the American prison in Guantanamo Bay, Cuba, and was repulsed by the interrogation techniques he witnessed. He refused to prosecute because the interrogation of Slahi was "morally repugnant." The American Bar Association gave him its Minister of Justice award for his commitment to ethics and legal standards.

Couch struggled to define the difference between torturing people and merely treating them cruelly and inhumanely. He resorted to baseball metaphors:

> [W]hat is torture? Where does torture pick up . . . where do you cross over that line? Cruel, degrading, inhuman treatment, and when does it cross that line over into torture? And I think that's almost like a [sic] that's almost like a strike zone for an empire [sic] in baseball. What is that empire's [sic] strike zone? And I think that's an issue that's going to be debated to the end of time. All I know is, for me, I had a strike zone. What I thought to be permissible and what I thought had to be impermissible. And whether or not I can be a part of a system, part of a process that utilizes that information or not. And me, it just went outside the strike zone.

The Value of a Soldier's Life

Roger Clemens announced in May 2007 that he would be returning to New York to pitch for the Yankees. A few weeks later Andrew Bacevich, a Vietnam veteran who opposed the war in Iraq, wrote an essay about politics, money, and war. Earlier that month his son, an American soldier, had been killed by a suicide bomber in Salah al-Din province. Bacevich recalled how after his son died, two people wrote to burden him with blame. They claimed his antiwar activism strengthened America's enemies. Bacevich had hoped by speaking out against the war in conjunction with other Americans, the nation's leaders would eventually do the people's will.

But after his son was killed, he wrote:

> This, I can see now, was an illusion. The people have spoken, and nothing of substance has changed. . . . Memorial Day orators will say that a G.I.'s life is priceless. Don't believe it. I know what value the U.S. government assigns to a soldier's life: I've been handed the check. It's roughly what the Yankees will pay Roger Clemens per inning once he starts pitching next month. . . . [Money] negates democracy, rendering free speech little more than a means of recording dissent. This is not some great conspiracy. It's the way our system works.

THE GHOST OF BILLY SUNDAY

Baseball stadiums are one of the few places where church and state mingle and hardly anyone notices. A Yankees fan left his seat to use the restroom during the seventh-inning stretch in August 2008. In the years since the 9/11 attacks, the Yankees had used the break to enforce a moment of silent prayer and blast the stadium with "God Bless America." A police officer stopped the fan, who explained he needed to urinate. Two officers then twisted his arms behind his back and ejected him from Yankee Stadium. One told the fan to leave the country.

The fan consulted the American Civil Liberties Union and sued both the police department and the Yankees. The ACLU described the fan's treatment at Yankee Stadium as "an abuse of authority and a violation of the constitutional principles that our country was founded on." The fan explained his own view:

"My issue is with the Yankees forcing people to stay in their seats and participate in it. . . . Forcing people to participate in an act of patriotism really devalues the freedom our country fought for in the first place."

As part of the settlement with the fan, the Yankees released a statement saying they "have no policy or practice at the new Yankee Stadium that imposes any restrictions on fans wishing to move about the Stadium during the playing of 'God Bless America' that do not also apply during the rest of the game."

Sun City, Arizona

The House That Ruth Built was replaced with a copy, a replica, a simulation of the original. It was a business decision. George Steinbrenner had wanted a new field for decades. When Yankee Stadium closed in 2008, old players and other notables came to visit the park one last time. Julia Ruth Stevens, Babe Ruth's ninety-two-year-old daughter, was one of those present for the final ceremony. She had given her approval for the team's move earlier in the day: "Daddy always said that records were made to be broken. So I think he probably would have felt this was O.K."

It turned out Babe Ruth's daughter had divided loyalties. She appreciated the Yankees because of her father's success in New York. She had also lived in New Hampshire for a long time and had become a Red Sox fan. On the night commemorating the end of Yankee Stadium, she also admitted that as a longtime winter resident of Sun City, Arizona, she had attended the 2001 World Series there and "wasn't exactly heartbroken" when the Yankees had lost.

Sun City is the planned community developed for seniors by former Yankees owner Del Webb. His first planned community, of course, was Poston, the Japanese internment camp.

NOW PITCHING, WOODY GUTHRIE

Woody Guthrie is known for writing "This Land is Your Land." Guthrie called the song "God Blessed America for Me" and intended it as a parody of the Irving Berlin song "God Bless America."

One version of Guthrie's song includes the stanza: "As I went walking I saw a sign there / and on the sign it said 'No Trespassing.' / But on the other side it didn't say nothing. / That side was made for you and me."

Woody Guthrie pitched nine seasons for the Delta Dragons in the Cosmic Baseball Association and had an impressive career as a right-hander, going 110–73 with a 3.91 ERA and 1025 strikeouts. Neil Young, Lou Reed, Frank Zappa, and Joan Baez have all played for the Delta Dragons.

SPECTATOR SPORTS

The Alphatown Ionians were a team of philosophers and thinkers in the Cosmic Baseball Association. Newton, Darwin, and John Dewey were pitchers, and their catcher was Noam Chomsky, who hit .288 in their only season. Chomsky, though a respected linguist, has also written books about American policy and history, and was prompted by an interviewer to talk about sports:

> [I]n our society, we have things that you might use your intelligence on, like politics, but people really can't get involved in them in a very serious way—so what they do is they put their minds into other things, such as sports. . . . And I suppose that's also one of the basic functions it serves in the society in general: it occupies the population, and keeps them from trying to get involved with things that really matter. In fact, I presume that's part of the reason why spectator

sports are supported to the degree they are by
the dominant institutions. And spectator sports
also have other useful functions too. For one
thing, they're a great way to build up chauvinism—you start by developing these totally irrational loyalties early in life, and they translate
very nicely to other areas. . . . But the point is,
this sense of irrational loyalty to some sort of
meaningless community is training for subordi-
nation to power, and for chauvinism. . . . All of
this stuff builds up extremely anti-social aspects
of human psychology. . . . [T]hey're emphasized, and exaggerated, and brought out by
spectator sports: irrational competition, irrational loyalty to power systems, passive acquies-
cence to quite awful values, really. In fact, it's
hard to imagine anything that contributes more
fundamentally to authoritarian attitudes than
this does, in addition to the fact that it just
engages a lot of intelligence and keeps people
away from other things. . . . But this stuff is a
major part of the whole indoctrination and propaganda system, and it's worth examining more
closely.

The Washington Presidents have played in the Cosmic Baseball
league since 1982. The official 2009 roster had a promising
rookie pitcher named Barack Obama, while George W. Bush
languished in right field.

SEDUCTION

The Yankees were in the postseason again. My girlfriend and I
stood in the 4 train somewhere between 125th and 161st, on
our way to the new Yankee Stadium to watch the playoffs. The
train was full of Yankees fans, of course. I gripped a metal rail-
ing above my head and swayed as the train jostled me. My

damp armpit was in a young woman's face. She was talking
with her father, who was on the other side of my body. I wore
a stocking cap, gloves, and a coat. I was sweating. Ten feet
away a giant man caught my eye. His body was thick, he was
a head taller than most people in the train, and a small black
transmitter was affixed to his wrist. An earplug with a spiral
coil protruded from his ear. The young woman said into my
armpit, "Bloomberg?"

I craned my neck and finally saw the rich little mayor standing between his two large bodyguards. The train arrived at
Yankee Stadium, and my girlfriend and I departed, walking
alongside Mayor Bloomberg. He wore a tan-and-blue leather
Yankees jacket. He stepped ahead and descended the stairs. I
felt like I had just seen a rare animal—a whooping crane or a
platypus.

We stepped out and to our right we saw Yankee Stadium—
the new Yankee Stadium—the one that had opened months
before. It shined. To our left was the old Yankee Stadium: dark,
empty, and surrounded by a tall blue mesh fence that looked
like a gauze medical bandage. Our tickets in hand, we walked
to the turnstiles.

Tall vertical banners hung from the ceiling: Babe Ruth, Lou
Gehrig, Joe DiMaggio, Mickey Mantle. Yankees players everywhere. Yankees fans everywhere. Eating hot dogs. Drinking
beer. Wearing coats, gloves, and stocking caps.

Our seats were the cheapest I could find. We were down the
right field line, halfway between first base and the fence, way up
in the highest deck, but the view was very good. The field
glowed green. The scoreboard was colossal. It was hard to turn
away from it and watch the real players on the real field as they
stretched and played catch. We were engulfed in light. "It's very
masculine," my girlfriend said.

Regina Wilson, a New York City firefighter, took the field and began to sing the national anthem. I knew I should take my cap off my head, but it was too cold. Very few people in our section removed their caps. It was in the midthirties and dropping. Wilson's image was projected on the monstrous screen as she sang. Down the right field line, I saw three flags: the Stars and Stripes, a POW-MIA, and a Purple Heart. The screen showed images of the Statue of Liberty as Wilson sang, "O'er the land of the free and the home of the brave!" The United States Navy Color Guard presented the colors, a ceremonial remnant from wartime traditions.

The scoreboard showed the Yankees' pictures as they announced the lineups, and my girlfriend observed that they were "surprisingly handsome." Most were clean shaven. Damon had a little stubble. Jeter, a spokesman for Gillette, had cheeks as smooth as a balloon. The theme from *Star Wars* played during the lineup call.

The game proceeded slowly. In the bottom of the second, the Yankees scored on a triple by Robinson Cano. In the third, Jeter hit a solo homer. The Angels tied the game in the fifth, and it remained tied for several innings. Between innings the giant TV screen showed clips of Yankees past and present. They were interspersed with taglines: "A new home in the Bronx recalls old traditions" and "We play for those who came before us," the latter while Babe Ruth radiated from the screen.

A shot of the fans in the stadium showed a man with an Uncle Sam top hat. He had affixed the Yankees "NY" symbol to the front and waved to the camera. During a montage of Yankees players, the screen flashed, "This is OUR house."

Regina Wilson took the field again during the seventh-inning stretch, and began to sing "God Bless America." The giant screen showed images of the Statue of Liberty and the

flag. Thousands of fans sang along with her: "From the moun-
tains, to the prairies, to the oceans, white with foam, God bless
America, my home sweet home." Immediately following "God
Bless America," a commercial ran on the screen urging people
to donate to a program for military families. The crowd sang
"Take Me Out to the Ballgame," but by then most fans had
already taken their seats and were no longer paying attention.

It began snowing in the eighth, and the strong wind swirled
the small flakes into the lights, making us feel like we were in
the center of a snow globe. I was taken in by the spectacle. I had
disparaged it from the outside while watching it on TV in a distant state, but on the inside, in real life, it felt good. And then
I felt guilty—I wasn't supposed to enjoy it. I was from Kansas
City. I was a Royals fan. What would George Brett think? I
risked committing the sin of Santiago in *The Old Man and the
Sea* by worshiping another winner while being a loser.

With two out in the top of the eighth, manager Joe Girardi
brought in Mariano Rivera, the Yankees' ace closer and one of
the best pitchers in the sport. As Rivera took the mound and
began warming up, the loudspeakers blasted "Enter Sandman"
by Metallica. The crowd cheered. Rivera rarely blew it. The
giant screen showed fans' reactions. One man with long blond
hair and an unbuttoned Yankees jersey sang along to the lyrics
and thrashed his head forward and back. The old headbanger's
yellow hair blurred across the screen. The crowd cheered as he
played air guitar. Rivera kept the Angels from scoring.

In the top of the ninth, Damon made a diving catch and
prevented a double or triple. Rivera retired the next two batters.
The frenetic tone and excitement continued in the bottom of
the ninth. "Welcome to the Jungle" echoed in the air. A-Rod
led off. The Yankees got a couple of hits, but failed to score. For
the rest of the game we stood every time the Angels had two

outs, and when a Yankees pitcher got two strikes on a batter. We stood every time a Yankees batter needed a boost. The fans in the right centerfield bleachers chanted, "A-Rod" and "Derek, Jeter."

We were in the extra innings then, and of all nights for it to happen, this was the coldest. But the crowd was excited. I was excited. By the top of the tenth, I was openly rooting for the Yankees to win. The stadium, the crowd, the game—it was overwhelming. My will melted away. I wanted to know what it felt like to win in New York. I tried to think—why did I ever hate the Yankees? After Jeter's home run, it was impossible to care about the Angels. Who could hate Derek Jeter? He came up through the Yankees farm system. He stayed with his team. He had never been caught taking steroids.

The Angels scored in the top of the eleventh, and I felt relief. I had been feeling guilty for wanting the Yankees to win. It was so cold we could barely sit still. The precipitation alternated between a blizzard and rain. I imagined our warm apartment, an hour away, and tried to will that warmth into the stadium. Then A-Rod homered to lead off the bottom of the eleventh, and the thrill was back. I pulled my stocking cap down over my face. My breath was trapped, the heat rose within, and I was finally warm. The fabric was thin, and I could see the green field far below. The last time a game was this exciting to me was the day Mark McGwire hit his sixty-first home run. The tension in Yankee Stadium felt the same. But here it never ended, and for the crowd, every batter was Mark McGwire.

As the Yankees prepared to bat in the bottom of the twelfth, the giant screen played clips from *Rocky II*. We saw Rocky training for his fights, we saw him by Adrian's bedside, we heard the inspiring music. The crowd roared. Shots of Rocky smacking

bags and walloping people were intercut with shots of the
Yankees. The grounds crew ran out and tossed quick-drying
dirt around home plate, the pitcher's mound, and in front of
second base.

It was almost one in the morning. A long train ride to
Brooklyn loomed. We were freezing. It was halfway through the
top of the thirteenth. My girlfriend went to the bathroom
where it was warm, joining other women who had taken refuge
there. I was freezing, and I realized the game could go on forever. I had a plane to catch in the morning. I wanted a hot dog.
I *really* wanted a hot dog.

I got up and walked to the concession area. My girlfriend
found me and we shared the hot dog, which warmed my stomach. We walked down the ramps and I paused to throw away
the wrapper and look back at a television. The Yankees had two
runners on base. Suddenly an Angel threw away the ball, it
rolled past third base, and a run scored. The Yankees won!
Hundreds, then thousands of Yankees fans appeared like a
school of fish and swarmed past us into the night. We joined
them, and I could not stop grinning.

FAN REACTION
The Yankees went on to beat the Phillies in the World Series,
and fans shared their opinions.

> To the Editor:
> We in Chicago would like to congratulate the
> New York Yankees as well as their extensive farm
> system in Kansas City, Texas, Seattle, Oakland,
> Cleveland and Toronto for their latest World
> Series win.

> To the Sports Editor:
> You might say Hideki Matsui's spectacular per-
> formance the [sic] World Series, leading the

Yankees to their 27th title and receiving a well-
earned Most Valuable Player award in the
process, shows how far Asian players have come.
Major League Baseball used to be a game of
only white ballplayers. Now they come from all
corners of the globe. So our championship
game is now truly a World Series.

The Size of Yankee Stadium

The military presence at Yankee Stadium—the color guard, the
flags, the advertisements on the scoreboard—echoed in my
mind during the weeks and months that followed. The stadium
holds 50,287 people. It is the essence of the American way of
life. It is the kind of luxury America goes to war to protect.

Though official combat operations ended in 2010, people are
still dying as a result of the chaos we caused in Iraq. The website
Iraqbodycount.org estimates noncombatant Iraqis killed since
the United States invaded total at least 111,840. That's enough to
fill Yankee Stadium twice with dead Iraqi *civilians*.

Patriotic Story

One Fourth of July, I drove from Chicago to Kansas City, hoping to get home in time to watch the fireworks with old friends
from high school. I got a late start, so I had to rush. I made
good time. The Royals were playing the Yankees, our natural
enemy, in Kansas City. I listened to the radio broadcast and
sped to get home.

Johnny Damon was still playing for the Royals, and he hit
a home run for the lead. I imagined the crowd loving it.
Everyone in the Midwest hates the Yankees. I glanced in my
rearview mirror and saw red and blue flashing lights. The
officer ambled up to my window to check my license. After the
ticket, I knew I had lost time. I doubted I would make it home

for the fireworks. I listened to the game, driving slowly to avoid another ticket. Innings passed. After a while, I realized it was the ninth and I was close to Kauffman Stadium.

The Royals won the game when I was ten minutes away. I pulled alongside the park just as the stadium launched its fireworks. The sky glowed above my car. Purple, red, blue, and green streaked across the sky. Minutes passed. I looked around and realized I had stopped dead still in the middle of the highway. But so had many other cars. We had stopped to watch the fireworks exploding all around us. I leaned my head out my window and stared as blue sparks floated down from the sky, closer and closer to the asphalt. The stadium's lights were dark. In thrall to the spectacle, the crowd sat in silence.

FREEDOM OF SPEECH

On Opening Day 2010, President Barack Obama continued the long tradition of American presidents throwing out the first pitch. He strode to the mound in a Nationals jacket, withdrew a White Sox cap from his pocket, and pulled it snug on his head. The crowd cheered, and he threw the first pitch, a ball. Commissioner Bud Selig issued a statement: "Opening Day of the baseball season is a special event for our country, and its importance has been reinforced by the 100-year history of presidential participation."

The next day, the paper reported that "the Obama administration has taken the extraordinary step of authorizing the targeted killing of an American citizen." The target was a bearded New Mexican named Anwar al-Awlaki, who was hiding in Yemen. Al-Awlaki said bad things, and used words to encourage others to do terrible things. The director of national intelligence said, "If we think that direct action will involve killing an American, we get specific information to do that."

An American president ordered the assassination of a citizen, without trial, for *speech*. But the news was swallowed up by the start of a new baseball season. A little more than a year later, U.S. drones flying in Yemen murdered the American and his sixteen-year-old son, who was also an American.

An owner of the Washington Nationals released a statement on the day Obama opened the baseball season: "It's a time of renewed hope and optimism for fans everywhere."

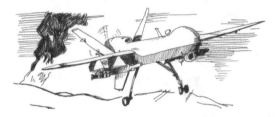

KIDS IN THE CAPITAL OF BASEBALL

On Good Friday in Cooperstown, a white schoolboy with a .22 rifle chased a black classmate in Cooper Park, near the Baseball Hall of Fame. The children ran across Main Street into the police station, where the white boy shot the black boy, and then shot himself in the chin.

The white boy pleaded not guilty to charges of attempted second-degree murder as a hate crime, first-degree attempted assault as a hate crime, and second-degree assault as a hate crime.

PROFESSIONALS

Following the custom for championship teams, the New York Yankees visited the White House, where President Obama greeted the assembled players and made a speech.

> Now, it's been nine years since your last title—
> which must have felt like an eternity for Yankees
> fans. I think other teams would be just fine with

a spell like that. . . . But this is a team that goes down to spring training every year expecting to win it all—and more often than not, you guys get pretty close. . . . That attitude, that success, has always made the Yankees easy to love—and, let's face it, easy to hate as well. . . . But what people tend to forget—especially after watching their teams lose—is that being a Yankee is as much about character as it is about performance; as much about who you are as what you do. Being successful in New York doesn't come easy, and it's not for everybody. It takes a certain kind of player to thrive in the pressure cooker of Yankee Stadium—somebody who is poised and professional, and knows what it takes to wear the pinstripes. It takes somebody who appreciates how lucky he is, and who feels a responsibility for those who are less fortunate. . . . The same spirit was on display today, when the team visited members of our Armed Forces recovering at Walter Reed. They spent time with soldiers and their families—bringing hope and joy to folks who really need it at a time of great difficulty. . . . In the end, that's what makes the Yankees special. . . . It's the players and coaches who shoulder a legacy unlike any other, but who share a belief that anybody blessed with first-class talent also has an obligation to be a first-class person. . . . That's what being a Yankee is all about. That's why I want to congratulate this team—for winning the World Series, and for showing every young person what it means to be a true professional.

1%

In 1975, just before free agency began, the average baseball salary was $44,676. By 2010 it was over $3 million, a raise of at least 6,600 percent. The professionalization of baseball—the

tendency to value quantification, venerate statistics above stories, and impose penalties for behaviors or opinions that could
damage brands and revenue—mirrors a pattern in the larger
culture. In baseball, as in the upper levels of the corporate
world, profits remain high. Average Americans have fared
worse. In 1975, the minimum wage was $2.10 per hour. By 2010
it had risen to $7.25. For much of 2012, I earned $7.50.

In Kansas City in the fifties, the worry had been that the A's
existed solely to increase profits for the Yankees. Decades later
this is the same predatory relationship the average American
shares with the 1 percent: we are hosts for parasites.

Bud Selig/Billy Sunday/B.S.

Bud Selig ordered Jackie Robinson's number, 42, retired among
all major-league ballplayers. It was a feel-good moment for the
league, which had alienated fans during the 1994 strike. Selig's
decree marked the first time the entire sport, rather than an
individual team, retired a number. It was a worthy tribute to
the honorable man who had integrated professional baseball,
and it was an effective public relations stunt.

In the aughts, when star after star was caught using steroids,
revealing anew that the game was anything but clean, Major
League Baseball adopted a pious stance by emphasizing Jackie
Robinson's accomplishments, and, in the wake of 9/11, using
baseball as a vector for nationalism. In 2010, Selig decreed *all*
players would be *required* to wear number 42 on April 15—
every season.

Selig's repeated use of the old ballplayer was a reaction
against the problems that occurred during his tenure as commissioner. In a bait-and-switch reminiscent of the way George
W. Bush used terror alerts to distract the public from Iraq's
nonexistent nuclear weapons, Selig used Jackie Robinson to

turn fans' attention away from steroids. This prefabricated self-righteousness failed to overshadow the steroid scandal, because player after player was caught using drugs, but it framed baseball owners and executives as benevolent rather than the more complex reality that they had benefitted from a culture of substance abuse for years. Selig's behavior was a lot like Billy Sunday's at the turn of the twentieth century. Even as Hal Chase was throwing games for financial gain, Sunday insisted on baseball's moral authority.

POSTMORTEM

The long white car from *Ghostbusters* sat in the gallery space, and a video flashed across its windshield. Ambulance or hearse? A woman narrated pictures and video from America's past. Joseph Beuys, wrapped in blankets, is nibbled by a coyote. President Obama hits a punching bag on a TV talk show. A man sits in flames, having doused himself with gasoline in protest. Klansmen ride horses. Pop stars sing in vain to end hunger in Ethiopia. President George W. Bush. Marlon Brando. Divine. Frankenstein. Dylan. Breasts. Crack. A group of police officers beat Rodney King with clubs as he cowers.

The narrator sounded mournful. She spoke in past tense, as though America were *over*. It was an elegy. She concedes, "Maybe we misrecognized her from the beginning." The hearse's windshield displays a short clip from *Stand by Me*. River Phoenix pulls a .45 from his bag and a scrawny kid wearing a Yankees cap stares. River Phoenix hefts the gun again and hands it to the kid, who smiles, extends his skinny arms, squints, and points. River Phoenix looks away, briefly, and then back to the kid in the Yankees hat holding the gun. The narrator says, "America was our best friend, whoever we were back then."

Déjà Vu All Over Again

Arizona passed a law in 2010 that allows police to demand papers from anyone they suspect of being in the country illegally, and to demand proof of citizenship at any time. The Major League Baseball Player's Association issued a statement opposing the law, in part because hundreds of professional baseball players are from countries other than the United States. The entire National League passes through Arizona during the season, and half of Major League Baseball has spring training there.

The Player's Association said:

> All of these players, as well as their families, could be adversely affected, even though their presence in the United States is legal. Each of them must be ready to prove, at any time, his identity and the legality of his being in Arizona to any state or local official with suspicion of his immigration status. This law also may affect players who are U.S. citizens but are suspected by law enforcement of being of foreign descent.

Native Americans, African Americans, Japanese Americans, Mexican Americans: it's déjà vu all over again.

The Pitcher's Mound

Pitchers are particular about the dirt on their mound, whether it's solid or pliable, piled high, or scooped low. Whether it's Mark Fidrych, Catfish Hunter, or a lesser hurler, they make it their own. A brash young pitcher for the Oakland A's was starting against the Yankees at home when A-Rod pranced across his pitching mound after chasing a foul ball. A-Rod's incursion into Dallas Braden's territory infuriated the younger player. One of baseball's unwritten rules is that a player from the opposing team should never step on the mound.

Through a combination of talent, hard work, and steroids, A-Rod has accumulated impressive statistics. In response to Braden's anger, A-Rod pointed out the younger pitcher only had a few career wins, as though the younger player's statistics, untainted by steroids, disqualified him from respect. Three starts later, Braden threw a perfect game against the Tampa Bay Devil Rays. It was only the nineteenth perfect game in Major League history.

Braden's grandmother, who was at the game, said: "Stick it, A-Rod!"

RUN

A Phillies fan jumped onto the field during a game and ran around like a fanatic, sprinting across the outfield grass while being chased by security guards. He was seventeen, an age when kids play childish pranks. He didn't resemble the bare-chested hooligans who had attacked a coach at Comiskey Park years before. The Phillies and Cardinals players watched. The boy broke the rules, trespassed, and frightened a few ballplayers. He did what drunk or immature baseball fans have been doing for decades: joining in the fun, creating a little ruckus. Celebrating a tradition.

The chase lasted thirty seconds, and then an officer shot the boy with a Taser. The boy collapsed. A police spokesman said: "From the preliminary look at it, it appears that the officer was within the policy. He was attempting to make an arrest, and the male was attempting to flee." The police chose not to recognize or admit that a boy joking around on a baseball field poses no threat. The police used language to soften their violence: he's not a boy, he's a "male"; he's not playing a prank, he's trying to "flee."

YANKEEDOM

A writer named Colin Woodard has recast the geography of the United States into regions named for their dominant beliefs. In *American Nations,* he argues that deep cultural and historical patterns unique to specific locations continue to influence American life. In an interview, he explained:

> Yankeedom was founded by radical Calvinists trying to create a religious utopia. And this is important for understanding the culture today because the idea was to try to make the world more godly, and actually do social engineering and create a more perfect place on Earth. And this was done through public institutions and governments. . . . This is a very different idea than in the midlands and netherlands, which were multi-ethnic and multi-religious and multilingual from the very beginning.

HAPPINESS

In midsummer I visited a farm in central Wisconsin for a weekend party away from the city to celebrate life. The bonfire blazed and popped. I tossed in my sunglasses and they incinerated in a cloud of foul smoke. The soles of my walking shoes smoldered. When I finally retired, I lay down on thick grass near the coals and slept. No tent, no bag, an extra shirt for a pillow. No dreams. I woke up early, the sun was rising, and the light smeared yellow. Mist hovered above the grass. It was quiet. The corn was tall, sturdy, and formed a green fence around the edge of the property.

Soon others were awake. There were taunts. A challenge was issued. A plastic yellow bat appeared. A game of Wiffle ball began. We made up the rules. It was an out if you hit it into the corn. Nobody but the dog wanted to go looking for it. There were spiders in there, and worse: insecticides, fertilizers, spliced genes, and soggy baseball nostalgia. A double if it bounced off the shingles atop the peeling, unsteady toolshed. A home run if it was over the roof. We threw wicked curveballs that started behind the batter's back and broke all the way down to his knees.

We threw knuckles, slurves, sliders, sinkers, and risers. We struck out, we hit line drives, we won. We won. We won.

THE HIT

When news leaked that Osama bin Laden had been assassinated, the New York Mets were playing the Phillies in Philadelphia. Daniel Murphy was batting when the first murmurs rippled through the crowd. "USA, USA, USA," the fans cheered. The players were the only ones who didn't know what had happened.

Mets manager Terry Collins said later, "You almost want to stop the game. You almost want to just stop the game and have that girl come and sing another beautiful rendition of 'God Bless America.' The first thing I thought of was, 'Well it's about time.'"

Phillies star Ryan Howard said, "It's kind of an uplifting moment."

The Two Minutes Hate played well on YouTube:

> Awesome! Truly a historic day for America. We
> will never forget those who tragically lost their
> lives on that fateful day in September. This
> moment will be remembered as a day that is
> held in honor to the men and women that sac-
> rifice unselfishly so we can enjoy a game that
> embodies the American spirit. And in no other
> game does that spirit resonate more than in the
> Great American Past-time, baseball.

> I was at this game. . . . Phillies and Mets have a
> long rivalry but on that night, the atmosphere
> of Citizens Bank Park when we all found out, it
> didn't matter what team you were rooting for.
> And coincidentally, we were all doing some-
> thing so American when the news broke:
> watching a baseball game, and the two teams,
> Philadelphia, the birthplace of our Independen-
> dence, and New York, where the events of 9/11
> took place. I still say it was the best loss I saw of
> my Phillies :-)

> if u didnt shed a tear on this day, than u werent
> a true american

The Man with the Golden Gun

Throughout the 2011 baseball season, much of the Middle East
was undergoing revolution—the Arab Spring. In Libya, the
brutal tyrant Muammar Gaddafi went into hiding, but in
October he was found crouching in a drainage pipe. His last
words were, "Do you know right from wrong?"

A young man named Mohammed al-Bibi took credit for
shooting the dictator, and was hoisted onto the shoulders of
men in the gathering throng. Al-Bibi wore a New York Yankees
cap and waved the dictator's gold-plated handgun. The crowd
chanted, "God is great! God is great! God is great!"

WAX MUSEUM

The Heroes of Baseball Wax Museum is a short walk from the Hall of Fame in Cooperstown. Entrepreneurs combined beeswax and petroleum byproducts, sculpted and painted the result, and now use the ghostly statues to tell an eccentric version of the history of baseball. Some of the statues are predictable: Mickey Mantle in midleap, Roger Maris with a bat dangling from his hand, Lou Gehrig at the microphone giving his famous speech at Yankee Stadium. But the museum, operating on the fringes of the sport and free of the burden of officialdom, has a strange and enjoyable curatorial viewpoint. Sometimes the displays are political, and other times they are designed to celebrate the Yankees above all other teams. Many are unabashedly silly. There are statues of lanky Randy Johnson towering over little person Eddie Gaedel, Shoeless Joe Jackson in a business suit, Pete Rose giving an induction speech at the Baseball Hall of Fame, and Wade Boggs circling Yankee Stadium on a stuffed horse, snuggling in the crowded saddle with a wax cop. Kevin Costner from *Field of Dreams,* clad in overalls and red-and-black plaid; George Costanza at a desk in shirt and tie, waiting for the Boss on *Seinfeld.* Presidents Reagan, Kennedy, Eisenhower, and Carter pay homage to the game.

Wax Rudy Giuliani and wax George W. Bush sit in stadium seats. The mayor wears a Yankees tie, and his right arm is bent at an angle across his chest as though he'd just thrown a base-ball. Giuliani is smiling, and the dome of his bald head looks to me like the bulging stomach of an overweight tomcat lying on its back. President Bush wears a dark jacket with "Yankees" written in white cursive across the front. He looks straight ahead and slightly toward the sky, as though watching a long fly ball arc toward the outfield fence, or scanning the clouds for Saddam Hussein's weapons of mass destruction. His hands rest in his lap. Limp.

Deeper inside the museum, two gentlemen wear antique garb. Alexander Cartwright looks like Moses. He stands tall with a long gray beard and curly gray hair, while dapper Abner Doubleday sits in a nearby chair. The plaque in front of Doubleday reads: "Civil War general, Cooperstown resident and forever known as the mythical inventor of baseball. He never claimed to have anything to do with baseball and may never have seen a game." It is a slight dig at the Hall of Fame, where the Doubleday myth was perpetuated many decades before. In reality, Doubleday is credited with taking the first shot in defense of the North at Fort Sumter during the Civil War. He was an American war hero.

Cartwright was a "real" inventor of baseball. He organized the Knickerbocker Base Ball Club in New York City in 1845, and published the first rule book in 1845. Cartwright went to California to mine gold in 1849, and according to legend intro-duced baseball wherever he traveled along the way.

In 1852 he relocated to the Kingdom of Hawaii—also known as the Sandwich Islands—where he became a suc-cessful businessman. He is said to have set up baseball fields and proselytized. Cartwright served as an advisor to the

Hawaiian monarchy before his death in 1892. The next year, American businessmen, missionaries, and plantation owners removed Queen Lili'uokalani from power and overthrew the Hawaiian monarchy. By then the Westernization of the islands was well underway, due in part to the popularity of American baseball.

THE UNOFFICIAL HISTORY OF BASEBALL

Once, during a rainout, I wondered how the sport would be different, how the history would be understood, if all those rainouts over the last hundred and twenty years had counted. I thought back to the time when manager Miller Huggins delayed a Yankees game during a rainstorm to avoid a loss. Home runs, strikeouts, wins, losses. They happened, but they don't count. It's strange to consider.

I called the Elias Sports Bureau. What happened during all the rainouts in Major League Baseball's history? How many home runs did Babe Ruth hit before the fifth inning during games that were canceled? Roger Maris? Alex Rodriguez? Would the Yankees have ever *lost* a pennant if rainouts had been counted? My question is unanswerable. Unknowable. Box scores were never produced for most of these games. The papers reported them as rainouts, and rarely, if ever, described what happened in them. No statistics exist. They are unofficial. It's as if the teams never met. The history of baseball has a shadow history, and it's the countless games that were rained out before the fifth inning. The game we know and understand is arbitrary. Its history is cited and built upon, but its ghost history is mysterious. Who won the batting title? Who won the game? Who won the pennant? Who decides? Without facts, we rely on stories to make sense of the game.

EXPLICATION

Over time I noticed the professional games I saw in the stadiums, on TV, in the papers, and online stopped feeling real to me. It felt like hype. Like stagecraft, static, soap opera. It was gluttony, but it left me hungry. It felt controlled, not free: the opposite of how it feels to actually play baseball. So I began playing again, with a Wiffle ball and bat rather than cowhide and wood. Removed from the daily box scores, pennant races, and hyperbole, baseball's constructed meanings evaporated. What remains—play—is the opposite of the official images the sport projects.

I have come to believe the history of baseball is a history of questions, and anecdotes and events that raise still more questions. Its boundaries have dissolved, and all the teams have merged into one that matters more than the rest—the Yankees. The game's original meanings have escaped and grown weird: wax statues of heroes plodding like zombies across America.

THE XXL CHALUPA

During the seventh game of the 2011 World Series, the Cardinals and some other team were battling for victory. Oh. It was the Rangers. It was the first baseball game I had watched on TV in several years, partly because I lacked a television. But my mom had been given a tiny digital television the size of a book as a reward for being a loyal customer somewhere. She passed it on to me.

There was a World Series at stake, so I sat at my kitchen table and stared intently at the little men in their tights and fancy shoes as they ran to and fro. A jug of Carlo Rossi's finest vintage, Paisano, was my companion. The wine was a viewing-enhancement drug, and induced the passivity necessary to sit and watch, sit and watch, sit and watch. The game dragged.

Someone was winning. It was the Cardinals, with Tony LaRussa at the helm. LaRussa was an indisputable genius of the sport, one of the winningest managers of all time. Though nobody mentioned it much anymore, he was also the manager at the helm during Oakland's steroid-infused victories of the late eighties, and again with the Cardinals when Mark McGwire broke home run records. That his players used steroids does not take anything away from LaRussa's intelligence—it was smart baseball to play dumb.

Innings passed. Millionaires threw balls, millionaires hit balls, millionaires ran. Millionaires in the dugout told millionaires on the field what to do. Millionaires in the executive suites put pressure on the managers. Millionaires fortunate enough to buy tickets to the game sat in the stands, drank beer, and talked on cell phones. Millionaires at the helm of giant corporations ran advertisements between innings and during pitching changes, and people excluded from the game watched passively at home.

An advertisement played on my little TV, which stood on my kitchen table amidst a clutter of empty mugs with tea bags stuck inside; old ATM receipts; coins for the laundry; stacks of unpaid phone, electric, gas, credit card, and student loan bills; crumpled drafts of resumes and cover letters; and a sickly jade plant growing horizontally toward the window blinds. The television commercial showed an extremely hairy baseball player sporting a dark black beard. An obscene bush, like an armpit from an old Buñuel film. I vaguely recognized the bearded player as Brian Wilson, the closing pitcher for the Giants, who won the World Series the previous year. Last season Wilson wore a Mohawk hairdo, the bushy black beard, and seemed to be proof of a real connection between hair, danger, and power. He also established college scholarships for the military.

In the ad, Wilson stands in a restaurant that serves a processed, frozen, reheated, Americanized version of Mexican food to obese, diabetic, xenophobic Americans. The baseball player was using the power of his beard to sell something called chalupas.

As the commercial begins, Wilson sits in a chair while an alluring young woman grooms his beard with a long golden comb. "Mmmm," he says. His beard and his cap fill the frame. The camera pulls back to reveal an actor representing the commercial's director, who says that the double XL chalupa is so big—when Brian Wilson stands and interrupts—"You need a closer to finish it."

Wilson takes control, and the commercial veers into dark territory, relying on television's strange ability to take what should disturb us, excise its meaning, and serve it back as humor. Wilson says, "New idea. Imagine this. I'm black ops. I'm gonna sneak up and finish these chalupas." He bites the air like a hungry coyote. "Where I show up, nobody knows. 'Cuz I'm black ops!" He crouches down and points at the chalupa. "But these monsters are stacked." A walkie-talkie appears in his hand. "I need to call my inner deliciousness. Hello? And that double XL chalupa—never happened."

The Paisanos were working inside me, clamoring for their say, and I wondered whether Wilson was talking about a chalupa, an immigrant pulled in by ICE, an Iraqi, an Afghani, or a nameless, faceless soul who had vanished into Abu Ghraib or Guantanamo.

In an interview, Wilson discussed the reasons why he points his right index finger into the palm of his baseball glove after he saves a game:

> What I've taken into my own belief is that this finger represents one man. I'm that one person.

And I can only go so far in life leaning on my
own understandings and my own strength. The
fist represents the power of the Holy Trinity:
the Father, Son, and Holy Ghost. The fist is
symbolic of a circle. It's never-ending. This
strength will only continue to grow. So here's
the strength of God and the strength of man.
And without him, I am nothing. I can only go
so far in this life. But when I cross, I now have
this one person with the strength of Christ, and
I can do anything through Christ who strength-
ens me. I can get over any battles in life. So I
basically give respect to the ultimate fighting
world and I also give respect to Christ, the
audience of one that I play for. I don't play for
anything else. I play to impress Him and only
Him and I must honor Him through defeat
and also successes because I wouldn't be here
today if it weren't for the strength that He gives
me. Talent only goes so far. But faith gets you a
little farther.

Baseball, animality, religion, xenophobia, and corporate and
military control: the XXL chalupa.

WinCards

I have been thinking about ways to make sure my teams—the
Cubs, the Royals, even the Twins—win more games. I'd also be
happy to make the Yankees lose. I have designed a new kind of
scorecard. First there was Henry Chadwick's box score, then the
card that Harry Stevens modified and made popular, and then
the Babe Ruth Baseball Scorer that gave fans the illusion of participating in the game from their seats. But statistics miss so
much of the game, and they often cause my teams to lose and
the Yankees to win.

That's why I invented the WinCard. I will sell them at every stadium in the country. The WinCard is guaranteed to produce the *feeling* of having won, even when everyone else thinks you've lost. It's a matter of rearranging perceptions, changing the rules, altering what counts and what does not. Who wants to be bound to the old way of scoring a game, dependent upon hits and runs, which caused so much anguish for those with fewer hits and fewer runs?

I got the idea at Wrigley Field several years ago, and it has been brewing ever since. Before the game, as usual, my friends and I stood for the national anthem. A young woman in a formal black dress and Cubs hat began to sing. I stood with my hand over my heart, impatiently waiting for the song to end so I could sit down and relax. I'd heard it at a hundred games, so I was shocked when she sang the lines "*No* bombs bursting in air / gave proof through the night / that our flag was still there." I'd always thought the lyric was "*the* bombs bursting." The song ended, everyone cheered, and I sat down.

But the singer had enunciated every word carefully and clearly. I had no doubt she sang "*no* bombs bursting in air." Was it a subtle protest? The friends I was with heard the normal version of the song. None of the fans around me seemed to have noticed. Was I just hearing what I wanted to hear? Or were they? The teams began to play, but my perception of the game had broken open, and I wondered what would happen if I chose to see only what I *wanted* at each game.

By the second inning, the Cubs were losing five to nothing. My scorecard was still blank because I had spaced out during the starting lineups. This happens to me a lot. I doodled on the scorecard while a pitching change was made. As the crowd cheered for the new pitcher, I drew a bear cub fighting a marlin. The great fish had stabbed the bear through its barrel chest and blood had spilled across the scorecard, pooling at the bottom of the Marlins' ninth- and tenth-inning columns. I heard cheering and looked up. The Cubs fans were applauding one of their own for tossing a Marlin homer back onto the field.

I drew a new category on the scorecard: Homers Tossed Back: 1. And then I drew another category: Time (in seconds) for Homer to be Tossed Back: 8. I was probably inspired by a credit card commercial I had seen. And suddenly it hit me: a way for me to transform the Cubs into a winning team, if not on the field or in the "real" record book, then at least according to *my own rules.* If the Cubs failed to win according to the usual definitions and statistics, I'd tabulate hot dogs and beers rather than hits and runs. A new way to define reality.

BROKEN RECORDS
The Beastie Boys sang about having more hits than Sadaharu Oh. He hit 868 home runs during his career in Japan.

Nobody knows how many Barry Bonds hit.

Hank Aaron hit 755.

Babe Ruth hit 714.

Willie Mays hit 660.

Ken Griffey hit 630.

Nobody knows how many Alex Rodriguez hit.

Nobody knows how many Sammy Sosa hit.

Jim Thome hit 612.

Frank Robinson hit 586.

Nobody knows how many Mark McGwire hit.

BUT
Sadaharu Oh used a bat of hard compressed wood that was illegal in Major League Baseball because it gave an unfair advantage to the hitter. It was later banned in Japan as well.

HISTORY

Does anybody know how many games old Pud Galvin really won?

Who's on first?

THE TRIALS

The whole country was bloated. Not just the players' biceps and their inflated faces. Cars grew into SUVs, houses grew into mansions, anxiety grew into fear, and cats and dogs went on diets. The military expanded, the pundits shouted louder, the players hit more home runs. Much of it was based on lies: bad credit, bad investments, bad habits, bad intelligence, bad legislators, bad presidents. Americans knew this. They had been telling lies to each other. They had chosen to deceive themselves. Instead of punishing the people who started the wars, instead of changing things that mattered, the public went after the easiest, most symbolic target: baseball players. Not even the owners, managers, or the commissioner. Just the players. At a time when Bush and Cheney should have been called before Congress to answer questions about Iraq, Congress instead called baseball players to testify about steroids. When some of them lied to the government about their use, they were charged with crimes and put on trial. It was a symbolic shift. The home run king could not be allowed to cheat and lie and get away with it because it tarnished the sport and, by extension, America. Neither could the Yankees pitcher.

But presidents and their staff can cheat, lie, torture, kill, and reengineer the legal system into a personal shield. The corporate world collects record profits at workers' expense, and when CEOs and financiers commit fraud they are protected from the consequences. We the veal watch it all on television, but a noble few take to the streets and protest in peace.

TAKE ME OUT OF THE BALLGAME

One night, friends and I piled into a car and meandered into the parking lot of the minor-league St. Paul Saints. It was the first beautiful evening of the summer. Sunny, warm, no humidity. The parking lot was crowded with others tailgating, playing catch, tossing beanbags. We arranged our lawn chairs, lit the grill, and cracked open local beers. Most of us had jobs, partners, kids, but this was to be a night of escape, a night of baseball, of clarity, of math, of defined winners and losers. Smoke billowed from the top of our little grill. Hot dogs split and blackened. Someone distributed another round as we heard the national anthem wafting over the fence and across the blacktop.

An hour later, we ambled over to the ticket counter. The general admission seats, which we hoped to buy for five dollars each, were sold out. A corporation had purchased the entire section. We debated whether to buy the regular seats for nine dollars, or drive downtown and watch the Twins. Majority ruled—since the Twins were terrible, we figured we could get into the new stadium for even less than nine bucks. We crammed the grill into the trunk and drove downtown.

The game was in the fourth inning by the time we parked and walked to the stadium. The cheapest seats from the ticket window were twenty-five dollars. The cheapest seats from scalpers were fifteen. Eh.

We walked to Fulton Brewery, a small local taphouse a few blocks away, and ordered a pitcher of its specialty, a pleasing IPA called Sweet Child of Vine. The Twins were on large TVs, and we glanced now and then, during the lulls in our discussion of the indignities of work and unemployment, of life and death. Later, on the way home, as we joked about having gone out for a night of live baseball without seeing either of the games we intended, I sat in the backseat and sensed that something had

shifted in our lives, or at least in mine. Four ardent baseball
fans, the kind that know the starting lineup, the kind that critique the minor-league prospects, the kind that know how to
keep score, did not care enough to pay their way into two local
stadiums.

MY FAVORITE VEGETABLES

Our lack of motivation to cross through the turnstiles into the
stadiums that summer might have been an anomaly. Might
have been, but was not for me. Deep into the same summer,
deep enough so that I was conscious of the need to start taking
advantage of the remaining light, deep enough so that at night
the birds had gone silent and been replaced by crickets, my
friends invited me to their neighborhood for a baseball game.
A local park was hosting an outdoor screening of game seven of
the 1987 World Series. Here in Minneapolis, that is a big deal.
It was a big deal for me as a kid, too, because my grandmother,
living in Elbow Lake, Minnesota, mailed me clippings from the
local paper about Dan Gladden, Kirby Puckett, and Frank
Viola. And a Homer Hanky, the genuine article, which I
pinned to a cork board on my bedroom wall.

At first it seemed like a perfect evening to watch baseball.
I envisioned lawn chairs, beer, friends, even a little harmless
nostalgia. But something held me back. I didn't want to go,
and I didn't know why. My friend called and taunted me, told
me to get up there and watch the game. Instead, I walked into
my backyard to the garden I shared with my neighbors. The
day's heat had broken and the light entered at an angle, cast-
ing long shadows. It was time to water the vegetables. The
zucchini leaves were forest green and as big as dinner plates.
A bee leaned deep inside a yellow flower, and when it crawled
out, I saw its shoulders were dusted with pollen. The squash

had stretched and thickened since the night before. Watermelon leaves sprawled haphazardly, and their green fruit was the size of my fist. Two cantaloupes, so well disguised among the leafy chaos that they had been invisible until this week, were a pale shade of green. All fourteen tomato plants were studded with green, yellow, orange, and red fruit. My feet were wet, my legs muddy, and mosquitoes perched on my arm and neck to drink. Not once, not once did I think to compare the small watermelon, cantaloupe, or tomatoes to the shape and size of a baseball. Not once did I spot a zucchini lurking under the canopy of leaves and think to compare it to a bat. Not once did I wish I was watching a replay of an old ball game.

Dissemination

More than most other professional sports, baseball has long been enjoyed by fans outside the stadium walls. Box scores, word-of-mouth, newspaper stories, ticker tapes, radio broadcasts, television, movies, and fantasy leagues have all stepped in to replace the actual experience of watching a game at the stadium. Baseball lives in the imagination, and the imagination is messy. Memories, stories, details, images, and associations jumble together. When a person writes or talks about baseball, what comes out is a story about the details of the game, flavored with whatever was lingering in their mind along with the pitch count, or who hit a triple into the right field corner. Meanings can be stretched and molded into something that is equal parts sport, religion, and political theater. When not directly participating, the fan is liable to be manipulated.

Playing is different. You have to focus on the pitch flying toward your head, the ball's angle off the bat, or the likelihood that you'll be thrown out by the catcher while trying to steal second. The experience itself fills your mind. You don't need to be told what happened, because you were there, you saw it, you helped make it so. The old cliché about baseball and democracy being similar really is true: they are best when you hustle onto the field rather than sit in the stands. The moment you become passive, meanings mutate and fester. The only solution is to play.

The Bullfighter

The Miami Marlins hired hot-tempered, opinionated, uncontrollable manager Ozzie Guillen to lead their team for the 2012 season. Attendance had been slipping, and the owners hoped he would appeal to the Latino population in Miami, many of whom are Cuban American.

"I love Fidel Castro," Guillen said. He explained that he admired the dictator for his ability to survive American attempts to kill him. It should not have been a controversial statement. Though it took nearly ten years after the 9/11 attacks to assassinate Bin Laden, Fidel Castro has managed to survive for over fifty years while living just ninety miles from the United States. But when the Cuban American community in Miami protested Guillen's comments—conflating Guillen's admiration for Castro's wily survival with Castro's repression of his people—the Marlins suspended Guillen for five games.

Imprisonment without trial, wiretapping, torture, and political murder were hallmarks of Castro's rise to power and tools he used to remain in control. They were why Cubans fled for the safety of Miami, and these crimes were a big reason why America wanted Castro dead. But in recent years, imprisonment without trial, wiretapping, torture, and political murder have also become key tactics of the American War on Terror. Just as Castro used them against Cubans, the United States uses them against anyone it chooses—even citizens.

An editorial argued, "The Marlins may be within their legal rights, but they should have thought harder before succumbing to the cries of a mob and punishing a political statement for business reasons."

In the din over Guillen's offhand remarks about Castro, other, more interesting statements Guillen made were obscured. He also told the reporter that he loved bullfighting. The reason was that "you're giving the animal an opportunity to kill you."

Anyone who voices an unusual opinion is like Guillen's bull-fighter. The corporatocracy is the bull.

Rewilding

Two coyotes traipsed through alleys, streets, and parking lots to visit Wrigley Field late one November night. They stared with reverence at a statue of Ernie Banks, and sauntered over to the VIP parking lot favored by players. A Chicago man working that evening at the Cubby Bear took their photographs and said, "It was kind of like they were looking for tickets. They went by the ticket window and unfortunately found it was closed, so they were ready to move on to the bar."

An Ugly Fish Imperiled by Extinction

After George Steinbrenner died at age eighty, a baseball fan summed up his feelings about the late owner and his team: "I would no more become a Yankee fan than I would become a coelacanth."

The Velvet Rut

Velvet harvested from the antlers of young deer is pulverized and mixed into a tincture rich in IGF-1, which can elevate blood levels of human growth hormone, which may increase the number of home runs a batter swats if he sprays it beneath his tongue.

Liquefied deer velvet sounds like a terrible thing to put in your mouth, but it is a big improvement in performance-enhancing drugs. Old Pud Galvin back in 1889 had injected himself with the pureed testicles of various mammals in order to improve his pitching. But at least he didn't have to put them in his mouth.

Aspiring sluggers, take heart! The "elixir" emitted from the penis of the Roosevelt elk during thrash-urination is a possible repository of powerful hormones undetectable by Major League Baseball's drug program. The danger of harvesting the fluid and the reticence of the elk have slowed the commercial market for this potion, which means the moment is nigh for you to slink through the woods, mouth agape, tongue lapping, and gain your advantage over Ryan Braun.

THE GLASSIAN SHIFT, OR, HOW I LEARNED TO STOP WORRYING AND HATE THE ROYALS

The past few baseball seasons, I have been harboring a secret: I want the Royals to lose. I'm eager for the day when the Yankees wallop them by fourteen runs. I feel relief when the Twins bury the Royals. The only anxiety I feel as a baseball fan happens during those rare periods when the Royals win two games in a row. When a star player leaves the Royals for a different club, I feel happy for them rather than angry at some abstract faux-betrayal. And I think what a fool Mike Sweeney was for squandering years with them, how misguided he was to put loyalty into a bloodless organization over opportunities to develop his talent with better teams. As a bleeding Kansan, these heresies came to me gradually, one by one, and I kept them to myself, even *from* myself.

It was not until I was surprised to find myself having fun in Yankee Stadium, even rooting for my archenemy, that I was forced to admit my change of heart over the Royals: I hate them, and I am glad that I hate them. I can't imagine ever again rooting for *any* baseball team, but especially not the Kansas City Royals.

When David Glass took over the Royals, his approach to running a baseball team was remarkably influenced by his long-time employer, Walmart. Their idea—Glass's and Walmart's—was to buy *cheap* materials, assemble them as *cheaply* as possible, and sell them to a public whose taste they had no respect for, a public they assumed would keep buying cheap *crap* because it was the only crap in town. Whenever quality appeared in the David Glass system, whether it was Johnny Damon, Carlos Beltran, Melky Cabrera, or Zack Greinke, his instinct was to get rid of it, lest it raise expectations for the rest of his operation and raise costs for himself. Walmart did not sell cashmere to people accustomed to synthetic fleece, and neither did David Glass.

During most of the David Glass era, I was blinded to the realities of what was going on with his team, and with baseball as a whole. I knew Glass was doing something wrong, that all of our young players were eventually shipped to the coasts for little in return. But instead of blaming Glass, or the structure of the overall compensation system, I instinctively blamed the New York Yankees. I complained about the Yankees, about Steinbrenner, about Jeter. I complained about the entire zoo of exotic talent their money allowed them to attract and retain.

But after I went to Yankee Stadium and watched them in the playoffs, my perspective gradually shifted. Under Steinbrenner, the Yankees were what every baseball team should be: a mix of athletes, managers, and moneymen who actually cared about winning. The Yankees knew their fans would not accept a shoddy product. If the Yankees went up for sale, a man like David Glass wouldn't even be allowed to bid. However rapacious, greedy, spoiled, and annoying the Yankees are, and have been for decades, it can never be said that they don't care about their sport, and don't care about their fans.

Put another way, George Steinbrenner was an old-school capitalist, in the flawed but comparatively human tradition of Henry Ford. At times he seemed to have an assembly-line approach to building his teams, because the best players eventually found their way to New York. But, like the system Ford created, the benefits of the Steinbrenner system were not limited to him alone. He became richer, and more powerful—and baseball owners *do* wield symbolic power—during his time at the helm of the Yankees. But his *players* also became rich, in fact richer than they could have been anywhere else. And if you overlook the late eighties and early nineties, when the team suffered losing streaks and Steinbrenner's behavior distracted him from the task of winning, Yankees *fans* were better off under Steinbrenner's system. Every year, Yankees fans knew they would be taken seriously. The owner respected them, if only for pragmatic reasons.

David Glass is an entirely different kind of capitalist. A kind of post-American capitalist, who seems to care more about accumulating money than about the quality of the product, or the success of the team. Whose vice is avarice rather than pride. The Glass model of baseball ownership has only one thing in common with the Ford model: money. And under the Glass model, the only one who benefits is Glass himself. Like Walmart workers, Royals players are acquired cheaply, are of underdeveloped talent, and when they are good are still grossly underpaid. Glass seems not to care about them. The same is true of Royals fans. Walmart's lack of respect for its customers and its underpaid workers—the very traits that enable its leadership to accumulate massive profits—are mirrored in the way David Glass runs the Royals. It's a profound shift in the history of baseball and a consolidation of a tendency that has been lurking within Americans throughout our history. Quality and respect replaced by an emotionless approach to interacting with one's fellow beings. I would call it inhuman, but it's common among humans. Maybe it is the future trajectory of the evolution, or devolution, of our species. It makes me want to join the coelacanth and sink beneath the Royals, beneath the Yankees, beneath America itself, and swim in weird waters with other obstinate fish who refuse to become extinct, with my fellow water-breathers of no commercial value, which is another way of saying: freely.

On the Beach

My family and I visited an isolated beach in Hawaii, where Alexander Cartwright moved later in his life. Cartwright may have helped spread baseball to the islands, which helped American culture take hold, which helped the missionaries and businessmen gain strength and overthrow the Hawaiian monarchy in 1893.

The sand was white and warm under my feet. A dark, severe cliff rose above the aqua water. I held a long piece of pale driftwood, broken and smoothed by the ocean. Grains of sand were stuck to the wood, and to the skin on my hands and arms. My younger sister stood twenty feet in front of me, a pile of hard brown seeds at her feet. They had fallen from a nearby tree and were the size of walnuts. She held one in her right hand. I steadied myself, raised the driftwood, kept my rear elbow up, and waited for her pitch.

A whale breached behind her. I pointed and she turned. The ripples from its splash dissipated, then its tail rose high above the waves, and it slapped down hard: crack! Again, crack! Crack! The beast sank beneath the water.

My sister and I took our places. Her sunglasses were orange and obscured her eyes and cheeks. The sun had bleached her hair. She grinned, wound, and threw. I swung but the seed was too small, too fast. She threw again. I was tempted by a pitch over my head, and I swung like I was chopping with an ax. Strike two. She wound again, threw, and I was out. We decided to snorkel.

Alexander Cartwright may have swum here.

Because of Cartwright we may swim here.

We stepped into the warm water and swam toward the world beneath the waves.

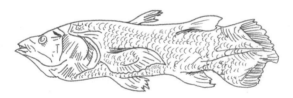

EPILOGUE
Saturday, March 30, 2013
Minneapolis, Minnesota

The first thunderclaps of spring woke me before sunrise today, and I was bounced from a vivid dream. It was past dusk, and I was standing on the grass at Royals Stadium waving to the bleachers at friends and family there to see my first game in the majors. On my head sat the mesh Royals hat I've had since the mideighties, and I was amazed our manager would allow me to wear a ratty plastic cap while everyone else donned new blue wool. I was happy. That's when I awoke.

The Major League Baseball season begins tomorrow, and on Monday morning, I will deliver this manuscript to Coffee House Press. The Royals went twenty-five and seven during spring training, and despite knowing better, it gives me hope for the season. Today I believe false hope is better than no hope. I sit at my kitchen table wearing the mesh cap from my dream, finishing my final edits. It was good to be part of a team that until this morning I thought I'd rejected. It was good to be playing the game and feeling free.

Extra
Innings

The Umpire's Rules

T've chosen to include notes on my methods and sources so that readers can assess for themselves what to make of *The Devil's Snake Curve,* and because I want to give readers new ideas for texts they might someday enjoy. One of the underlying subjects of *The Devil's Snake Curve* is the ways in which baseball has been represented in the United States, and how these representations can be understood in the context of American history. Apart from my own personal experiences and observations, everything in this book came from outside sources. As I have viewed it, my job as a researcher and writer has been to analyze, interpret, highlight, and *skew* what I have learned about baseball's role in American culture and *bend* it toward my current vision of the sport and of the nation. The result is my subjective retelling of the sport's history. In this project, my interests, methods, and aims have more in common with a curator in a wax museum than a historian in a university.

Depending on whether I was writing a personal or historical anecdote, I used differing approaches while researching raw material. I reconstructed my personal stories purely from memory. I deliberately did very little research to learn whether my memories were verifiably accurate because I learned early on that if a given memory was demonstrably flawed, it would force me to write a version of my own history that I did not subjectively experience. The "truth," in such a case, would paradoxically cause me to write a "false" version of what I remember living through. Sanity is contingent on forgetfulness, and meaning is only possible through reconstruction.

One of the subjects of this book is the oddity of public trust in statistics. I view them, as did the late sportswriter Shirley Povich, as an imperfect tool for representing realities that are more complicated than numbers convey. I feel the overreliance on statistics in documenting baseball history is an outgrowth of the religious heritage of the United States, which has instilled in people an obsession with documenting, and accounting for, their behavior, and with viewing texts as being capable of inerrancy. The result of these impulses is our strange cultural moment in which many Americans simultaneously expect books to be literal representations of an objective reality, in the same way they view their chosen holy text as being "perfect," while these same people often deny things that are demonstrably true: dinosaurs lived millions of years ago, human behavior is changing the climate, Iraq had nothing to do with the 9/11 attacks, and religious books have internal contradictions and historical flaws. I remained scarred by the certainty with which politicians and news outlets drummed up support for the invasion of Iraq in 2003, and I long ago came to see the value of doubt, uncertainty, and skepticism. Evidence can be falsified. Statistics can lie. I view the increasing use of statistics as a way to tell stories about the game of baseball as an outgrowth of underlying cultural beliefs and trends in the United States, and it is my impulse to work against hubris. Admitting my subjectivity and searching within my memory for the deeper meaning of a given story or anecdote seems a better approach than false bravado.

I have chosen to indulge this point of view as I've written the personal sections of this book. Although one of my former little-league teammates read several drafts, I have chosen not to conduct much research on whether my memories are perfectly in line with other people from my past. And in some instances, I have doubts about the literal accuracy of my stories. Others are entitled to their own versions of scenes in which, for them, I was just one of many participants. A couple of examples will illustrate what I'm talking about.

Long after I wrote and revised the passage titled "Obsession," my dad and I talked about Baseball Nut ice cream. He told me that *I* was the one who was obsessed with it, not *him,* and that *he* only ate it because *I* wanted it. This is not at all how I remember it. I distinctly remember disliking the ice cream's raspberry swirl. So whose version of the memory should I use in my book? I chose to use my own memory because it felt true, and it served my overall purposes as a fragment in the larger collage. But maybe my dad's memory is true and mine is false. Who cares? Only the pedant.

In the "Mental Toughness" passage, I report rumors about a teammate's proclivity to shave his body. I never saw him during his shaved phase, and I have no idea whether the rumors were true. But for my purposes, it does not matter whether the rumors were true, because they reveal a tiny splinter of meaning about human anxiety over its relationship to the fur that sprouts on certain parts of our bodies. The rumors *existed,* and that's all that matters. As with my overall approach with this book, it is the representation, the memory, and the constructed image that interests me as much as literal, objective reality. It would be absurd to try to find and document the veracity of this passage, to track down long-lost friends and find out whether one of them really did shave his entire body.

To paraphrase Werner Herzog's "Minnesota Declaration," in sharing my personal stories I have been more interested in visceral and emergent meanings than in an accountant's version of truth. Gabriel García Márquez advised taking notes while researching a story, and then throwing the notes away before sitting down to write. The meaning will stick with you, while the trivial details, the truth of the accountant, will fall away and be forgotten. While constructing the personal anecdotes in *The Devil's Snake Curve,* I often saw value in the methods of Herzog and Márquez. By temperament, training, and intellect, I'm usually more interested in what things mean than what is strictly factual, although when possible I like to know the difference. I have no interest in deliberately confusing the issue for myself or my readers.

There are exceptions to my insistence on a memory-based approach to the personal stories I tell about baseball. In some cases I happened to be taking notes, and I ignored Márquez and went back to them while writing. The passage "Whaling" is one example. As unlikely as it may seem, I was indeed taking notes while watching game seven of the 2003 National League Championship Series at the Billy Goat Tavern, and I wrote down the phrases uttered and shouted by people in the bar, including my conversation with the man bearing a harpoon. And I'm glad I double-checked my memory in this case, because until I went back to my notes, I thought there was a chance I'd dreamt the whole thing.

I also chose an approach that might disappoint Herzog and Márquez while researching and citing sources for the purely historical sections of this book. I was as careful, cautious, and scrupulous as I could be. When in need of statistics and general information about baseball history, I used http://www.baseball-reference.com/, http://www.baseball-almanac.com/, and *Total*

Baseball by John Thorn. I even spent money I'd reserved for indulging in beer and "smelt fries" at the Red Stag in Northeast Minneapolis to hire a fact-checker named Clifford Blau who freelances for the *Baseball Research Journal* of the Society for American Baseball Research. Even when history is contested, there is often a version accepted by consensus as the most accurate. I view the existence of consensual reality as a good thing, and it has been my goal to use facts and accurate details as the starting point in my book's historical anecdotes. The reader may dislike or disagree with the implications, meanings, and arrangement of the facts, but unless I've made accidental mistakes, the reader will not be able to argue that I'm fabricating history itself.

I have made choices that my fact-checker advised against. I use "Senators" for the Washington Senators of the twentieth century even though their official name was apparently "Nationals." Many references, including *Total Baseball,* consistently refer to them as "Senators," and I found it impossible to call them anything else. It's also true that calling them the "Senators" worked better thematically. I use "buffalo" rather than "bison," because I like "buffalo" better. And I use "Hilltop Park," a nickname, rather than American League Park, the proper name for where the Highlanders played in their early years. The underlying theme is that when it served my purposes as the writer and curator of this book, I chose the words I felt had the most impact, even if one could quibble with them. But where there were no gray areas, I tried, with Clifford Blau's help, to use facts drawn from consensual reality. He may think I'm insane.

The information in my historical sections came from secondary and primary sources. I read countless newspaper articles dating between 1885 and 2013. I came to wonder whether baseball

reporters become bored with their subject over the course of a
long season, and therefore begin to write about things like facial
hair as a way to deal with the otherwise repetitive nature of
their jobs. Whatever the cause, I found that across several
decades, the best and most interesting writing about baseball
has come from daily sportswriters working for major newspapers. Their stories, which imbue baseball and its history with
deadpan humor, outright silliness, and a touch of humanity,
have influenced my book more than anything else. I'm not sure
whether they would be glad to know it, but the newspaper writers whose work has influenced my thinking include: Dave
Anderson, Harvey Araton, Ira Berkow, Thomas Boswell,
Murray Chass, Jack Curry, John Kieran, Leonard Koppett, Joe
Posnanski, Shirley Povich, William C. Rhoden, Irving
Vaughan, George Vescey, Arch Ward, and many, many others
whose stories ran without bylines or whose work I came across
just once or twice.

Other secondary sources—books about baseball—were less
important to me. I have read and enjoyed many of the classics
of the genre, including Eliot Asinof's *Eight Men Out,* and W. P.
Kinsella's novel *Shoeless Joe.* But for research purposes, I preferred newspaper accounts. One of the exceptions was *The
Catcher Was a Spy* by Nicholas Dawidoff, which directly
influenced both my impulse to write *The Devil's Snake Curve*
and my sections on Moe Berg. Another was the work of anthropologist and former minor-league ballplayer George Gmelch,
especially his essay "Baseball Magic," which I read a few years
before I started this book. Older books written about the sport
were a pleasure to read, and thanks to a perfectly timed sale in
St. Paul, I discovered several gems in the final stages of my writing. They include *A Pennant for the Kremlin* by Paul Molloy
and *Me & The Spitter* by Gaylord Perry (with Bob Sudyk).

Apart from newspapers, the secondary sources I preferred were books unrelated to baseball. I have no idea how it happened, but while trying to study the history of the sport very early in this project I found myself reading *Producing Hegemony: The Politics of Mass Production and American Global Power* by Mark Rupert. I tried to stop myself because it felt so far off the path I thought was relevant to baseball, but it was riveting and influenced how I came to view the game. This was typical. There are several other examples of books that had nothing to do with baseball but influenced *The Devil's Snake Curve*. I loved finding references to baseball in unexpected places, and when I found them by chance in books like *The 9/11 Commission Report, The Bin Ladens: An Arabian Family in the American Century, Bush at War, Total Cold War: Eisenhower's Secret Propaganda Battle at Home and Abroad,* and *The Cold War and the United States Information Agency,* I was always thrilled and joyfully included them in my own pastiche about the sport's role in American history.

Although I loved reading secondary sources, my most important work drew from special collections. I traveled to the New York Public Library to peruse their Yankees collection and the Baseball Hall of Fame to study scrapbooks, newspaper clippings, and photographs. Later, they sent me television commercials and films. I received materials from the Truman Presidential Library about the Psychological Strategy Board and Lefty O'Doul, and Ike's comments on Iran's nuclear program are from files at the Hoover Presidential Library. Even in cases where I chose not to include what I learned in this book, my readings of undigested history informed and emboldened my overall project.

It's worth mentioning a couple of examples to convey how I handled the history-making portions in this book. Because

I'm interested in other people's subjective representations of baseball, I've included details in my book that I do not necessarily take at face value. In the passage "Baseball at Los Alamos," I tried to confirm the detail that "Yankees" was the code for overwhelming success during the testing of the atomic bomb, but I found no evidence for it. Neither did my professional fact-checker. Rather, my information comes from a letter to the editor of the *New York Times*. For all I know, the person who wrote the letter to the editor could have been mistaken, making a joke, delusional, or completely accurate. The reason I left it in my book is that it reveals something about how the man viewed the world. Something that's a little bit complicated, actually. Did the man think the Yankees were the best, and that the atom bomb was the best? Or did he hate the Yankees, and hate the bomb? It is interesting that somehow baseball teams and atomic weapons became linked, and it doesn't matter, for the sake of my book, whether the government created the code or a random man was off his rocker. I have tried to tip my hand in those rare instances where I report details that may be flawed but nevertheless are interesting. Myths and legends, for example, are not technically factual but reveal more about a set of circumstances than dry historicity. Anything uttered by Mark Twain should be understood as a lie, but a lie that he intended to use to tell the truth.

I followed a similar principle with the passage "A Testament Betrayed." While writing an early draft, I happened to re-read *The Old Man and the Sea* by Ernest Hemingway. Such was my immersion in my own research into baseball history that I couldn't see the short novel as anything but the story of the dominance of the Senators by the Yankees. Later, I read *Testaments Betrayed* by Milan Kundera, which bashes the distortion of authorial intent by literary critics. I momentarily agreed, and felt ashamed of myself for my lunatic baseball-centric interpretation of *The Old Man and the Sea,* but then decided my interpretation was *fun* and that the question of whether it was accurate or fanciful was beside the point. I feel the same about my analysis of *The Hustler* and other aspects of pop culture that I included in the book. Over time, I couldn't help but read the Yankees *into* all sorts of "texts," including lines of Arthur Rimbaud's written before the Yankees even existed. This cohesion of vision was a residual effect of the mefloquine I gobbled during trips to hot climates. I eventually cut some of these eccentric interpretations from my book, but I feel those that remain, while perhaps not technically "true," wrestle with issues in the culture.

My point is that even though I've been scrupulous with regard to the facts and details of baseball history—I have no interest in having my book attacked for getting George Brett's batting average wrong—I've indulged in a feverish kind of radical subjectivity while assembling these factual pieces into a larger whole. There are an infinite number of ways to write a book, an infinite number of ways to read a book, and an infinite number of ways to be a fan of baseball and of America.

The story of how and why I created *The Devil's Snake Curve* is long and strange. For a period of years it was a 350-page novel starring eccentric protagonists who held barely sane views of baseball and America, but I will reserve that story for another time and oversimplify to reveal a few sources that inspired the version Coffee House Press published. My first memory of wanting to use an episodic, sporadic, and narrative-thwarting structure in a book dates to a couple of years before I began writing, when I happened across a friend's copy of *The Arcades Project* by Walter Benjamin. I flipped through it a few times, reading passages, skipping others, and developed a persistent obsession with thinking about the underlying meanings of seemingly banal aspects of daily life (the Paris arcades and Major League Baseball). And I loved the way Benjamin's unfinished book, clogged with long quotes and under-theorized bits of information, left me alone to direct my own thinking. *The Arcades Project* stuck with me over the years. I no longer feel this way, but back then I became fixated on the notion that narrative itself was somehow dictatorial and claustrophobic, and that reading a traditional story was akin to spending a weekend in a cave with Joseph Stalin.

I discovered several other books, movies, and albums whose collage-like or episodic approach to making meaning struck me as interesting. A partial list (alphabetical by artist) includes *Paul's Boutique* by the Beastie Boys; *Notes from No Man's Land: American Essays* by Eula Biss; *In Patagonia* by Bruce Chatwin; *Mrs. Bridge* by Evan S. Connell; *About a Mountain* by John D'Agata; *Let's Get Free* by Dead Prez; *The Impossible Leap in One Hundred Simple Steps* by From Monument to Masses; *71 Fragments of a Chronology of Chance* by Michael Haneke; *Wisconsin Death Trip* by Michael Lesy; *Collected Works: Volumes I–III* by Paul Metcalf; *The Way to Rainy Mountain* by N. Scott Momaday; *Fast, Cheap & Out of Control* by Errol Morris; *Why Did I Ever* by Mary Robison; *Owl* by William Service; *Cat's Cradle* by Kurt Vonnegut, and *Holy Land* by D. J. Waldie. I continue to enjoy many of these texts.

Though the form and structure of *The Devil's Snake Curve* may seem unique to baseball writing, there's a tradition within the genre of trim, anecdotal books laden with facts, jokes, trivia, and sometimes drawings. There are countless examples, good and bad, but the ones that have spent time on my shelf include *Baseball . . . A Laughing Matter!* by Warner Fusselle; *Baseball Lite: The Fine Sport of Running, Throwing, Hitting and*

Catching While Stealing, Sliding, Bunting and Scratching by Jerry Howarth; *Baseball Confidential* by Bruce Nash and Allan Zullo; and *O Holy Cow! The Selected Verse of Phil Rizzuto* by Phil Rizzuto.

In the same way that "Born in the USA" functions like a Trojan horse by cloaking its critique of post-Vietnam America in the sounds and signifiers of patriotism, I deliberately used the language and history of baseball as a palette through which to convey my deeper concerns about contemporary life. Thank you, Mr. Springsteen. *I'm Keith Hernandez,* the brilliant short film by Rob Perri, accomplishes a similar feat.

The drawings in *The Devil's Snake Curve* were created by the one and only Andy Sturdevant, a well-bearded man-about-town and a fellow Coffee House Press author, after the work of E. Franklin Wittmack, who illustrated *Joe Below Zero: A Story of Mystery and Adventure in the North Woods* (1943), a novel written by my great-uncle Vermund Ostergaard.

SOURCES

REPOSITORIES & INFLUENCES ⌒

ARCHIVES
• National Baseball Hall of Fame and Museum, A. Bartlett Giamatti Research Center
• Herbert Hoover Presidential Library and Museum
• National Security Archive at George Washington University
• New York Public Library
• Harry S. Truman Presidential Library and Museum

EXHIBITIONS, CONFERENCES, LECTURES
• *Baseball as America,* February through July, 2003, the Field Museum.
• Sixteenth Cooperstown Symposium on Baseball and American Culture, June 2004.
• Eighteenth Cooperstown Symposium on Baseball and American Culture, June 2006.
• George Grella, "Cartoons and Cinema—The Cultural Contexts of Baseball Movies," June 8, 2006.
• Bill Staples, "From Internment to Hope: Arizona Honors a Japanese-American Baseball Legend," June 7, 2006.
• Kerry Yo Nakagawa, "Baseball and the Multicultural Experience of the Negro and Nisei Leagues," June 7, 2006.
• NINE Spring Training Conference on the Historical and Sociological Impact of Baseball, 2004.
• *Rare Films from the Baseball Hall of Fame,* curated by Dave Filipi and screened at Block Cinema, Northwestern University, June 28, 2007.

FRONT MATTER ⌒

• Phil Pepe, *The Wit and Wisdom of Yogi Berra* (New York: Hawthorn Books, Inc., 1974), 133.
• Mary Robison, *Why Did I Ever* (New York: Counterpoint, 2001), 8.

CHAPTER 1: ORIGINS ⌒

HE'LL SAVE CHILDREN, BUT NOT THE BRITISH CHILDREN
• Title from Brad Neely's animated film, *Washington,* available on You Tube, http://www.youtube.com/watch?v=l7iVsdRbhnc.
• Micah Cohen, "Washington Shed Here: A Collectible," *New York Times,* September 5, 2007.

- "This card contains": Quote from the back of Washington's 2007 Allen and Ginter (Topps) baseball card.
- "This and the fact": Dobby Gibson, "Beware of False Friends," *It Becomes You* (Minneapolis: Graywolf Press, 2013), 15. Copyright © by Dobby Gibson. Reprinted with the permission of The Permissions Company, Inc., on behalf of Graywolf Press, www.graywolfpress.org.

QUANTIFICATION

- Notes on Henry Chadwick are from a plaque at the National Baseball Hall of Fame and Museum.
- "Amusement Business spotlights 100th anniversary of Harry M. Stevens Inc." and "Leland's Harry M. Stevens live auction 1996, May 11, including historical sports memorabilia and vintage baseball cards" are both items at the National Baseball Hall of Fame and Museum.

THE RULES

- "Mark Twain," *Los Angeles Times,* July 16, 1887; "Mark Twain as an Umpire," *Los Angeles Times,* July 22, 1887.

TECHNOLOGY

- Christopher Klein, "Baseball's First Fountain of Youth," last modified April 5, 2012, http://www.history.com/news/baseballs-first-fountain-of-youth; Robert Smith, "A Different Kind of Performance Enhancer," National Public Radio, last modified March 31, 2006, http://www.npr.org/templates/story/story.php?storyId=5314753.

HORACE WILSON'S SEEDLINGS

- Noel Perrinn, *Giving up the Gun: Japan's Reversion to the Sword, 1543–1879* (Boston: David R. Godine, Publisher, 1979).
- Sayuri Guthrie-Shimizu, *Transpacific Field of Dreams: How Baseball Linked the US and Japan in Peace and War* (Chapel Hill: University of North Carolina Press, 2012).

ACCUMULATION AND CONSTRUCTION

- "Watches and clocks": Mark Rupert, *Producing Hegemony: The Politics of Mass Production and American Global Power* (Cambridge: Cambridge University Press, 1995), 63.
- "a clean, sober": Henry Ford quoted in Rupert, *Producing Hegemony,* 66.

Hot Air
- "Ball Tourists Banquet," *Chicago Daily Tribune,* April 9, 1889; "Depew's Curves," *Boston Daily Globe,* April 9, 1889; "Now Play Ball," *Minneapolis Tribune,* April 9, 1889; "Welcomed Home," *Los Angeles Times,* April 9, 1889.

The Devil's Snake Curve
- "'Striking Out' Satan," *Chicago Daily Tribune,* February 18, 1889.

Sampson and the Yankees
- "Sampson's Test of Strength," *New York Times,* April 3, 1896.

Evolution
- I initially learned this history through http://www.hot-dog.org, which quoted Bruce Kraig of the Culinary Historians of Chicago. I learned more by speaking with Kraig on the phone on March 6, 2007.

The Facts
- Oliver E. Allen, *The Tiger: The Rise and Fall of Tammany Hall* (Reading, Massachusetts: Addison-Wesley, 1993), 200.
- "Betting Incidents at the Up-Town Hotels," *New York Times,* November 3, 1901; "Devery Speaks to Ninth District Voters," *New York Times,* July 15, 1902; "'Have a Drink' is Devery's Slogan," *Chicago Daily Tribune,* July 20, 1902; "Devery's Dictionary," *New York Times,* September 7, 1902; "Rain Does Not Stop Devery's Campaign," *New York Times,* September 14, 1902; "Thousands Wagered at Hoffman House," *New York Times,* November 4, 1902; "'Big Bill' Devery Sore at Heart," *Chicago Daily Tribune,* November 4, 1903; "Yankees Made $90,000 in 1906," *Washington Post,* December 11, 1906.

The Farrell Colt
- "Clark Griffith Won in Real Stake Style," *New York Times,* April 21, 1906; "Refuses Picture: Rich Woman Sued," *Chicago Daily Tribune,* April 25, 1906; "Frank Farrell Hurt," *New York Times,* April 25, 1906; "Clark Griffith Won Toboggan Handicap," *New York Times,* May 13, 1906; "Wide World of Sport," *Washington Post,* January 16, 1907.

Cleanliness and Democracy
- "Rev. Billy Sunday Picks All-Star Ball Team from Major Leagues," *Minneapolis Tribune,* October 21, 1908.

"Luck"
- Anthony Papalas, "Lil' Rastus Cobb's Good Luck Charm," Society for American Baseball Research, accessed September 22, 2013, http://research.sabr.org/journals/lil-rastus-cobs-good-luck-charm.

KNOTHOLE
- "White Hose Suspicious of Sign Tipping at Yanks' Park," *Chicago Daily Tribune,* July 13, 1910.

HAL CHASE
- "• Hal Chase Must Go or Stallings Will," *New York Times,* September 21, 1910; "Chase Will Lead Yanks Next Year," *New York Times,* September 22, 1910; "Hal Chase Exonerated," *New York Times,* September 24, 1910.
- Eliot Asinof, *Eight Men Out: The Black Sox and the 1919 World Series* (New York: Henry Holt and Company [an Owl Book], 1987).

TEAM SPIRIT
- Edward Mott Woolley, "The Business of Baseball," *McClure's Magazine,* July 1912.

CASH MONEY
- W. J. L., "A Lucrative Profession," *New York Times* (letter to the editor), March 24, 1914.

CHAPTER 2: MACHINES

THE WAY FORWARD FOREVER AMEN
- "To See 'Billy' Sunday," *New York Times,* January 8, 1915; "Sunday Tried Out by Capital Throng," *New York Times,* January 19, 1915; "Sunday Gets $25,000 and Charity $6,000," *New York Times,* May 24, 1915.

OH, TO BE A HAIRY HELLION
- Arch Ward, "Talking it Over," *Chicago Daily Tribune,* July 19, 1934; Arch Ward, "In the Wake of the News," *Chicago Daily Tribune,* July 16, 1940.
- Terry Lefton, "Gillette's Century of Close Shaves in Baseball," *Street and Smith's Sports Business Journal,* June 22, 2009, http://www.sportsbusinessdaily.com/Journal/Issues/2009/06/20090622/SBJ-In-Depth/Gillettes-Century-Of-Close-Shaves-In-Baseball.aspx.

WINNERS
- Ruppert Brewery advertisements are from the *New York Times.*
- "It will be constructed": Henry Ford quoted in Rupert, *Producing Hegemony,* 63.

NICE, VERY NICE
- John J. McGraw, "French Turn Out to See Giants Play," *New York Times,* February 17, 1914.

Protectorate
- "Play Ball with Palestine Army," *Chicago Daily Tribune,* August 14, 1918; "Reports Arabs are Making Fair Progress with Baseball," *New York Times,* January 24, 1923; "4th in Jerusalem Brings Out Throngs," *New York Times,* July 5, 1929.

Pay Attention
- "'Big Bill' Devery Dies of Apoplexy," *New York Times,* January 21, 1919.

Babe Ruth
- "Red Sox Pound Yankee Pitcher," *New York Times,* October 3, 1914; "High and Cook Spill Red Sox in 13th," *New York Times,* May 7, 1915; "Left-Hander Ruth Puzzles Yankees," *New York Times,* June 3, 1915; "Red Sox Rehearse for World's Series," *New York Times,* October 7, 1915; "Ruth Lets Yanks Have Three Hits," *New York Times,* June 23, 1916; "Yanks Stage Weird Comedy of Errors," *New York Times,* April 20, 1918; "Babe Ruth is Hero, Though Yanks Win," *New York Times,* May 5, 1918; "Babe Ruth Menace Breaks Out Again," *New York Times,* June 26, 1918; "Ruth Knocks Out His 26th Homer," *New York Times,* September 9, 1919.

Dominant Dogs
- Edward Grant Barrow and James M. Kahn, *My Fifty Years in Baseball* (New York: Coward-McCann, Inc., 1951).

Mr. Bob
- Stephen Warren, *The Shawnees and their Neighbors, 1795–1890* (Urbana: University of Illinois Press, 2009).

An Errant Pitch
- "Ray Chapman Dies; Mays Exonerated," *New York Times,* August 18, 1920.

A New Home
- Yankee Baseball Collection (1913–1950), mss Col 3403, New York Public Library.

Entrapment
- Barrow and Kahn, *My Fifty Years in Baseball.*

Ruth's Logic, or the Evening Redness in the West
- Christy Walsh, "Babe Back on Buffalo Meat Diet," *Tacoma Ledger,* undated; Babe Ruth scrapbooks at the National Baseball Hall of Fame and Museum (1921–1935), assembled by Christy Walsh (ba scr 44).

ICON
- "Babe Ruth Cigar (Partially Smoked)," the Baseball Reliquary, Inc., accessed September 22, 2013, http://www.baseballreliquary.org/cigar.htm.

THE IMPORTANCE OF ETYMOLOGY
- I learned the name of Ruth's ancestor in Mary Anne Hess's article, "The House That Ruth Filled," *Washington Post,* March 30, 1990.

PARTICIPATION
- Babe Ruth scrapbooks at the National Baseball Hall of Fame and Museum (1921–1935), assembled by Christy Walsh.

HIPPODROMING
- Sid Mercer, "Yanks Once More Up On Carpet Before League Chief," (paper and date unknown) in the Babe Ruth scrapbooks at the National Baseball Hall of Fame and Museum (1921–1935), assembled by Christy Walsh.

THE SANDLOTS
- "White Sox Smash Cleveland's New Pitching Idol, 10 to 2," *Chicago Daily Tribune,* May 12, 1919; "Indians Beat Yanks Twice and in First Game Caldwell Sets Them Down Without a Hit," *New York Times,* September 11, 1919; James R. Harrison, "Uhle Tames Yanks, Indians Winning, 6-2," *New York Times,* July 13, 1926; John Kieran, "Sports of the Times," *New York Times,* May 10, 1928.

CHERRY BLOSSOMS DO NOT LINGER
- "Japanese-Americans in baseball," Scrapbooks 1 & 2 (1927), assembled by Irene Masayo Enokida, National Baseball Hall of Fame and Museum (BA SCR 39).

THE BIGGEST CHEW
- "Player File for Charles Arthur Shires, 1928- / compiled by the National Baseball Hall of Fame and Museum Library, Cooperstown, N.Y." Many of its original clippings were not fully sourced.
- "Man Dies From Injury Sustained at Hands of White Sox Player, *New York Amsterdam News,* January 2, 1929; "Jury Exonerates Shires of Blame for Fan's Death," *Chicago Daily Tribune,* March 29, 1929; Irving Vaughan, "Shires Crowds Action of a Lifetime into a Few Years; You Wouldn't Believe He's Only 22," *Chicago Daily Tribune,* June 30, 1929; "Shires, Calm, Sober, Ponders Latest Melee," *Chicago Daily Tribune,* September 15, 1929; "Shires is Back! Writing Poetry and Fighting—For Coin," *Chicago Daily Tribune,* November 30, 1929; "The Great Shires—How He Proved It," *Chicago Daily Tribune,* December 10, 1929; "Shires to Fight Spohrer," *New York Times,* December 23,

1929; "Landis Calls Art Shires on Green Carpet," *Chicago Daily Tribune,* January 16, 1930; "Shires Traded to Washington," *Los Angeles Times,* June 17, 1930; "Art Shires, 60, Ex-First Baseman," *New York Times,* July 14, 1967; "Art 'The Great' Shires Dies," *Chicago Daily Tribune,* July 14, 1967.

CLEAN-CUT BOYS
• Advertisement in *Minneapolis Tribune,* October, 1930.

CHAMPIONS OF THE WORLD
• Barrow and Kahn, *My Fifty Years in Baseball.*

THE CONVEYER BELT
• Alva Johnston, "Beer and Baseball," *New Yorker,* September 24, 1932.

JACKIE MITCHELL STRIKES OUT THE YANKEES
• "Girl Pitcher, 17, Fans Ruth, Gehrig, Walks Tony, Quits," *Washington Post,* April 3, 1931; William Brandt, "Girl Pitcher Fans Ruth and Gehrig," *New York Times,* April 3, 1931; Ring Lardner, "When Girl Pitcher Struck Out Babe," *Chicago Daily Tribune,* April 6, 1931; "House of David Nine Gets a Girl Pitcher," *New York Times,* July 15, 1933; Bryan Field, "Here and There in Sports," *New York Times,* July 23, 1933.

MOE BERG
• Nicholas Dawidoff, *The Catcher Was a Spy: The Mysterious Life of Moe Berg* (New York: Pantheon Books, 1994).

MR. NAGASAKI
• "'Patriot' Stabs Noted Publisher in Tokyo for Sponsoring Babe Ruth's Tour in Japan," *New York Times,* February 22, 1935; "Japanese Praises Ruth," *New York Times,* February 24, 1935; "Japan and Babe Ruth," *New York Times,* March 4, 1944.

FRENCHY'S REBELLION
• Arch Ward, "Talking it Over," *Chicago Daily Tribune,* July 19, 1934.
• Russell Wolinsky, "Frenchy Bordagaray: Mustache Man," National Baseball Hall of Fame and Museum, accessed May 22, 2006, http://www.baseball halloffame.org/library/columns/rw_041201.htm.
• John Kieran, "The Man with the Mustache," *New York Times,* March 27, 1936; John Kieran, "Hits, Runs, and Errors," *New York Times,* April 14, 1936.

WHAT REMAINED OF RUPPERT
• "Museum Shows Ruppert's Art," *New York Times,* July 16, 1939.

They Say Pigeons Are Inbred Doves
- Donald Davidson and Jesse Outlar, *Caught Short: The Amusing and Amazing Escapades of a Little Man Who Walked Tall among the Giants of Baseball* (New York: Bantam Pathfinder Editions, 1972).

Chapter 3: War ⌒

The Oddity of the Everyday
- "He faced death": Damon Runyon in *The Pride of the Yankees,* directed by John Ford, 1942.

Yankee Doodle, Do or Die
- *Yankee Doodle Dandy,* directed by Michael Curtiz, 1942.

Dirt in the Skirt
- *A League of Their Own,* directed by Penny Marshall, 1992.

Motivation
- "Japan and Babe Ruth," *New York Times,* March 4, 1944.

Standard Operating Procedure
- "I honestly feel": *Baseball as America,* the Field Museum, 2003.
- Richard Rutter, "Personality: Boss in Baseball and Building," *New York Times,* July 9, 1961; "Man on Cover: Del Webb," *Time,* August 3, 1962; "Del Webb Buying Las Vegas Hotel," *New York Times,* September 19, 1964.
- Del Web's history, accessed March 15, 2006, http://www.delwebb.com /about/history.aspx.
- Sally Denton and Roger Morris, *The Money and the Power: The Making of Las Vegas and its Hold on America, 1947–2000* (New York: Alfred A. Knopf, 2001).
- "Webberization": Margaret Finnerty, Tara Blanc, and Julian DeVries, *Del Webb: A Man. A Company.* Edited by Julian DeVries and Robert Gryder (Phoenix: Heritage Publishers, 1991).
- Jay Feldman, "Baseball Behind Barbed Wire," *Whole Earth Review,* Winter 1990.
- Alexander Leighton, *The Governing of Men: General Principles and Recommendations Based on Experience at a Japanese Relocation Camp* (Princeton: Princeton University Press, 1968).
- Iwata went to Poston: "Special meeting of rep's Unit I, II, III re: net factory project," University of California Calisphere, accessed September 22, 2013, http://content.cdlib.org/ark:/13030/ftoj49n5d9/?query=Harvey%20Iwata& brand=calisphere.
- Zenimura, who'd been: Bill Staples and Kerry Yo Nakagawa, the Cooperstown Symposium on Baseball and American Culture at the National Baseball Hall of Fame and Museum, June 7, 2006.

- "We seek the softness": Anonymous, "That Damned Fence," in Paul Bailey's *City in the Sun: The Japanese Concentration Camp at Poston, Arizona* (Los Angeles: Westernlore Press, 1971).
- Poston closed: Richard Shigeaki Nishimoto and Lane Ryo Hirabayashi, *Inside an American Concentration Camp: Japanese American Resistance at Poston, Arizona* (Tucson: University of Arizona Press, 1995).
- pitched the shutout: "Yankees Blank Red Sox, 5–0, on Stirnweiss Day," *Chicago Daily Tribune*, September 30, 1945.
- "Both the wisdom": Joe David Brown, "The Webb of Mystery," *Sports Illustrated*, February 29, 1960.

On the Trail of Heisenberg
- Dawidoff, *The Catcher.*

Baseball at Los Alamos
- Garry Michael Buff, "Bronx Bombers, or Nonbombers." *New York Times* (letter to the editor), July 29, 1990.

The Joke
- *The Atomic Café,* directed by Pierce Rafferty, Jayne Loader, and Kevin Rafferty, 1982.

Good-Will Should Be Exploited
- Harry S. Truman Papers, Staff Member and Office Files: Psychological Strategy Board Files. Dates: 1951-53. GORDON GRAY CHRONOLOGICAL FILE, 1951. Box 30, 353.8
  - Memorandum for the Record, "Activities of "Lefty" O'Doul in Promoting U.S.-Japanese Friendship Through Sports Activities." October 14, 1952, Truman Papers, Truman Library.

Mea Culpa
- "Play by Play Story of 4th Series Battle," *Chicago Daily Tribune,* October 2, 1955; photograph caption reads, "Webb Uses Head."
- "Big Crowd Greets Yankees in Tokyo," *New York Times,* October 21, 1955.
- I learned of the film by Yankees players Elston Howard and Andy Carey at Dave Filipi's screening, *Rare Films from the Baseball Hall of Fame* at Block Cinema in Evanston, Illinois. I later obtained a copy of the entire film from the Hall of Fame.

Warrior
- John Findlay, *Magic Lands: Western Cityscapes and American Culture after 1940* (Berkeley: University of California Press, 1992), 177. Findlay, in turn, was quoting an interview with Webb published in *Arizona Highways.*

Major
- Richard Sandomir, "Kubek Says Battlefield Made Houk a Leader," *New York Times,* July 22, 2010.

Politics
- "Fiery Shires Enters Texas Political Race," *Chicago Daily Tribune,* May 18, 1948; "Alter Murder Charge Against Shires to Aggravated Assault," *Chicago Daily Tribune,* February 1, 1949.

Public Relations
- Kenneth Osgood, *Total Cold War: Eisenhower's Secret Propaganda Battle at Home and Abroad* (Lawrence: University of Kansas Press, 2006).

Business as Usual
- Gillette television commercial, National Baseball Hall of Fame and Museum collection.

Intelligence
- Timothy Weiner, *Legacy of Ashes: The History of the CIA* (New York: Doubleday, 2007).
- Miles Copeland, *The Game of Nations: The Amorality of Power Politics* (London: Weidenfeld and Nicolson, 1969).
- "To the people of Iran:" Lewis L. Strauss Papers, 1914–74; Atomic Energy Commission Series; Box 422, "Bilateral Agreements, 1955–57," Herbert Hoover Presidential Library and Museum.

Parasite and Host
- John E. Peterson, *The Kansas City Athletics: A Baseball History, 1954–1967* (Jefferson, North Carolina: McFarland & Company, Inc., Publishers, 2003).
- "Yankees Trade Larsen for Maris," *Los Angeles Times,* December 12, 1959.
- "Yanks' So-Called Farm Burns a Wayward Bus," *New York Times,* February 5, 1961.

Loyalty
- *The Day the Earth Stood Still,* directed by Robert Wise, 1951.

The Rescue
- *Ace in the Hole,* directed by Billy Wilder, 1951.

Billy Sunday's Children
- "Pledge," accessed September 22, 2013, http://www.littleleague.org/learn/about/pledge.htm.

LaRussa
- Bruce Webber, "The Slow Pitch Ambassadors to Cuba," *New York Times,* November 25, 2011.

Billy Martin
- "Billy Martin Tops with Polio Victim," *New York Times,* October 4, 1953.

Willard Nixon's Monkeys
- "Nixon Blanks Yankees, 1 to 0," *Chicago Daily Tribune,* April 25, 1955; Louis Effrat, "Yankees Shut Out Red Sox in Boston," *New York Times,* May 9, 1955; Joseph M. Sheehan, "Three Hit Effort Tops Bombers, 7–3," *New York Times,* May 30, 1956; Joe Reicler, "Nixon Can't Explain Jinx Over Yanks," *Washington Post and Times Herald,* August 18, 1956; Richard Goldstein, "Willard Nixon, 72, A Pitcher Known for Beating the Yankees," *New York Times,* December 14, 2000.

Goofs
- Charles McGrath, "Another Side of Kerouac: The Dharma Bum as Sports Nut," *New York Times,* May 15, 2009.

Holiness
- *Pull My Daisy,* directed by Robert Frank and Alfred Leslie, 1959.

Stern Advice
- Gillette television commercial, National Baseball Hall of Fame and Museum collection.

Lew Burdette's Blarney Stone
- Lew Burdette, "Blarney Stone Aids Burdette Victory," *Los Angeles Times,* October 4, 1957; "'Burdette Never Really Worried Me'—Haney," *Los Angeles Times,* October 11, 1957.

Nexus
- George Dugan, "Throng Sets Arena Record—Nixon is Platform Guest," *New York Times,* July 21, 1957; Harold Hutchings, "100,000 Crowd Yankee Park, Hear Graham," *Chicago Daily Tribune,* July 21, 1957; "Nixon Guest of Graham in Huge N.Y. Rally," *Los Angeles Times,* July 21, 1957.

The Milwaukee Effect
- Nicholas J. Cull, *The Cold War and the United States Information Agency: American Propaganda and Public Diplomacy, 1945–1989* (Cambridge: Cambridge University Press, 2009), 149–160.

Frank Strong Lary

- Gordon S. White, Jr., "Lary Sets Back Bombers, 8 to 1, With 3 Hit Pitch at Stadium," *New York Times,* May 3, 1956; "Lary Hurls 4th Straight Win Over Yanks, 6–3," *Los Angeles Times,* June 2, 1956; "Yanks Beaten by Lary Again, 6 to 2," *Chicago Daily Tribune,* September 16, 1956; Louis Effrat, "Tigers, Behind Hurling of Lary, Crush Yankees With Early Drive at Stadium," *New York Times,* July 16, 1958; John Drebinger, "Lary of Tigers Beats Yanks 7th Time With 3-Hitter," *New York Times,* September 17, 1958; "Pitchers' Pet Teams Are Mystery," *Washington Post and Times Herald,* May 27, 1961; "Lary Again Works Hex on Yankees," *Los Angeles Times,* April 14, 1962; "'Yank-Killer' Lary Sent to Minors," *Washington Post and Times Herald,* May 9, 1963; S. Lee Kanner, "Question Box," *New York Times,* February 1, 1982.

Obsession

- "Fun Facts," accessed September 22, 2013, https://www.baskinrobbins.com /content/baskinrobbins/en/funfacts.html.

Gasoline

- Louis Effrat, "Bombers Feel 'Playboy' Fines Will Put Club in 'Playball' Mood," *New York Times,* June 5, 1957; Shirley Povich,"This Morning . . . With Shirley Povich," *Washington Post and Times Herald,* June 5, 1957; "Yanks Trade Billy Martin," *Washington Post and Times Herald,* June 17, 1957; Shirley Povich, "This Morning . . . With Shirley Povich," *Washington Post and Times Herald,* June 18, 1957; Louis Effrat, "Silence! Bobby Richardson at Work," *New York Times,* June 25, 1957.

Infidel

- Roberto González Echevarría, *The Pride of Havana: A History of Cuban Baseball* (New York: Oxford University Press, 2001).
- R. Hart Phillips, "Castro 'Waiting' to Get U.S. Base," *New York Times,* January 14, 1961.
- David Wise and Thomas B. Ross, *The Invisible Government* (London: Jonathan Cape, 1965).

Exports

- Michael A. Barnhart, "A Secondary Affair: American Economic Foreign Policy and Japan, 1952–1968," Working Paper No. 9, National Security Archive, accessed February 5, 2010, http://www.gwu.edu.~nsarchiv/japan/barnhart.html.

Psyche-Outs

- Gaylord Perry and Bob Sudyk, *Me & The Spitter: The Candid Confessions of Baseball's Greatest Spitball Artist (or How I Got Away With It),* (New York: Signet, 1974), 40.

TO BE OWNED
- *The Hustler,* directed by Robert Rossen, 1961.

CHAPTER 4: ANIMALS

THE CYCLE
- *Never Cry Wolf,* directed by Carroll Ballard, 1983.

HUNTING THE COW
- I heard this story from my fishing guide at Lake of the Woods, a man named Big Mike, who worked on the grounds crew for the Kansas City Athletics and Royals. Billy Martin himself told a version of the story to David Letterman in 1985.

HAIR (OF THE MULE)
- "Athletics Hope to Dazzle Win from Yankees," *Chicago Daily Defender,* April 9, 1963; Arthur Daley, "Sports of the Times," *New York Times,* May 18, 1965.

THE HALF-PENNANT PORCH
- Peterson, *The Kansas City Athletics.*

THE BULL GOOSE LOONY
- *One Flew Over the Cuckoo's Nest,* directed by Miloš Forman, 1975.

CHANCE DAMNS THE YANKEES
- Leonard Koppett, "Yanks 2 in 15th Beat Angels, 2–0," *New York Times,* June 7, 1964; Braven Dyer, "Angels Need Punch; Haney Goes After It," *Los Angeles Times,* June 8, 1964; Joseph Durso, "Chance Allows Bombers 2 Hits," *New York Times,* July 29, 1964; Leonard Koppett, "Adcock Connects for a 3-Run Homer," *New York Times,* September 3, 1964; Braven Dyer, "Angels Leave it to Chance, Win 4–0," *Los Angeles Times,* September 3, 1964; Braven Dyer, "Chance Has NY Number 000 000 000," *Los Angeles Times,* September 16, 1964; "Chance Beats Yanks Fifth Straight Time," *Washington Post, Times Herald,* April 25, 1965; Bill Becker, "Angel Home Run Downs Yanks, 1–0," *New York Times,* September 1, 1965; "Old Chance Magic Puts Yanks Under Spell Again, 1–0," *Los Angeles Times,* August 24, 1966.
- Maury Allen, *Bo: Pitching and Wooing* (New York: Dial Press, 1973).

SOLUTIONS
- "90,000 at Stadium Attend Papal Mass and Hear a Homily," *New York Times,* October 5, 1965.

STEINBRENNER SAVES THE YANKEES
- Leonard Koppet, "Ruth! Gehrig! DiMaggio! Mantle! Etc!," *New York Times,* October 2, 1966.

CHARLIE FINLEY'S REVENGE
- "Oakland to Spend Day in the Handlebar Era," *New York Times,* May 28, 1972.
- Wolinsky, "Frenchy Bordagaray: Mustache Man."
- Chris Jaffee, "40th Anniversary: Mustache Day," *Hardball Times,* last modified June 18, 2012, http://www.hardballtimes.com/main/blog_article/40th -anniversary-mustache-day/; Bruce Markusen, "Thirty Years Ago......Birth of the Mustache Gang," the Oakland Athletics Fan Coalition's *Historical Hot Stove,* last modified March 14, 2002, http://www.oaklandfans.com/columns /markusen/markusen134.html.

THE MASTER
- Perry and Sudyk, *Me,* 24–25 & 27.

TRADITION
- Joe Donnelly, "Steinbrenner: The Yankees' Dandy Doodler," *Los Angeles Times,* July 4, 1976.

TIGERS TRY SAMSON APPROACH
- George Minot, Jr., "Tigers Try Samson Approach," *Washington Post and Times Herald,* March 25, 1973.

BILLY MARTIN COULD BE A PRETTY GOOD GUY
- "Billy Martin, Tiger Farmhand Arrested," *Los Angeles Times,* March 29, 1973; "People in Sports: No, Thanks," *New York Times,* March 29, 1973.

LEFLORE
- Thomas Rogers, "People in Sports: Tigers Change Convict's Stripes," *New York Times,* July 3, 1973.

FIRST BLOOD
- Lesley Oelsner, "Steinbrenner Pleads Guilty to Two Counts," *New York Times,* August 24, 1974; Joseph Durso, "Steinbrenner Suspended 2 Years," *New York Times,* November 28, 1974; Murray Chass, "Yankees Owner is Reinstated by Kuhn," *New York Times,* March 2, 1976; Richard Sandomir, "Pursuing Pardon, Steinbrenner Aided FBI," *New York Times,* May 9, 2011.

BEYOND THE SPORTS PAGES

- "Béisbol Diplomacy," National Security Archive, accessed September 22, 2013, http://www.gwu.edu/~nsarchiv/NSAEBB/NSAEBB12/nsaebb12.htm; Document 9, "Additional Talking Points on Sending a Baseball Team to Cuba," February 19, 1975, National Security Archive, http://www.gwu.edu/~nsarchiv/NSAEBB/NSAEBB12/docs/doc09.pdf; Document 6, "William Rogers to Henry Kissinger," February 13, 1975, National Security Archive, http://www.gwu.edu/~nsarchiv/NSAEBB/NSAEBB12/docs/doc06.pdf.

MOSES

- Richard Goldstein, "Marvin Miller, Union Leader Who Changed Baseball, Dies at 95," *New York Times*, November 27, 2012.

HOME-FIELD ADVANTAGE

- Big Mike, Lake of the Woods.
- "Groundwork to Foil Hunter and Yanks in Kansas City Being Laid by Toma, the Royals' Nonroster Asset," *New York Times*, October 5, 1976.

PRIDE

- Murray Chass, "Steinbrenner Rule on Hair Splits Yanks," *New York Times*, March 23, 1976; "More Pride, Less Hair: Owner Bearding Yanks in their Den," *Los Angeles Times*, March 24, 1976; Joe Donnelly, "Steinbrenner: The Yankees' Dandy Doodler," *Los Angeles Times*, July 4, 1976.

CACHING THE KILL

- Mark Fidrych and Tom Clark, *No Big Deal* (New York: J. B. Lippincott Company, 1977).
- Kare Elgmork, "Caching Behavior of Brown Bears (Ursus arctos)," *Journal of Mammalogy* 63(4) 607–612, 1982.
- Micheline Maynard, "Mark Fidrych, Baseball's Beloved 'Bird,' Dies at 54," *New York Times*, April 14, 2009.

PROXY WAR

- Dave Anderson, "Billy Martin's Liver Ailment," *New York Times*, July 16, 1978; Murray Chass, "Martin Resigns; Bob Lemon to Manage Yankees," *New York Times*, July 25, 1978.

BEAST

- Deane McGowen, "Zahn, Marshall Help Twins Beat Yankees," *New York Times*, August 17, 1979.
- Marc Bekoff, "Ground Scratching in Male Domestic Dogs: A Composit Signal," *Journal of Mammalogy* 60(4) 847–848, 1979.

PEACE
• Francis X. Clines, "Closes First of 2 Days at a Mass for 80,000 in Yankee Stadium," *New York Times,* October 3, 1979; "Excerpts from Talk at Yankee Stadium," *New York Times,* October 3, 1979.

WHAT'S GOOD FOR THE HORSE
• Murray Chass, "Yankees Beaten 9–8; Ken Clay is Berated," *New York Times,* September 2, 1979.

CUD
• Big League Chew packaging.

BUGS
• "Martin Version Bugs Yankees," *Chicago Tribune,* July 21, 1980; "Yankee Official Denies Phone Tap," *Los Angeles Times,* July 21, 1980.

ANOTHER TAKE ON HAIR
• Robert Whiting, *You Gotta Have Wa: When Two Cultures Collide on the Baseball Diamond* (New York: Macmillan, 1989).

OCTOBER SURPRISE
• Les Carpenter, "Safe at Home," *Washington Post,* January 20, 2006.

THIRD BECOMES FIRST
• "Issue in Baseball Dispute," *New York Times,* June 12, 1981; "Strike: The Fans," *Los Angeles Times,* August 1, 1981; George Vescey, "The Game is Back," *New York Times,* August 11, 1981; Stuart Wolpert and Joanne Curran, "Morning Briefing," *Los Angeles Times,* August 11, 1981.
• "Really, What Is the Cosmic Baseball Association?" accessed September 22, 2013, http://www.cosmicbaseball.com/really.html.

THRASH URINATION
• Eric Malnic, "Two Knockdowns in an Elevator," *Los Angeles Times,* October 26, 1981; Jane Gross, "Steinbrenner Cheerful Despite Wounds," *New York Times,* October 27, 1981; Bob Verdi, "Dodgers' Fortitude Led to Series Win," *Chicago Tribune,* October 29, 1981.
• Terry R. Bowyer and David W. Kitchen, "The Significance of Scent-Marking by Roosevelt Elk," *Journal of Mammalogy* 68 (2) 418–423, 1987.

SUCCESS NEVER COMES
• "Edwin Dodson, 54; Antiquities Dealer Turned Prolific Bank Robber," *Los Angeles Times,* February 26, 2003; Manny Fernandez, "Crime Blotter Has a Regular: Yankees Caps," *New York Times,* September 15, 2010.

HUEVOS

- Dave Anderson, "The .680 Hitter," *New York Times,* October 10, 1976; "Martin's Needle Pierces Gura and Brett on Field," *New York Times,* October 10, 1976; Shirley Povich, "A Big Yank, A Long Pull," *Washington Post,* October 15, 1976; "Brett Bats Royals Over Yanks," *Washington Post,* June 14, 1977; Ken Denlinger, "Royals Yield to Smash By Munson, 6–5," *Washington Post,* October 7, 1978; Thomas Boswell, "Brett's Bat is Red Hot," *Washington Post,* July 23, 1980; Murray Chass, "Royals' 21 Hits Back Gura in 13–1 Romp Over Yankees," *New York Times,* July 19, 1980; Murray Chass, "Royals Rout Yankees 14–3, Scoring 7 Runs off Guidry," *New York Times,* July 21, 1980.
- Thomas Boswell, *How Life Imitates the World Series* (New York: Penguin Books, 1982), 178–183.
- Steve Cameron, *George Brett: Last of a Breed* (Dallas: Taylor Publishing Company, 1993).

THE RULES BEHIND THE RULES

- Murray Chass, "Brett Homer Nullified, So Yankees Win," *New York Times,* July 25, 1983; William C. Rhoden, "Fans Savor Game's Fine Print," *New York Times,* July 25, 1983; Scott Ostler, "Answer Man Helps Explain Pine Tar Rule," *Los Angeles Times,* July 26, 1983; Sydney H. Schanberg, "Something You Can Count On," *New York Times,* July 30, 1983; "Reversal on Brett Has Martin Upset," *New York Times,* July 30, 1983; Murray Chass, "Finale of Game in Doubt," *New York Times,* August 18, 1983; Thomas Boswell, "First Court, Then Royals Beat the Tar Out of Yankees," *Washington Post,* August 19, 1983; "Resumed Game Ends in 5–4 Yankee Loss to Royals," *New York Times,* August 19, 1983.

KNOW YOUR ENEMY

- Laura Ruel, "Eye Tracking Points the Way To Effective News Article Design," *Online Journalism Review,* last modified March 12, 2007, www.ojr.org /stories/070312ruel/; Julie Deardoff, "Sizing up Where Men Look," *Chicago Tribune,* April 23, 2007, http://featuresblogs.chicagotribune.com/features _juliieshealthclub/2007/04/when_men_gaze_a.html.

THE KISS

- Randy Covitz, "Always a Winner; Hank Bauer 1922–2007," *Kansas City Star,* February 9, 2007.

SIDE EFFECTS

- Mark Fainaru-Wada and Lance Williams, *Game of Shadows: Barry Bonds, BALCO, and the Steroids Scandal that Rocked Professional Sports* (New York: Gotham Books, 2006).

- "Tetrahydrogestrinone," Wikipedia, accessed September 22, 2013, http://en
  .wikipedia.org/wiki/Tetrahydrogestrinone; "Hirsutism," Wikipedia, accessed
  September 22, 2013, http://en.wikipedia.org/wiki/Hirsutism.

Chapter 5: Nationalism

Militia
- Charles M. Robinson III, *The Men Who Wear the Star: The Story of the Texas Rangers* (New York: Random House, 2000).
- Dave McNeely, "Looking at Bush's Words and Deeds," *Austin American Statesman,* October 30, 1994; Simon Kuper, "Baseball: America's Game Launches George W. Bush: Ruthian Rise of Dubya: He Might Well Be the Next US President but George W. Bush's Career Details Are Strictly Minor League," *The Observer,* December 3, 2000.

The Importance of Character
- Plaque, National Baseball Hall of Fame and Museum, 2004.

Progress Steamrolled West
- *Field of Dreams,* directed by Phil Alden Robinson, 1989.

Whimsy
- The eccentricities and math in this section are my own. I also read Ira Berkow, "Remembering Billy Martin, Battler," *New York Times,* December 30, 1989.

Fanatics
- Murray Chass, "Spira Guilty of Attempting Steinbrenner Extortion," *New York Times,* May 9, 1991.
- Ira Berkow, "Contrasts Fill the Life of Steinbrenner," *New York Times,* July 20, 1990; Ira Berkow, "Reorganizing the Yankees: Horse Breeder at the Ballpark; Racing Has Been a Focus for Steinbrenner's Son," *New York Times,* August 1, 1990.
- Fan mail received by the Office of the Commissioner: letters, 1990–1992, National Baseball Hall of Fame and Museum (BA MSS 31).

Impeached
- Murray Chass, "Mattingly Flap: Hair Today, Gone Tomorrow?" *New York Times,* August 16, 1991; Jack Curry, "Mattingly Chooses Seat on Yanks Bench Over Barber's Chair," *New York Times,* August 16, 1991; Jack Curry, "No More Split Ends as Mattingly Rejoins Yanks," *New York Times,* August 17, 1991; Ira Berkow, "The New Yankee Clippers Aren't Very Sharp," *New York Times,* August 18, 1991.

TRIUMPHALISM
- "Indians Stage Protest Outside the Dome," *New York Times,* October 20, 1991.

WARNING
- "Wahoo! Indians Take on Indians Cleveland Mascot Burned in Effigy," *Cincinnati Post,* April 11, 1998; American Indian Movement, "The Anti-Racist Five." Press Release by Grand Governing Council, August 1, 2001, http://www.aimovement.org/moipr/CleveLawsuit.html.

HOW IT HAPPENED
- Kuper, *The Observer,* December 3, 2000.

UNITED 93
- National Commission on Terrorist Attacks Upon the United States, *The 9/11 Commission Report: Final Report of the National Commission on Terrorist Attacks Upon the United States* (New York: W. W. Norton & Company, 2004).

INTENTIONAL WALK
- Steve Coll, *The Bin Ladens: An Arabian Family in the American Century* (New York: The Penguin Press, 2009).

BASEBALL HAS A MAGIC VALUE
- These clips are on YouTube, including: http://www.youtube.com/watch?v=UXuxCqPKflo.

RALLY
- Bob Woodward, *Bush at War* (New York: Simon & Schuster, 2002), 277.

PEOPLE WERE COWED
- Ira Berkow, "The Hall of Fame Will Tolerate No Dissent," *New York Times,* April 11, 2003; Ira Berkow, "Hall of Fame President Acknowledges Mistake," *New York Times,* April 12, 2003; "Cooperstown Muffs One," *New York Times,* April 12, 2003.

FATHER AND SON
- Associated Press, "'I Was Stunned': Royals First Base Coach Assaulted by Father-Son Duo," SportsIllustrated.com, last modified September 19, 2002, http://sportsillustrated.cnn.com/baseball/news/2009/19/royals_whitesox_ap/.

RAINOUT
- "Take Me Out to the Ball Game," Baseball Almanac, accessed September 22, 2013, http://www.baseball-almanac.com/poetry/po_stmo.shtml.

- Sam Roberts, "A Song's Forgotten History, Complete with Cracker Jack," *New York Times,* May 4, 2008.

War Games
- "Baseball Donations from u.s. Military in Afghanistan Find a Home in the Hall of Fame," Press Release, National Baseball Hall of Fame and Museum, October 19, 2004.

Horace Wilson's Seedlings Bear Fruit
- Jeff Z. Klein, "Selling Matsui," *New York Times,* April 4, 2004; Colin Joyce, "Hero's Welcome; Yankees' Matsui Gets Grand Reception in Exhibition Game at Tokyo," *Los Angeles Times,* March 29, 2004.

Purity
- Dan Gordon, "Japan: Changing of the Guard in High School Baseball," In *Baseball Without Borders: The International Pastime,* edited by George Gmelch, (Lincoln: University of Nebraska Press, 2006), 3–21. The student who killed his mother appears to have done so in the early 2000s, judging by the context, but no date is given in the chapter and its notes do not appear to cite a specific source for that incident, which took place at Oku High School in Okayama Prefecture.

Damon and Ortiz
- Jackie MacCullen, "Johnny on the Spot; Damon Has Made the Sox Go— Now He Must Get Going Again," *Boston Globe,* October 15, 2004; Susan Slusser, "Unprecedented/Four-Gone Conclusion/Damon, Lowe Spark Red Sox to Historic Win Over Yankees," *San Francisco Chronicle,* October 21, 2004; John Powers, "A Revival Meeting; After Falling Behind, Sox Kept the Faith and Stunned Yankees," *Boston Globe,* October 31, 2004.

Submission
- Lee Jenkins, "Idiot is Not the Only Role Damon Knows How to Play," *New York Times,* December 23, 2005.

Progress
- Ty Young, "From Internment to Hope: Arizona Honors Japanese Baseball Player Held at Gila River," *Arizona Republic,* November 10, 2005; Tom Singer, "Baseball Cast Light in Shadow of War," *Mlb.com,* March 7, 2008 (accessed May 18, 2010).

Massive Retaliation
- This clip is available on YouTube, http://www.youtube.com/watch?v=HgqbCq _sxmo.

An Idea Is the Hardest thing to Kill
- Joe Frisaro, "Girardi Sets Clean-Shave Policy; Manager Brings Yankee Influence to South Florida," last modified January 27, 2006, http://mlb.mlb.com/news/article.jsp?ymd=20060127&content_id=1301754&fext=.jsp&c_id=m%2520lb.

Reminder
- Mark Gonzales, "Hair Police Strike Again: Garcia, Cotts Nabbed," *Chicago Tribune*, April 19, 2006.

On the Uses of a Baseball Bat, according to an American Intelligence Agency
- "A Study of Assassination," National Security Archive, accessed March 10, 2013, http://www.gwu.edu/~nsarchiv/NSAEBB/NSAEBB4/ciaguat2.html.

The Truthiness of Metaphors
- *Torturing Democracy,* accessed September 22, 2013, http://www.gwu.edu/~nsarchiv/torturingdemocracy/interviews/stuart_couch.html.

The Value of a Soldier's Life
- Andrew J. Bacevich, "I Lost my Son to a War I Oppose. We Were Both Doing our Duty," *Washington Post,* May 27, 2007.

The Ghost of Billy Sunday
- Sewell Chan, "On Yankee Stadium Restroom Dispute, the City Settles," *New York Times City Room Blog,* July 7, 2009. http://cityroom.blogs.nytimes.com/2009/07/07/on-yankee-stadium-restroom-dispute-the-city-settles/ (accessed May 15, 2010); C. J. Hughes, "At Stadium, Trip to Bathroom Signals Free Choice," *New York Times,* July 20, 2009.

Sun City, Arizona
- Harvey Araton, "Ruth's Daughter Greets Finale with a Smile," *New York Times,* September 21, 2008.

Now Pitching, Woody Guthrie
- "This Land is Your Land," accessed September 22, 2013, http://www.woodyguthrie.org/Lyrics/This_Land.htm. Words amd music by Woody Guthrie. WGP/TRO-© Copyright 1956, 1958, 1970 and 1972 (copyrights renewed) Woody Guthrie Publications, Inc. & Ludlow Music, Inc., New York, NY. Administered by Ludlow Music, Inc. Used by permission.
- "Woodrow Wilson Guthrie," Cosmic Baseball Association, accessed September 22, 2013, http://www.cosmicbaseball.com/wguthrie06.html.

SPECTATOR SPORTS
- "Noam Chomsky," Cosmic Baseball Association, accessed September 22, 2013, http://www.cosmicbaseball.com/chomsky8.html.
- Peter R. Mitchell and John Schoeffel, eds., *Understanding Power: The Indispensible Chomsky* (New York: New Press, 2002), 100.

FAN REACTION
- Y. Hillel Crandus, "Letters: Yankees Win, To Glee and Grumbling," *New York Times,* November 5, 2009; Kenneth L. Zimmerman, "In Box: Letters to the Editor," *New York Times,* November 7, 2009.

THE SIZE OF YANKEE STADIUM
- "Iraq Body Count," accessed March 31, 2013, http://www.iraqbodycount.org.

FREEDOM OF SPEECH
- Bill Ladson, "Obama to Throw First Pitch at Nat's Opener," *Mlb.com,* March 29, 2010; Tyler Kepner, "From Taft to Obama, Ceremonial First Pitches," *New York Times Bats Blog,* April 5, 2010, http://bats.blogs.nytimes.com/2010/04/05/from-taft-to-obama-ceremonial-first-pitches/; Scott Shane, "U.S. Approves Targeted Killing of American Cleric," *New York Times,* April 6, 2010; Laura Kasinof, Mark Mazzetti, and Alan Cowell, "U.S.-Born Qaeda Leader Killed in Yemen," *New York Times,* September 30, 2011.

KIDS IN THE CAPITAL OF BASEBALL
- Tom Grace and Michelle Miller, "2 Injured in Cooperstown Shooting," *Daily Star,* April 3, 2010.

PROFESSIONALS
- Ken Belson, "At White House, It's Good Politics to Play Ball," *New York Times,* April 25, 2010; the White House, "Remarks by the President Honoring the 2009 World Champion New York Yankees," press release, the White House Office of the Press Secretary, April 26, 2010.

1%
- Annalyn Censky, "How the Rich Became Uber Rich," February 22, 2011, accessed November 15, 2011, http://www.money.cnn.com/2011/02/22/news/economy/income_inequality/index.htm; "Characteristics of Current Minimum Wage Workers: 2010," Bureau of Labor Statistics, accessed September 8, 2013, http://www.bls.gov.cps/minwage2010.htm; Cork Gaines, "Chart of the Day: Baseball Salaries Up by 6,600% Thanks to Free Agency," *Business Insider,* last modified January 21, 2011, http://www.businessinsider.com/chart-of-the-day-major-league-baseball-salaries-since-1970-2011-1; "Major League Baseball

Salaries," Baseball Almanac, accessed September 22, 2013, http://www.base ball-almanac.com/charts/salary/major_league_salaries.shtml.

POSTMORTEM
• Bruce High Quality Foundation, *We Like America and America Likes Us.* Screened at the Whitney Biennial, 2010, and on Vimeo, http://vimeo.com /9768610.

DÉJÀ VU ALL OVER AGAIN
• Major League Baseball Players Association, "Statement of MLBPA Executive Director Michael Weiner Regarding Arizona Immigration Law," press release, April 30, 2010; "Diamondbacks Caught Up in Debate on Immigration," *New York Times,* May 2, 2010; Erin Einhorn, "Snub Arizona's Baseball All-Star Game to Protest Immigration Law, WFP Urges Yankees and Mets," *New York Daily News,* May 4, 2010.

THE PITCHER'S MOUND
• Tyler Kepner, "No One Crossing this Mound; 27 Up, 27 Down," *New York Times,* May 10, 2010.

RUN
• "Phillies fan Tasered after running onto field," *Sporting News,* May 4, 2010, http://aol.sportingnews.com/mlb/story/2010-05-03/phillies-fan-tasered-after-running-field; Patrick Walters, "Philadelphia Chief Backs Officer Who Tasered Fan," *Washington Post,* May 4, 2010 http://www.washingtonpost.com /wp-dyn/content/story/2010/05/04/ST2010050403731.html; "Couldn't they Just Tag Him?" *New York Times,* May 7, 2010.

YANKEEDOM
• Interview of Colin Woodard by Margaret Warner, "Author Takes Fresh Look at Shaping of U.S. Cultural, Political Landscape," *PBS NewsHour,* air date November 24, 2011. Transcript accessed November 29, 2011, http://www .pbs.org/newshour/bb/entertainment/july-dec11/colinwoodard_1124.html?print.

THE HIT
• Video of Philadelphia fans on You Tube, http://www.youtube.com/watch?v =kXvjz7KkkEM.
• Patrick Berkery, "Phillies Fans, Players React to the News of Osama Bin Laden's Death," *Phils-Ville,* May 2, 2011, http://www.phillyburbs.com/sports /phillies/phils-ville/phillies-fans-players-react-to-the-news-of-osamabin/article _95a8c7aa-74c6-11e0-8abe-0019bb30f31a.html; Gabe Lacques, "Nationals to Honor Military at Tonight's Game," *USA Today,* May 2, 2011; Todd Zolecki,

"Philadelphia Freedom: Game Takes Backseat," *Mlb.com,* May 2, 2011, http:
//mlb.mlb.com/news/article.jsp?ymd=20110501&content_id=18479234&c_id
=mlb; George Vescey, "Mets Thanked Troops; Nation Should, Too," *New York Times,* May 4, 2011.

THE MAN WITH THE GOLDEN GUN

- Tom Kelly and David Williams, "Is this the Yankees Fan who Shot Gaddafi?," *Daily Mail Online,* last modified October 21, 2011, http://www.dailymail .co.uk/news/article-2051784/Gaddafi-dead-Yankees-fan-Mohammed-al-Bibi -claims-killed-dictator.html.
- Benjamin Hoffman, "Yankees Hats Are Everywhere, Even North Korea," *Bats: The New York Times Baseball Blog,* last modified December 29, 2011, http://bats .blogs.nytimes.com/2011/12/29/yankees-hats-are-everywhere-even-north-korea /#postComment.

WAX MUSEUM

- I wrote this section from memory, based on a visit to the Heroes of Baseball Wax Museum in 2006. The extent to which Cartwright helped baseball develop in Hawaii is an unsettled issue. For more information, read Guthrie-Shimizu, *Transpacific Field of Dreams.*

THE XXL CHALUPA

- The Taco Bell commercial is available on YouTube, http://www.youtube.com /watch?v-iLsDZjIH7sE.
- Andrew Baggarly, "At Long Last: Brian Wilson Reveals the Meaning Behind his Crossed Arms Gesture After he Saves a Game," *San Jose Mercury News* "Giants Extra" blog, last modified July 14, 2008, http://blogs.mercurynews .com/giants/2008/07/14/at-long-last-brian-wilson-reveals-the-meaning-behind -his-crossed-arms-gesture-after-he-saves-a-game/.

THE BULLFIGHTER

- Sean Gregory, "Big Fish," *Time,* Monday, April 9, 2012; Editorial, "The Marlins Punish Political Speech," *New York Times,* April 10, 2012, http://www .time.com/time/magazine/article/0,9171,2110450,00.html.

REWILDING

- Barbara Rodriguez, "Wild Coyotes 'Kind of Chilling' by Wrigley Field," *Salon,* last modified November 28, 2012, http://www.salon.com/2012/11/28 /wild_coyotes_kind_of_chilling_by_wrigley_field/.

AN UGLY FISH IMPERILED BY EXTINCTION
• David Dyte, *New York Times City Room* blog, July 14, 2010, http://cityroom .blogs.nytimes.com/2010/07/14/will-yankee-haters-have-a-change-of-heart/.

THE VELVET RUT
• Tyler Kepner, "Baseball Warns Players About Deer Antler Spray," *Bats: The New York Times Baseball Blog,* August 6, 2011, http://bats.blogs.nytimes.com /2011/08/06/baseball-warns-players-about-deer-antler-spray/; Tom Verducci, "MLB Trying to Curtail Use of Deer Antler Spray as Steroid Alternative," *si.com,* August 5, 2011, http://sportsillustrated.cnn.com/2011/writers/tom _verducci/08/05/deer.antlers.arod/index.html.

THE GLASSIAN SHIFT, OR, HOW I LEARNED TO STOP WORRYING AND HATE THE ROYALS
• Harvey Araton, "Restoration Project; Once Proud Royals Prepare to Host All-Star Game in Kansas City," *New York Times,* July 8, 2012.

Acknowledgments

*I*t would be impossible to thank everyone who helped make this book a reality. Countless people have given me encouragement, ideas, and research leads, and many read early drafts and provided valuable feedback. My family and friends were supportive without exception. Jeff Snowbarger and Paul Lindblade deserve special thanks for their contributions. Andy Sturdevant created the wonderful drawings. Chris Fischbach, publisher of Coffee House Press, instantly recognized the value of this eccentric book, and his work as a reader, editor, and promoter has been exactly what the project needed. The entire staff of Coffee House Press did an amazing job, and I'm proud to have been able to work with them.

I'd also like to thank: Ted Adamson, Big Mike, Eula Biss, Clifford Blau, Alex Bolyanatz, Kit Briem, Virgil Brower, Anitra Budd, Claudette Burke, Sarah Caflisch, Caroline Casey, Mark Charon, Ivan R. Dee, Mary Doi, Russ Elliott, Steve Fiffer, Dave Filipi, Jim Gates, Dobby Gibson, George Gmelch, my colleagues at Graywolf Press, Craig Griffin, Patricia Hampl, Art Hansen, Benjamin Harry, Ying Huang, Michael Jauchen, Kayla Kohanek, Linda Koutsky, Bruce Kraig, David LeGault, Meganne Lube, Hesse McGraw, Ed McConaghay, Edward McPherson, Heather McPherson, Chris Messenger, Josh Morsell, Roberta Newman, Caroline Oh, Nathan Peeke, Kate Petersen, Jacob Pomrenke, Adam Robinson and Publishing Genius Press, Julie Schumacher, Kelsey Shanesy, Madelon Sprengnether, Matt Spurgin, Bill Stanley, Bill Staples, Erika Storella and the Gernert Company, Cecilia Tan, Rob Taylor, Margaret Telfer, Jessica Trent, my classmates and faculty at the University of Minnesota MFA program, Celine Vaaler, Jonathan

Westmark, Hans Weyandt, Tim Wiles, Kerry Yo Nakagawa, and all my former teammates.

Thanks also to the research staff at the New York Public Library, the Harry S. Truman Presidential Library and Museum, the Herbert Hoover Presidential Library and Museum, and the National Baseball Hall of Fame—particularly its Giamatti Research Center.

Colophon

The Devil's Snake Curve was designed
at Coffee House Press,
in the historic Grain Belt Brewery's
Bottling House near downtown Minneapolis.
The text is set in Garamond.

COFFEE HOUSE PRESS

The mission of Coffee House Press is to publish exciting, vital, and enduring authors of our time; to delight and inspire readers; to contribute to the cultural life of our community; and to enrich our literary heritage. By building on the best traditions of publishing and the book arts, we produce books that celebrate imagination, innovation in the craft of writing, and the many authentic voices of the American experience.

Visit us at coffeehousepress.org.

FUNDER ACKNOWLEDGMENTS

Coffee House Press is an independent, nonprofit literary publisher. Our books are made possible through the generous support of grants and gifts from many foundations, corporate giving programs, state and federal support, and through donations from individuals who believe in the transformational power of literature. Coffee House Press receives major operating support from Amazon, the Bush Foundation, the National Endowment for the Arts, the Jerome Foundation, the McKnight Foundation, from Target, and in part from a grant provided by the Minnesota State Arts Board through an appropriation by the Minnesota State Legislature from the State's general fund and its arts and cultural heritage fund with money from the vote of the people of Minnesota on November 4, 2008, and a grant from the Wells Fargo Foundation of Minnesota. Support for this title was received from the National Endowment for the Arts, a federal agency, and through special project support from the Jerome Foundation. Coffee House also receives support from: several anonymous donors; Elmer L. and Eleanor J. Andersen Foundation; Mary & David Anderson Family Foundation; Around Town Agency; the E. Thomas Binger and Rebecca Rand Fund of the Minneapolis Foundation; the Patrick and Aimee Butler Family Foundation; the Buuck Family Foundation, Dorsey & Whitney, LLP; Fredrikson & Byron, P.A.; the Kenneth Koch Literary Estate; the Lenfestey Family Foundation; the Nash Foundation; the Rehael Fund of the Minneapolis Foundation; Schwegman, Lundberg & Woessner, P.A.; the Archie D. & Bertha H. Walker Foundation; the Woessner Freeman Family Foundation; and many generous individual donors.

To you and our many readers across the country,
we send our thanks for your continuing support.

The Publishers Circle

THE PUBLISHERS CIRCLE is an exclusive group recognizing those individuals who make significant contributions to Coffee House Press's annual giving campaign. Understanding that a strong financial base is necessary for the press to meet the challenges and opportunities that arise each year, this group plays a crucial part in the success of our mission.

Kathy and Dean Koutsky
Gerry Lauter
Jim and Susan Lenfestey
Carol and Aaron Mack
George Mack
Leslie Maheras
Gillian McCain
Mary McDermid
Sjur Midness and Briar Andresen
Glenn Miller and Jocelyn Hale
Peter and Jennifer Nelson
Rebecca Rand
Sam Savage
John Sjoberg and Jean Hagen
Kiki Smith
Marla Stack and Dave Powell
Stewart Stone
Jeffrey Sugerman and Sarah Schultz
Nan Swid
Patricia Tilton
Marjorie Welish
Stu Wilson and Mel Barker
Warren Woessner and Iris Freeman
Margaret Wurtele
Betty Jo Zander and Dave Kanatz

For more information about the Publishers Circle and ways to support Coffee House Press's books, authors, and activities, please visit coffeehousepress.org or contact us at: info@coffeehousepress.org.

Josh Ostergaard holds an MFA in creative writing from the University of Minnesota and an MA in cultural anthropology. He has been an urban anthropologist at the Field Museum and now works at Graywolf Press.